"You know Alan Patricof as a legend, but now you'll know why. AOL, AAPL, and Apax are among the many things he's helped back and build, and those are just the ones starting with the letter 'A.' It's like reading a real-life version of *Mad Men* except it's about venture capital and Don Draper is still going strong."

—**Chris Fralic**, Board Partner, First Round

"*No Red Lights* is an amazing thesis on building a life while building a business. What Alan Patricof has done in this memoir is to explain by specifics that success is about ethics, hard work, personal research, perseverance, and honest relationships, all with the understanding that 'life is cumulative.'"

—**Michael D. Eisner**, Chairman, The Topps Company;
Former CEO Walt Disney

"Alan Patricof's *No Red Lights* is an invitation to adventure—in growing businesses, helping others, and leading a life where all roads lead in one direction: forward."

—**Michael Bloomberg**, Founder of Bloomberg L.P. and
Bloomberg Philanthropies; Mayor of New York City, 2002–2013

"A great read. Alan Patricof shows that, whether in business or in your personal life, perseverance wins the day!"

—**Eric Hippeau**, Partner at Lerer Hippeau Ventures

"This delightful memoir is a journey through all of Patricof's incarnations, from a modest upbringing by hardworking immigrant parents, to the early days of venture capital, the founding of *New York Magazine* and the glittering heyday of media, canvassing for Biden in the nascent days of his candidacy, and the stellar rise of Greycroft, which has backed some of the most game-changing companies in our lifetime. At the crux of it all is Patricof's prescience, curiosity, and humor. He's as brilliant a storyteller as he is an investor."

—**Gwyneth Paltrow**, Founder of Goop

"Alan Patricof is the youngest eighty-seven-year-old on the planet: more energy, bigger dreams, passion, and commitment than all of us slightly younger folk. He came into my life through my late audio pioneer husband over four decades ago, and never ceases to dazzle. This book will make you gasp at how Alan still reaches for 'fashion and edge' and properly defines some of his many chapters as 'audacious.' His fan club will need vitamins as we watch and applaud his next moves."

—**Jane Harman**, Former Congresswoman; Author of *Insanity Defense: How Our Failure to Confront Hard National Security Problems Makes Us Less Safe*

"This book is invigorating, informative, and essential for anyone who dreams of being an entrepreneur…that also comes over very appealingly is how Patricof's natural gregariousness makes him form so many fascinating relationships. It's a particularly important lesson for the young today who are often stuck behind screens and don't understand the value of personal connections. He really is a marvel."

—**Tina Brown**, Author and Journalist

"*No Red Lights* is a brilliantly written and compellingly documented account of why Alan Patricof is one of the smartest, boldest, most imaginative, and most successful financers and venture capitalists of our era. It describes not only how he built his outstanding career, but also how he forged partnerships and teams with others who supported his success and whose successes he likewise supported. For anyone in the financial world, or any other profession, this is must, and constantly captivating, reading on how to begin, nurture, and grow great companies and a fulfilling career and life—one driven by competitive determination, high levels of integrity and commitment to the very best of human values, scintillating curiosity, and a constant quest for innovation."

—**Robert Hormats**, Managing Director, Tiedemann Advisors, LLC

NO RED LIGHTS

NO RED LIGHTS

REFLECTIONS ON LIFE,
50 YEARS IN VENTURE CAPITAL,
AND NEVER DRIVING ALONE

ALAN J. PATRICOF

Post Hill
PRESS

*To all the entrepreneurs and venture capitalists
who dream big and have the courage
to stake their careers on untested ideas.*

Contents

Preface

When Alan Patricof, my friend and business partner of thirty years in building Apax Partners, was raising his first venture capital fund in 1969, the world had a limited understanding of the important role ambitious entrepreneurs and fast-growing small businesses play in society and the broader economy. Investors and the average citizen firmly believed that large, traditional firms would be the ones to bring technological innovations to the market, create employment, and experiment with new ways of doing things.

Now we can see for ourselves. Small businesses exemplify all the excitement and potential of pursuing new ideas and bringing them to life. Venture capital investing has exploded. From the tiny, $2.5 million funds of the 1960s, a typical venture fund now raises hundreds of millions—and many reach more than a billion.

Venture capitalists no longer spend their time proverbially looking under rocks to find opportunities. Now they sift through hundreds of direct approaches by entrepreneurs each week to pick the gems that can bring new high-potential products and services to the world—and grow at 50 percent a year.

Entrepreneurs, with fire in their bellies, face more competition today than ever before. Every business school across the world teaches a well-attended entrepreneurship track. At least half of MBA candidates, when asked, say they want to start their own business. Many end up ultimately replicating an idea that already exists, but some strive to build huge sustainable businesses that improve both lives and the environment.

Alan Patricof has thrived through the growth and change of the past five decades, which saw the launch of the personal computer, the cellular phone, the internet, digital media, fintech, and podcasting. He has seen and helped spur all of them to mainstream adoption. The fundamentals of good investment decisions have not changed throughout Alan's career. He still continues to place his bets on entrepreneurs and exciting business ideas with sky-high potential.

Alan is a role model—a staunch supporter of the power of innovative entrepreneurs willing to take a step into the unknown.

Despite the uncertainty of the COVID pandemic, there are new and exciting investing opportunities related to climate change, space exploration, self-drive vehicles, medicine, and changing values that propel us into a more equitable world. The view stretches far and wide, and there is no better person than Alan Patricof to emulate as we navigate these new realities. He is proof that life offers us many opportunities to renew ourselves as we contribute to and try to improve our ever-changing world.

Sir Ronald Cohen
Co-Founder, Apax Partners, Chairman, Global Steering Group for Impact Investment (GSG)

CHAPTER 1

You Get Where You're Going from Where You've Been

A typical mix of conversation was underway in the Greycroft venture capital offices one day in early 2020—back before we all decamped to our pandemic home offices. In the conference room, two partners talked about the recent IPO (Initial Public Offering) of one of our portfolio companies, the luxury consignment brand The RealReal. In one of the offices, two other employees reviewed the market projections for a start-up that builds logistics systems for grocery stores hoping to offer home delivery. An investor sat in one of the phone pods conducting due diligence on an eSports start-up, while another rushed out to watch a driverless car demonstration for Optimus Ride at the Brooklyn Navy Yard. Amidst all that bustle related to our portfolio companies—current and prospective—my partner Ian eased open the glass door to my office to talk about paint.

Paint *colors*, that is. We'd outgrown our offices on the twentieth floor of a Madison Avenue building blocks from Grand Central Station. New Yorkers like me refer to this part of Manhattan as "midtown," a warren of tired fifty-year-old structures with some newer glass-and-steel monsters mixed in. Ian, between meetings with entrepreneurs and prospective investors, was overseeing the renovation of a new space on the eighth floor. Yesterday, we'd seen the designer's first ideas, and my response was not enthusiastic. Salmon pink at the entrance, bright blues on the walls. I couldn't see how we got there from here.

Greycroft's twentieth-floor offices have a downtown, industrial look. When we first moved into the space in 2013, I'd wanted to capture the fashion and edge of downtown neighborhoods like Union Square and Tribeca, where New York's venture capital firms have clustered since the 1990s. My plan was to headquarter the firm in that part of town, and I looked for more than a year, but couldn't find anything that suited us.

Madison Avenue was a necessary compromise to get Greycroft out of a subleased suite eighteen blocks north, near Central Park, where we'd made do for five years. Even that had been an upgrade after the two years we'd spent in the offices at Apax Partners, the $60 billion private equity firm that evolved from my first venture capital business, Alan Patricof Associates. But if it was going to be Madison Avenue, I wanted to bring downtown to midtown by using exposed AC ductwork and metallic support beams in our office design, and refining it with natural cement floor, glass walls, earthy colors, and modern art.

"If it were up to me," I said to Ian, "She would replicate exactly what we have here down there. Keep it the same."

Ian didn't react. He didn't have to. Even as the words left my mouth, I knew I didn't mean them—not exactly. I'd built my career on the ability to recognize and take advantage of change. That doesn't mean change is easy. But it is necessary. And inevitable. Like the move to the eighth floor. Like the move I made sixteen years ago when I left Apax Partners—which no longer emphasized venture— to found Greycroft. Like the biggest, highest-impact move of my life: leaving my salaried Wall Street job in 1970 to start a venture capital business—Alan Patricof Associates (APA)—one of the first in New York.

It's hard to get across in today's tech-heady world how audacious that move was. The investment portfolios of the '50s, '60s, and '70s were filled almost exclusively with the stocks and bonds of large, reputable public companies in traditional industries like commodities and manufacturing. I'd made my young reputation with four respected investment firms as a value investor, the approach espoused in the investor's bible *Security Analysis*, by Benjamin Graham and David Dodd, and made famous by Warren Buffett and Charlie Munger at Berkshire Hathaway. I became known for making recommendations based on disciplined due diligence—a reputation I still carry with me to this day.

Yet I was also interested in young, private companies from my first days on Wall Street, beginning in 1955. I gained a high profile in the 1960s as the founding chairman of *New York Magazine*, and for raising money for a start-up cardiac medical device company called Datascope. Start-ups like *New York Magazine* don't have financials to evaluate, and for entirely new ideas like Datascope (or, for that matter, AOL or FedEx, two of APA's earlier portfolio companies) the market didn't exist yet; the company had to create it.

Nonetheless, as I set out to start my own business, I knew there were exciting, early-stage companies looking for capital to grow, and private investors in 1970 could neither find them nor manage the investments once they were made. I saw a gap in the market and moved in to fill it. Through my Wall Street contacts, I was able to raise an initial $2.5 million fund.

As January 1, 1970, dawned, I stamped my Alan Patricof Associates nameplate to the entrance of One 53rd Street. My landlord was Bill Paley, the former chairman of CBS, and my downstairs neighbor was the Paley Center for Media. In the upstairs space, Frank Thomas, CEO of the Ford Foundation, kept his private office. Outside our window sat the Paley vest pocket park, and on warm days, the smells from Paley's public hot dog stand wafted through our open windows.

Venture capital wasn't much of an industry in 1970. It was more like an activity, its adherents a few scattered firms—most of them on the West Coast—making small investments in innovative start-ups. The National Venture Capital Association (NVCA) formed in 1973, and it was another five years until VCs had their first big fundraiser of a reported $750 million in 1978. In contrast, by the end of 2020, there was more than $548 billion in venture capital assets under management, according to the NVCA.

The environment for start-ups in 1970 was also, correspondingly, a world away from what it became in just a few short decades. Tech-focused small businesses were beginning to cluster around Stanford and UC Berkeley, many of them incubated—formally and informally—by Fairchild Semiconductor. Here on the East Coast, we didn't have anything like that kind of concentration. It was catch-as-catch-can until the early 1980s, but by then, Alan Patricof Associates was established and investing in companies like Apple, AOL, Cellular Communications, Inc., and Tessera Technologies, among many others inside and outside tech.

More moves happened as APA matured and expanded. In the late 1970s, I met Ronald Cohen, who became my partner in the international expansion and eventual rebranding of APA as Apax (which stood for Alan Patricof Associates Cross-Border). In the late 1980s to the early 1990s, the US arm—which had always focused on providing early-stage growth capital—began doing later-stage deals. We financed companies like Sunglass Hut and Life Time Fitness, and Chevys restaurants. Those experiences gave many people on our team a taste for private equity finance. Apax moved permanently out of venture after the dot-com bubble burst.

Moves carry a lot of symbolic weight, but they're also literal. We move on from experiences that have lived out their time, and we take on the next opportunity. I founded Greycroft in 2006, with offices in New York and Los Angeles, after the dot-com dust had settled. I still believed in a core model of providing start-up and growth capital to early-stage companies, and I wanted to realize it with a new company focused exclusively on the venture capital opportunities coming online in the new-millennium digital age. My two founding co-partners, Dana Settle and Ian Sigalow, stood at each of my shoulders as we raised the first Greycroft fund of $75 million from investors I knew trusted my instincts.

Our next major move in New York, to our current building in 2013, came at a moment when Greycroft was seven years old and closing its third fund. The firm had passed through venture infancy into adulthood, our reputation made with investments in companies like *The Huffington Post*, Axios, Venmo, and Buddy Media. Our move into a permanent home conveyed for us, our investors, and our portfolio companies the stability of an institution built to last. Dana and Ian also played larger roles in 2013, when we raised our third fund. In 2018 they would take the lead in management and fundraising, stepping forward as I began to step back.

Our preparations to move again came as Greycroft began its sixteenth year in business. Ian and Dana raised the sixth core fund and the third growth fund, both the largest in their categories. The size of our firm and the size of our latest funds are signs not just of Greycroft's growth, but of a new era of change in the technology start-up environment. Research-dependent companies building AI solutions, virtual reality, gaming systems, new transportation technologies, and any variety of digital platforms have longer development timelines and multiple rounds of funding before they turn a profit, go public, get acquired, or otherwise enable an exit for their investors. Some investments are larger and involve more institutions. We've moved into a new era.

Yet many of the investment and start-up practices I established during my fifty years in venture still guide how we make investments as a firm and how we advise our portfolio companies. We abandoned practices that were no longer relevant or adapted them for changing circumstances. I'm often invited to share my perspectives on start-ups and investing in panel discussions, speeches, or television appearances, and I've had people with vastly different

backgrounds suggest I write them down to share with young entrepreneurs and investors who'd like a cheat sheet for how to build or
invest in high-growth businesses.

This book is my answer to their request.

Fifty years on, I'm still here and casting my vote for the start-up
companies that get me excited and keep me working. In late 2020, at
eighty-six years of age, I started a new venture firm, Primetime Partners, with an initial $50 million fund to invest in entrepreneurial
ideas to do with aging and wellness, and to encourage older entrepreneurs to start again. What could be more exciting than investing
in the fastest-growing segment of the population, the one with the
most money to spend? This is really a white space that's relatively
untouched. I'm excited by this next move, and I'm really going for
it—no red lights. That's the spirit I've brought to every move for
the last fifty years. Here, I share it with you: entrepreneurs, venture
capitalists, business students, the perennially curious, or anyone
who's preparing for their next move.

CHAPTER 2

Sitting Shotgun

I always knew I wanted to go into finance. When I was a teenager, my father worked as a Wall Street stockbroker, and every day on the way home he'd pick up a copy of the *New York World-Telegram* so he could read the end-of-day stock prices. That's how it was done in the days before Bloomberg or the internet. I can still see my father sitting on the sofa, paper open, a cigarette hanging from his mouth with the ash clinging to the burned end until it dropped into his lap. He'd light his next one off the last cinder of the first, the definition of a chain-smoker.

He showed me how to read the stock pages, with the start-and-closing prices for each of the thousands of companies trading on the various exchanges. It fascinated me to see the prices move up and down, day-over-day, often for no reason. My teenaged obsession was so complete I wallpapered my small bedroom with the front pages of corporate annual reports. When I got to college at Ohio State, I adopted finance as my major, convinced that I wanted to work on Wall Street like my father. There were other opportunities, but nothing I considered for long.

Though I did flirt. At that time, few companies made the rounds of colleges to recruit new graduates, and those that did concentrated on the Ivies. None of the Wall Street firms came out to Ohio, but I was invited to interviews at Caterpillar in Peoria, Illinois, and the National Bank of Detroit—they were the few big names in town. Through my own efforts, I also interviewed for a job with USAID in Brazil. The safe choice would have been to go with one of those options, but I couldn't see myself building a life in any of the places I would have had to live.

I'm a New Yorker through and through. My buddies and I treated Central Park like it was our backyard when I was a kid. The noise, the people, the neighborhood feeling on the Upper West Side with the ice trucks and the coal trucks unloading through the chutes to the underground storage, and the man on the street ringing a bell and calling, "I cash clothes!"

I had no idea what that meant then or now, but somebody did, because he was there every single day. We played stickball with broom handles on the street, and stoopball off the edge of the stairs of the brownstones. All that, plus of course Wall Street, represented New York to me. After three years away at college on an accelerated program that allowed me to graduate early, I couldn't wait to get back home.

That's how I found myself in the hot weeks of July 1955 wearing out shoe leather in the buildings of Lower Manhattan looking for a job. I started at 110 Wall Street—the bottom of the block—and went building to building, riding the elevator to the top floor and stopping in each office all the way down to ask the receptionist if there were any job openings. Day after day for about a month, all I heard was "no"—no openings and no interest.

Then one morning in early September I arrived at 63 Wall Street and rode to the thirty-fifth floor, where I knocked on a door with the nameplate Naess & Thomas. I'd never heard of them. Once inside, I learned that Naess & Thomas designed and managed investment portfolios for high-net-worth clients. I didn't know the Wall Street lexicon yet, and none of the investment advisory firms were famous—certainly not at the level of a J.P. Morgan or Lehman Brothers. I had no idea that "Naess" referred to Ragnar Naess, an esteemed Oslo-born economist who'd built his reputation as the head of research at Goldman Sachs. Nor did I realize until much later that Naess & Thomas was a prestigious place with a high-quality client list. All I knew was I was in the right place at the right time, because they happened to be looking for a securities analyst trainee.

That morning I sat for an interview with one of the three partners. Ramsay Wilson was a Yalie with a New England accent and a crisp blue button-down shirt with bright suspenders. He was tall and well-coiffed, the perfect person to deal with clients, while the other partners—the older, academic Ragnar, and the head of research, Dave Rosenberg—focused on the portfolios. I was terrified the three of them would think I didn't have the credentials for the firm. I answered Ramsey's questions and met the other partners with all the confidence I'd learned selling favors to Ohio State fraternities, though part of my brain ran a parallel program measuring the distance between 63 Wall Street and the business schools of Columbia, Penn, or Harvard. The partners could have gone to any of those places to find a trainee for the firm. They didn't, though. They hired me. At that time, it felt like the beginning of something big, and it was.

To UNDERSTAND WHAT A BIG deal it was for me to get a job at a prestigious firm like Naess & Thomas, it helps to know a little bit about where I came from.

Both my parents were immigrants. My father, Martin, came to the US with his five siblings in 1907 as a four-year-old orphan. From Smiela, Ukraine, sixty miles from Kiev and so tiny it wasn't even on the map, they walked to Antwerp, Belgium, pushed west by a wave of pogroms. Once there, they traveled steerage class on the SS Zeeland to Ellis Island. When I hear that story now, I picture the scene in *Fiddler on the Roof* when Tevye and his family are forced to flee their village of Anatevka. Today the more apt image might be of Central American refugees walking through Mexico to the US border. The difference is my father and his siblings were let in.

They continued by train to Middletown, Ohio, where their maternal aunt Jenney and her husband, Max Arnovitz, waited to receive them. The Arnovitzes adopted all six Patricof kids, an event so momentous for sleepy Middletown that the town paper chronicled it with a front-page headline.

Jenney and Max also adopted Jenney's brother's two children, plus another orphan Arnovitz family of four. Adding their own biological children made a total of sixteen people in their house.

My father was lucky to have a place to go, but to call his upbringing "difficult" would be an understatement. Jenney and Max had decency, but few resources. Pennies made the difference between eating that day or going without, and work for my father

SIX LITTLE IMMIGRANTS ARRIVE IN MIDDLETOWN

Notice in the Middletown Ohio Press of six orphans when Martin Patricof, including siblings in 1907, came from Smelia, Russia.

Youthful Orphans From Smelia, Russia Will Make Their Home With Mr. and Mrs. Max Arnovitz

Six little orphans arrived in the city this morning from Smelia, Kieff, Russia, and will make their home with Mr. and Mrs. Max Arnovitz, cor. Clinton and Vail.

The group of children range in ages from four to eleven years, and notwithstanding their long trip of three weeks duration, they looked hale and hearty. The immigrants are the orphan children of the late Joseph and ... Patricoff. The father died in the ... 1906, while the mother passed away Christmas Day, 1905.

The youthful immigrants were accompanied by their uncle and aunt, Mr. and Mrs. Hyman Patricoff and their two children, Jacob and Solomon. The party left Smelia three

The authorities were notified that the would be cared for by Mr. and Mrs. Arnovitz.

As soon as permission was grant... they left New York and ar rived o nthe early C. H. & D. ... from Dayton this morning. At the station they were met by Mr. and Mrs Arnovitz and a few friends. Tears of mutual joy streamed down their cheeks as the immigrants met their ...

Mr. Arnovitz's home and given a hearty welcome. They will reside for the present at his home.

The names and ages of the youthful Russians are as follows: Esther, aged 11 years; Clara, aged 9 years; Jacob, aged 8 years; Rebecca ...

Alan Patricof with Sal and Jenny Arnovitz (Mima) at the 1939 NY World's Fair.

quickly became far more important than school (though he did eventually attend and graduate from college). He did any job he could, from delivering newspapers in the dark of night to helping anyone who needed an extra hand. By the age of fifteen, he'd left Ohio to set out on his own. Only once can I remember a reunion with the Arnovitzes, when they came to New York in 1939 to attend the World's Fair.

For a decade my father chased jobs around the country: he worked on a tramp steamer to Catalina Island off the California coast, picked limes and oranges, and shoveled coal to stoke furnaces. In 1930, during the depths of the Great Depression, he arrived in New York to go in with his brother Jack and a cousin in a "remnants" business. "Remnants"—or *shmatas* in Yiddish vernacular—are scrap pieces of cloth left over after a tailor cuts the main pieces for an item of clothing. My father bought the remnants cheap and resold them to be used for lining or edges or filler. It was a low-level business involving much schlepping of merchandise in burlap bags on the end of a baling hook to the small businesses engaged in manual clothing manufacturing in the old loft buildings of SoHo with cast-iron details over the windows.

Six days a week my father went to his tiny basement shop at 48 Bond Street between Lafayette Street and the Bowery. Saturdays I joined him and carried a bale on my back while we made the rounds to his customers. That neighborhood got an upgrade in the '00s with renovations and new construction converting the old tenements and brownstones, or replacing them altogether with fancy restaurants and stores occupying their ground floors.

He would have had a heart attack if he saw what happened to the neighborhood. The famed Il Buco restaurant now occupies the building right across from my father's old store, which disappeared, along with the building that housed it and the whole remnants business, since no one needed to use scraps anymore once the rations lifted after WWII. My father was long gone by the time the glitterati arrived, having traded the remnants shop for a stockbroker's desk at Gruntal & Co. For a few years in the mid-1960s, he even sat next to Carl Icahn, who ran the options desk for a time.

My father would have died at that desk if Gruntal hadn't taken it from him in the early 1990s. Work was that important to him. My father was in his late eighties by then, and his sales numbers had dropped too low to justify keeping him. I tried at one point to "buy" his desk by guaranteeing a certain dollar amount of commissions for him, but it didn't fly. In his final working days, when he couldn't walk the stairs of the subway anymore, he took the bus from his apartment on 92nd Street to Wall Street, a ninety-minute trip. I eventually forced him to take a car, which I paid for, and which cost more than he earned in a day.

All my father knew was work, not because he wanted to get ahead or improve his social status, but because work for him equaled survival. I share this to make clear the kind of job my father had on Wall Street and the kind of money it earned: namely, low level and not much. There was no upward mobility. He worked "on Wall Street," but that fact wasn't going to help me when my time came to start my career. On the contrary, my father's view was that *I* should help *him*. When my mother gave birth to my sister Marcia, twelve years my junior, my father said he was too old at forty-seven to parent her and told me to do it. I was to chase after her and make her practice the piano; I was to scold her when she misbehaved. When I started working, he asked me to call in the orders for Naess & Thomas to him so he could earn the commission. I declined. I didn't want to start my career like that.

My father didn't understand that. He was tough—tough on me, and tough on the world.

My mother, Dorine, was my father's opposite in approach, personality, and ambition. Her family came to the United States in 1905 from Mogilev, which at that point in history was part of Tsarist Russia (now it's the third largest city in Belarus). My grandfather, Isadore, had been a watchmaker in the Old Country. He settled his family in Waterbury, Connecticut, and subsequently opened a small store in New York on Broadway and 146th Street.

I remember him as a small man with a white starched collar sitting at his workbench with a magnifying glass attached to his glasses. He was formal and a bit cold with my grandmother, Bessie, who was as sweet as could be. For as long as I knew her, she spoke only Yiddish and broken English that she desperately wanted to improve, so she'd ask me to take her to the movies. On weekends there was always a double feature along with the Movietone News with Lowell Thomas and the Pluto cartoons. We sat in the front rows so she could see and hear better and read the actors' lips. A single run took three or four hours. When it was over, she'd ask to stay and see it again!

Taking my grandmother to the movies seems like a wholesome and simple activity, but these were post-WWII years marked by a lot of geopolitical turmoil. Whenever the Movietone News discussed some complex issue, my grandmother would break it down to a simple question: "Is it good for the Jews or bad for the Jews?" She meant it sincerely, but I still ask that question out loud today in all kinds of contexts when conflicting priorities and complex facts are clouding an issue. I do it to add a bit of levity (because it's taken that way now) but also to keep us focused on foundational questions.

My mother's family was not affluent, and my grandfather had very little desire to be—it was enough for him to be in the United States and to have his little shop. But my mother and her siblings wanted more. One of her brothers was a good student, went to law school at City College, and ultimately became a New York State Supreme Court justice. My mother, for her part, finished school and immediately moved to the city to take part in what she viewed as the glamour and excitement of New York. She got a job at Hearns Department Store, where my father saw her through the window one day and thought she was a model.

They married in June 1933. My father always said that he married my mother for her money: he had five dollars and she had ten dollars. In truth, most people were living on the edge during those long years of the Depression. They made it through on my father's work ethic and my mother's ingenuity. She took care of everything to do with the household and their children—me, my sister Jaclyn, and my much younger sister Marcia. Mom was the sweetest person you could imagine, but she cared about superficial appearances, and my father, who was the tough one, reluctantly went along for the ride.

In my earliest memories we lived at 444 Central Park West, at 104th Street, but when I was six years old, we moved downtown twelve blocks to 92nd Street because my mother thought we should. Moving downtown in those days was code for moving up in the world—92nd Street was better than 104th, 86th would have been better still, and 72nd Street would have been nirvana.

Our new building had a name—The Ardsley—which also signaled its superior quality. Located at 320 Central Park West, it had three banks of elevators associated with three tiers of apartments. The front elevator bank served apartments at the front of the building with windows overlooking the Park; the middle bank served apartments facing 92nd Street; and the rear bank served apartments facing the rear courtyard. Our small apartment was at the back, but we had a terrace facing 92nd Street, and if you were willing to risk your life and lean far enough over the railing, you could catch a flash of green from the Park. For that, my mother told people we had a "Park view."

Later, our building became famous for the fact that Barbra Streisand owned a penthouse duplex there and kept it through the early '00s (front bank, of course). Mom liked that. It helped with her ongoing efforts to construct a picture of our family for the outside world. She aimed high and made it look like we were already at the top by shopping for school clothes at Ohrbach's and then cutting out the labels to replace them with Macy's, which was upscale by comparison.

Don't misunderstand—Mom wasn't frivolous with money. I never saw her in a dress that cost more than fifteen dollars, and I vividly remember her doing all the housework herself, on her knees washing the floor to make it shine. But she didn't want us to work like that, and was willing to sacrifice personally to give us opportunities. After we were all grown and gone, she took an administrative job at Chase Manhattan Bank, a secret she kept from us for the rest of her life. I'm pretty sure she and my father needed the money to live.

And me? I am their son, equal parts my father and my mother. My father valued work and encouraged me at the age of six to

15

launch my entrepreneurial career selling *The Saturday Evening Post* outside the 103rd Street, 8th Avenue subway station. When the United States entered WWII, I went door-to-door in our apartment building collecting tin cans and newspapers for the war effort, as well as selling war bonds. I was so good at it I won an award.

But my mother valued education and saw it as a path away from the kind of work she saw as low-end and low-status. As a result of her saving and machinations, I started seventh grade at Horace Mann, one of the most prestigious boys' private schools in the city. Sending me there was a sacrifice, especially with my sister Jaclyn two years behind me attending the private Calhoun School. For six years I boarded the subway each day in my jacket and tie, a habit of dress and schedule that has stayed with me to this day.

LIKE MANY ELITE SCHOOLS, Horace Mann had a strong culture of school pride. Students were taught to expect great things from themselves and from each other, and we did. I still keep in contact with local graduates in my cohort, and a group of us meets about four times a year for lunch in Manhattan. Among them are my friends Richard "Dick" Eisner, who started a now-large New York accounting firm, and Larry Goodman, who started and ran what grew to be a large law firm. I was the first client for both of them, and through multiple mergers and iterations on both sides, my firm was still a client until recently. These kinds of relationships—forged and maintained for years—are an ongoing theme for me in my career and life.

For better or worse, Horace Mann also gave me a certain entitlement about my future prospects. The Ivy League was the ultimate goal for college, but I was rejected from Princeton, my first choice. I'd put all my eggs in that basket and was left, come graduation, with no college to go to. I scrambled, reapplied to a handful of places (which you could do then), and by August, had acceptances in hand from Brandeis, Columbia, Ohio State, and the University of Pennsylvania.

I initially opted for the first. Brandeis was only in its fourth year since its founding by a group of American Jews, who were responding to the discrimination they saw from elite universities. Today, Brandeis University is a top-ranked liberal arts college with a diverse student body, but it was just getting started back then. For me, it was an unenthusiastic choice, and I was feeling uncertain the night I headed alone to the Sherry-Netherland hotel in New York City, where the school was holding a pre-term orientation meeting. Once there, I found myself surrounded by young men and their parents speaking Yiddish, wearing black hats and coats, and sporting long beards. I knew immediately it wasn't for me.

I was raised Jewish, too, but of the reform tradition. Being "Jewish" for me meant going to synagogue on the High Holidays and having holiday dinners. Needless to say, I was very uncomfortable seeing so many Orthodox people around. It gave me the impression that Brandeis—which at the time had only a few hundred students—had a more religious bent than I had bargained for. I panicked, rushed home, and literally slapped an Ohio State address label on my trunk before sending it off on the Railway Express Agency (the forerunner to American Express).

I followed my trunk a few days later feeling hurt, angry, and disappointed. I'd imagined a totally different start to my college life, and it was hard to let go. But during the two-day drive west I managed to convince myself that Ohio was going to be okay. A Big Ten college experience could be fun, and with my academic background, I'd be ahead. By the time I turned onto Ohio State's Fraternity Row in the slightly used 1952 white Oldsmobile convertible my father had bought a few weeks before, I was ready to start the next phase of my life.

Step one was to pledge a fraternity. OSU was top-to-bottom a Greek school, and joining a fraternity was one sure way to peel off from the anonymous crowd of twenty thousand students and join a band of "brothers." Rush Week starts before the semester kicks off: seven days of parties, drinking, gorging, and everything else you can imagine. The fraternities compete for the pledges they want, and I found myself in demand. My connection to Horace Mann came in handy after all, as did my semi-new convertible and the modicum of comfort I had discussing world events and sports— and chatting up girls. I chose Zeta Beta Tau (ZBT), as much for the new, modern frat house and parking space for my car as for the organization itself. It beat living in the dorms.

As I settled in, life at OSU became a cycle of classes and studying, capped by Friday night bonfires, pep rallies with the marching band, and Saturday football games. My parents paid my tuition of a few hundred dollars a year (yes, a few *hundred*), but I was responsible for my living expenses, which I met by juggling multiple jobs. It occurs to me now that I was walking in my father's shoes by trying different kinds of work. I wrote a column for *The Columbus Citizen-Journal*; I did consumer research for the Brown Shoe Company; I worked for Burlington Industries scraping the cylinders from the Dictaphone machine so it could be recorded over again; I delivered telegrams for Western Union.

I even started a small business selling striped "rep" ties and fraternity "favors," like pins and scarves and keychains imprinted with the fraternity logo and given away at parties. I went around to all the fraternities with my samples and called on the social director, who placed the orders. In a school with tens of thousands of people, selling favors made a decent high-volume low-value business, and I became established enough that I was able to sell it to an under-classman for a small sum of money when I graduated.

Those jobs served my needs while I was in Ohio, and they also showed me plenty that I didn't want for my life. Trudging up and down Fraternity Row with my favor samples, beholden to the whims of the fraternity social directors, made me think of my father selling *shmatas*, or later, stocks—something he was adamant I not do. It was better to be on the buying side, my father said, not the selling side.

That mantra was on my mind in the summer of 1955 on the return trip to New York from Ohio with a BS next to my name.

Thanks to my AP credits and a few extra courses, I had managed to graduate in three years, long enough to be away in my view. I was going home, and I couldn't wait to start my life.

I SPENT ABOUT THREE MONTHS going door-to-door in the buildings along Wall Street before I received the offer from Naess & Thomas. I moved back in with my parents and Marcia (Jaclyn was studying at Boston University). I'm probably not the first to say that the post-college return home felt like wearing shoes that had been broken in by someone else. It was a relief to have somewhere to live for free while I was getting my bearings, but the place didn't fit me anymore. I was almost grateful when, a month after I started my new job, my father began charging me rent. It was the gust of wind I needed to blow out and rent my own place with a fellow I knew from Ohio State.

In my day-to-day job at Naess & Thomas, I analyzed the securities of public companies that the partners were considering for a portfolio. Ragnar, the economist and firm founder, spent his time making estimates and predictions about industry trends, and Dave Rosenberg, the head of research, followed up by identifying companies likely to benefit if Ragnar's predications came true.

Once they agreed on companies of interest, I got a list to investigate. At my desk I had a Keuffel & Esser slide rule, a Marchant calculator, and arms-reach access to the most current editions of *Standard & Poor's Guide* and *Moody's*—these were like the Wikipedia of publicly-traded companies in the days when information traveled by post and paper, not bits and bytes. *S&P* and *Moody's* had reams of historical information about every company trading on a US exchange, which at that time represented just over four thousand stocks and bonds and totaled just over $300 billion in market value. To give a sense of scale, Amazon, Apple, and Microsoft are each individually worth around $2 trillion, more than six times the value of all publicly traded firms in 1955.

When I couldn't find the information I needed on a company, I dug into the brokerage reports produced by Argus Research, or by Goldman Sachs and the other sell-side firms who could afford to do their own research and give it away to entice investors.

I also attended the New York Society of Securities Analysts luncheons held on the second floor of Schwartz's Restaurant next to the New York Stock Exchange. Believe me, no one went for the food or the service, delivered by surly waiters who practically threw the dishes at you. Instead, those lunches were the place to hear public company CEOs give presentations disclosing the current quarter results and projecting the likely results for the year. I vividly remember the creak and rustle of movement as members rose from their chairs to slip out and use the bank of pay phones in the lobby to call in a buy or sell order in response to what we heard— all perfectly legal in the years before "forward-looking statements" were forbidden by the SEC (the U.S. Securities and Exchange Commission). I learned a good deal at those meetings, and I met a lot of people, too, some of whom became friends and connections I would later call on—and who would call on me.

On my walk back to the office I would stop outside the New York Stock Exchange and spend a few minutes watching the market ticker count off the current stock prices. I had already started to do some trading on my own—everyone who worked on Wall Street did. Friends I made at those luncheons would tell me about a pending new issue and offer me allocations to buy a certain number of shares at the IPO price—all completely aboveboard and legitimate. Today the same system is in place, except most of the allocations are much larger and earmarked for institutional investors. Getting an allocation for a hot issue in those days was tantamount to instant profit, because almost every issue went from the list price to a premium in the first few minutes of trading. The money I earned in the market at that time helped supplement my salary of just fifty-five dollars a week. I was able to live on the Upper East Side of Manhattan and have more fun than I could have had with my salary alone. I was fortunate as well to avoid any major losses, though I also took pains to avoid too much risk. I didn't have the stomach for it.

I learned that I'm not a gambler the one time I experimented with short-selling a stock. I made the call to my broker one Friday during the summer to short Polaroid and then got on the bus to Long Beach Island, New Jersey, where I had rented a summer cottage. I sweated buckets during the two-hour ride. Since there were no cell phones back then, I was out of touch for that time. When the bus stopped at the rest area in Manahawkin, New Jersey, I rushed to the pay phone, called my broker, and as soon as he picked up yelled, "Cover!"—Street-speak for buying shares to cover an open short. I never forgot that feeling of panic from being out of contact and exposed, and never shorted again.

New fuel was just starting to feed the revving metabolism of Wall Street in those years. New investment banking firms came to be that would later play an important role in the wave of new issues that began in the late '60s and '70s. Among the most famous firms were Carter, Berlind, Weill, & Levitt (CBWL), otherwise known on the Street as Corned Beef with Lettuce; Marron Eden & Schloss; Faulkner, Dawkins & Sullivan; Donaldson, Lufkin & Jenrette (DLJ); and the so-called "four horsemen"—Alex Brown, Hambrecht & Quist, Robertson Stephens, and Montgomery Securities.

The leaders at the helms of these companies would rise to become the top financiers in New York City and Silicon Valley, among them: Sandy Weill, CEO of Citigroup; Arthur Carter, Publisher of *The New York Observer* and today a successful sculptor; Roger Berlind, a Broadway producer; Arthur Levitt, famed Chairman of the SEC; Don Marron, the former CEO of Mitchell Hutchins and Chairman of The Museum of Modern Art; Bill Hambrecht, one of the best known financial executives in tech; Bill Donaldson, who served as Chairman of the SEC and as Dean of The Yale School of Management; Dan Lufkin, Environmental Commissioner of the State of Connecticut; and Dick Jenrette, CEO of Equitable Life Insurance Co.

These people and their firms were poised to leap on the opportunities that would emerge. I was there working with them, learning from them, and bringing them promising companies when I came across one. They all became longtime friends.

Ragnar Naess was my primary mentor at that time. He was an advocate of "value investing," the approach described by Columbia University professors Benjamin Graham and David Dodd in their famous book, *Security Analysis*. Warren Buffett and Charlie Munger at Berkshire Hathaway are probably the most famous (not to mention successful) value investors on the planet. Naess & Thomas mostly bought stocks of established companies in traditional industries that for some reason or another were undervalued compared to what Ragnar saw as their potential. Diversification was a major priority for the portfolios, and applied to types of assets, as well as to industry exposure. Ragnar regularly said that he loved a particular company, and when the stock price went down 50 percent, he loved it twice as much.

Among the companies I was asked to analyze at that time were Rohm and Haas, a chemical company founded in Germany in 1909 and now owned by DuPont, and Premier Industrial Corporation, an electronics and vehicle parts dealer. But the one that really sticks in my mind was a little company in Rochester, New York, called Haloid Corporation, which had developed a process known as thermography to let office workers make a copy of an image or a sheet of writing. Back then we all used carbons to create duplicates, but Haloid quickly brought about the end of that with their "Thermofax Copies." Later, the company branded its product "Xerox" and renamed the company Haloid-Xerox and then just Xerox. I like to believe that I experienced a tingle of premonition when I did the analysis that resulted in us purchasing stock in this early technological pioneer. Haloid was the first firm I ever saw dabbling in unexplored territory.

Between the lessons I learned from Ragnar and David and from the lunch meetings I attended, you would think my head would have had its fill of new information, and it did. But I still jumped at the chance to get my master's degree when—through Ragnar's urging and with his support—I applied to and was admitted to Columbia Business School. Ragnar and the other partners let me restructure my schedule to leave early to attend afternoon classes. I graduated in the spring of 1957. Columbia (where today I sit on the Board of Overseers) played a critical role in solidifying my understanding of Graham and Dodd and their ideas. I learned to appreciate the value of "net-free cash flow," to understand the burden debt can put on a young company, and how to evaluate earnings and dividends as determinants of business value.

In today's world, valuations are determined primarily based on multiples of revenues, with less consideration given to immediate profits. There is a definite trend towards extrapolating growth rates and making assumptions about how fast and for how long a company will grow. This pattern is apparent in the valuations given to companies like Zoom and Peloton, which will require fifty years of earnings to justify current prices. Valuations were less grounded in wishful thinking when I was coming up, and I learned to calculate them based on the core practice taught at Columbia.

Grad school also introduced me to my first wife, Bette, who I met on campus when she was a graduate student at The Columbia University School of Dramatic Arts. We married in February of 1958 and went to London for our honeymoon, where we strolled the sites and joked each night in our too-cold second-floor room in the Cavendish about the hotel's rumored side door that Edward VII reportedly used to visit his mistress—the prior owner—for a rendezvous. The room was unheated, requiring a hot water bottle to warm the bed.

The marriage lasted seven years before Bette and I mutually decided that the relationship was not working. Like many young couples, we didn't know each other very well when we decided to get married, and we quickly found that we were incompatible. Every day of our marriage brought a new argument, each less important than the last. When we started fighting in front of our eighteen-month-old son, it became clear that continuing the marriage wouldn't benefit any of us, and we decided that I would leave.

Despite our conflicts, Bette was very supportive of my early career, as I was supportive of hers (she was part of the team at the Met that set up the department responsible for making reproductions of famous works, now a major source of revenue for the museum). We also had a wonderful son, Mark, who we continued to raise together after our marriage ended in 1966.

NAESS & THOMAS GAVE ME a prestigious start in the investment business, and it also gave me the tools to understand industry trends and to evaluate the potential value of a company. But after two years I started to feel like I was making only right turns, covering the same ground in varying intervals. The process used to analyze a public company doesn't change much from firm to firm, and I had learned all I could from doing it.

I was ready for a new challenge.

I was also wary of the fact that there was an active draft in place. I was fit and healthy and in the right age bracket, and I knew if I got called up it would mean two years of active duty. To avoid it, I could *volunteer* for six months of active duty, and then eight years in the reserves, which involved weekly meetings and two weeks every summer of active duty at Fort Drum in Watertown, NY—all this to legitimately get out of two full years of active-duty service. I took that route and joined the US Army in the 411th Quartermaster Corps based in Fort Dix, New Jersey, Company N, Third Training Regimen. Ultimately the joke was on me, but not until later.

Basic training was exactly as it's depicted in every military movie ever made. I crawled through mud and scrambled over fences. The friendships I made were also as strong as you see in those buddy films. I occasionally got an overnight pass to leave the base, handed out at 7:00 p.m. with no advance warning. On those rare occasions, I scrambled to catch the bus into the city to see my wife for a few hours before scrambling back to base again in time for reveille the next morning.

I was discharged in September, and shortly after returning to the city, I got a call from a headhunter who suggested I'd find it worthwhile to meet with an innovative "development finance" firm—a term I had never heard. Curious, I went one morning to 2 Wall Street, the Morgan Stanley headquarters building in those days, to meet and eventually accept a position from Jean Lambert, of Lambert & Co.

Jean Lambert was in his late thirties or early forties at the time, debonair and well-dressed in that distinctly European way that shows up in the cut of the suit or the pattern and color of his tie—all of it more vivid than is typical in a Wall Street banker. Jean spoke English with a strong French accent that got thicker when he talked about building companies and trying out new ideas. That he got his money from a divorce settlement from his wife, Phyllis Bronfman—an architect and one of the sibling inheritors of the Seagram's fortune—added to his celebrity. But even without that cachet, Jean was charismatic and on the move. He'd already established offices in London and Paris, and when I met him, he was building his office on Wall Street in New York.

And what an office! Jean had fashioned it to resemble his vision of the most successful firms of the time—Morgan Stanley, Lazard, and Milbank Tweed—with heavy green carpet, wide corridors, mahogany rolltop desks, and antique chairs made of walnut with green leather seats. The employees had their desks in a wide hall framed by a line of doors to the outer offices, which were always kept closed. Most of those offices were empty, but visitors didn't know that. The combined effect of all that bustle in the hallway and the line of closed doors gave the appearance of a firm at the height of demand. Coupled with the rich furnishings, Lambert & Co. *looked* like money. Its aura stated it was a place that had been and would be there for years.

Jean reinforced that image by signing with the best service providers. He used Sullivan & Cromwell as his lawyers, Price Waterhouse as his accountants, and wrote his checks off a JP Morgan account. There was morning coffee and afternoon tea service brought to each employee by a tuxedoed butler and a maid named Winnie, who wore a black dress with a white apron and gloves. We also had lunch served in the wood-paneled dining room, prepared by the kindly full-time chef and served by Winnie on porcelain china with sterling silver platters and cutlery. I often invited friends to join me, as there weren't enough of us in the office to use all the table settings. Guests were the point, anyway—the place was there to show off. We felt like kids playing on a stage set.

The team at Lambert & Co. consisted of Jean and his three boring senior partners, all of whom had come from name-brand firms, including Price Waterhouse, Sullivan & Cromwell, and The Bank of Montreal. There were two other mid-level employees, and I was the lone junior researcher.

Whereas Naess & Thomas was about investing in established, solid companies, Lambert & Co. was about creation—the ideal outlet for Jean's innovative sensibility. In the short time I worked there, Lambert & Co. established an oil company, a finance company called Atlantic Acceptance, and a Canadian real estate company called Royal York Development. We also spent months trying to win a deal with the government of Portugal to finance a bridge across the Tagus river. Jean had conceived of the idea of using Portugal's gold reserves as collateral to raise funds, since the country's economy was weak. I traveled to Lisbon with the annual reports and financial statements of the leading central banks in the world stashed in my suitcase, so I could compare their gold reserves with Portugal's. However, nothing ever came of it.

Something did come, however, of work I did with a small telecommunications company serving auto parts manufacturers in Hancock, Michigan. This company landed on my desk because no one else was interested. With the exception of Jean, the employees at Lambert were a flat lot. Jean was the brains, the heartbeat, and the soul of Lambert & Co. When he was around, life breathed through the place, and when he wasn't…well, let's just say he wasn't around much, as he spent long stretches of time in Europe. By some trick of luck, I got to look into Hancock Telecontrols, which was working on solutions to automate the flow of goods through a manufacturing plant, monitor work-in-process, and improve employee productivity. I'm not sure that I fully understood the potential of Xerox when I had first seen it years before, but with Hancock, I had no doubt I was looking at a technology innovation poised to explode. Lambert did some work with the company and Hancock Telecontrols did okay, though they were probably too early to market. As it happened, it would be another two decades before industrial "automation" was widely embraced.

As much satisfaction as I had with Hancock and Portugal, there wasn't enough of that going on at Lambert & Co. to keep me busy, and no real mentorship with Jean coming and going as much as he did. I ended up staying for around two years, until 1960, when my friend Bob Menschel, a partner at Goldman Sachs and a regular guest at my fancy Lambert lunches, told me about a position with Central National Corporation, the investing vehicle for the Gottesman family. I took the job and left Lambert for what would become the next major phase of my investing career.

There's an odd coda to the Lambert story. Lambert & Co. actually blew up several years after I left when a fraud at Atlantic Acceptance pushed that firm under and Lambert, overexposed, went with it. I hardly thought of Jean Lambert and my time with his company until one day in the early 1970s, when he called and asked me to meet him at his suite at the Plaza Hotel. I went and found him much changed from the sophisticated and debonair man who had been my boss. During our short reunion, he asked me for a loan of $100,000, which he said he would secure with some of his new wife's jewelry. I was in no position to make such a loan and declined with as much gentleness as is possible while being direct. I walked away from the Plaza sad and disturbed, and swearing I would never let that happen to me.

Rules of the Road: Lessons from My Early Career

My departure from Lambert & Co. marked a turning point in my early career. From the time I started as a kid at Horace Mann to the time I left Lambert & Co—from roughly 1946 to 1960—I was a student. Literally so during high school, college, and graduate school, and effectively also in my jobs as a researcher. I was learning the foundations of finance and building a career. Looking back, there are three core themes that emerge for me.

The first is that life is cumulative. By 1960, when I left Lambert & Co. to take the position at Central National Corporation, I was the product of two parents, of Horace Mann, Ohio State, and Columbia University, of Naess & Thomas, of the US Army, and of Lambert & Co. All of these experiences gave me information and context, and thereby revealed pathways for my future. I don't know what would have happened to me without them, but I do know that everything I learned in those years prepared me for the higher-profile and higher-responsibility environment I stepped into upon leaving Lambert. It added up. Take one of them away and I don't know if I would have been ready for what came to me or able to make what I did of it. I feel that way about all the experiences in my life and what they allowed me to see and embrace later.

Once I started working after college, I needed five years to move through the first learning phase of my career. Some people take longer. Others far less. There is no universal formula that applies for everyone, but if I was forced to take a position, I would say that it is worthwhile to spend some amount of time working for someone else to see the mistakes they make and what they do right. It never hurts to learn on someone else's nickel.

I recognize that is an unpopular position today. Whenever I am invited to give a talk at a business school, I ask members of the audience to raise their hand if they plan to start their own business directly after graduation. My caution for those pursuing that path is that unless you have prior experience in a particular area, or passion for an idea, you are better off working as someone's employee for a period. This is particularly true if you can work under a strong mentor. Doing so gives you the substance and exposure that increases your chances of success should you choose later to launch your own company.

For how long should you do this, though? The answer is you stay as long as necessary to learn all you can from the environment. You'll know that you've reached full saturation when all the scenery starts to look the same. In the meantime, and if you have the luxury, try to be selective and choose high-quality organizations from which you can learn and where there are good people with knowledge and a willingness to mentor. Stay only as long as you're still learning.

Another theme is don't drive alone. I can't stress enough how important people are to the trajectory of a career—and of a life. Friends I made at Horace Mann and at those Wall Street lunches stayed close to me for decades, and some of them became business contacts and friends I still have today. We helped each other. I wouldn't be where I am without them, and I believe the feeling is mutual.

Importantly, I didn't make these friends by keeping to myself and eating lunch at my desk. I got out there, attended events, and met people for breakfast, lunch, or coffee. This is particularly important early in a career. The people in your graduate school study group or who start working at around the same time you do will experience some of the same life and career milestones as you will, good and bad. You'll appreciate having them around to cheer you on or help wipe your tears. These people may be the future heads of banks, start-ups, unicorns, innovative nonprofits…you name it. Their careers will grow with yours. Nurture those relationships. Introduce them to others you know who can help them. Let them introduce you, too. Do it because you care about them, and because you want to see them grow and succeed.

Nor should you stop being open to new people in your mid-career phase. To this day when I attend a conference, I make it a point *not* to sit surrounded by people from my firm. Instead, I sit with an anonymous group and introduce myself to the person to my left and to my right and across the table. I don't do this with any ulterior motives. For example, I don't angle to sit with someone who looks "important," whatever that means. This is magic, not science, and I've met hundreds of people this way. With some of them I simply pass a pleasant meal, and with others, I end up making a new best friend. You never know, but I always hope for the friend. What I'm *not* doing is simply adding to my contact list or LinkedIn connections.

Don't limit yourself to people in your industry, either. I know many people in the finance arena, but I have also learned as much and enjoyed the connections with the people I have met in the art world, education and film, journalism and healthcare, and engineering and politics. Start early to expand your horizons, and build relationships with people in a range of fields.

Here, too, everything is cumulative, and it does comes back to you. It's a rare event I attend today when I don't have someone approach me and say, "You don't remember me, but…" and then share a conversation we had, a letter I wrote, or a speech I gave that helped them in some way. While it's true that I don't always remember every person who approaches me in this way, the fact that so many remembered *me* as someone who treated them with respect means a lot. Just last week—in late summer, 2021—I was at a cannabis convention, where two entrepreneurs and a former venture capitalist separately approached me to share a "You don't remember me, but…" anecdote about how I had helped them in the past. Neither of the entrepreneurs had received funding from my firm, but the money wasn't the issue.

They remembered that I had commented thoughtfully and that I gave them reasons for the rejection. The way you treat people defines your reputation. Whether it's a formal meeting or a brief handshake at a conference, I make it a point to treat all of the many people I meet over the years with the same attention I would like to receive. It's about creating an image and a reputation through your behavior that you can leave behind. I always feel a burst of pride when people approach me to share that I had some small impact on their lives, and I think they're genuine when they say it made a difference for them.

Yet another theme is to understand and apply the fundamentals of whatever business you're in. I learned that many times from Ragnar Naess, and I learned it again through the negative example of Jean Lambert and his fall with the crash of Atlantic Acceptance.

Net-free cash flow is one of the most important fundamentals I learned as it applied to finance and business growth in the context of the public companies on which I focused in my early career. Put another way, no company can rely on investor capital forever. Eventually a company needs to make money selling its products and serving its clients. That day should come sooner rather than later, for if it takes too long, the investors will conclude the company is an emperor with no clothes.

I realize that point may seem retrograde in today's market, given the way commentators like to cite Amazon, Tesla, Uber, and others as evidence that traditional metrics like net-free cash flow are dead. I also acknowledge that the metrics I use now to evaluate an early-stage company are different from the ones that I originally applied to established, public companies. But the idea that a business exists to serve a market, and that its growth potential is connected to demand for its product, coupled with effective operations and management, has always framed how I approach investing.

I find it difficult to maintain limitless faith in a company that churns through multiple rounds of capital without making progress toward defined milestones. I don't assume it will eventually emerge to become the next Amazon, and am more likely to assume such a firm will instead go the way of Webvan, Kozmo, or the many disk drive companies that received multiple rounds of funding during the dot-com boom before investors decided "the dogs were not eating the dog food."

Kozmo in fact offers an illustrative example—as well as an illustration of how I believe an investor should get hands-on when conducting due diligence. Back in the summer of 1998—long after I learned the fundamentals of the investing business from Ragnar Naess—I got a call from the private placement department of Goldman Sachs asking to set up a meeting about Kozmo.com, a "hot" new online delivery company that would bring customers a rented movie (pre-Netflix and streaming) and dinner from a range of locales—think Uber Eats plus VHS tapes for the '90s. Two young investment bankers had started the company in New York City in March 1998, and by the next year, Joseph Park and Yong Kang had established Kozmo enough to bring in $3.5 million in revenues, though they ended the year with a net loss of around $25 million, while eating through $280 million in venture funds. When I met them in 1998, it was early in the process, when Kozmo was only raising their second round.

I met the Kozmo principals and their Goldman Sachs representatives in the Apax Partners conference room. They explained how their system worked, and I said I wanted to test it out for myself. That night I used a POT (plain old telephone—you could still reach a live service person in those days) to call in my order for two videos, *A Raisin in the Sun* and *The Third Man*. Rental costs for each were $3.95 for delivery, overnight viewing, and subsequent pickup at my apartment building.

About an hour after I called in the order, the doorman rang our bell and gave me a package with the Kozmo branding on it. But instead of *Third Man* and *Raisin*, however, the package contained two candy bars and a copy each of *Meet Me in St. Louis* and Alfred Hitchcock's *Rope*—not exactly what I had planned. I politely called Kozmo, and they apologized and said they would send over the correct tapes. I waited another hour, which the deliveryman spent retrieving mine from the person on 86th Street to whom they'd been mistakenly delivered, and to whom he had to return once he received their films from me.

After I was settled at home with my movies, I began to think about the costs of the transaction: a delivery person had to bike from the Kozmo central office to my house twice, and then twice to the other customer's house. He or someone else would then come back to pick up the movies the next day. When I calculated the time involved in six delivery trips plus all the central handling, I concluded that Kozmo at its core was just a very low-margin logistics business with a lot of perils. The coup de grace occurred when I asked the doorman of my building what the delivery person looked like—Did he come on a special branded bike or scooter? Did he have a uniform? My doorman said, "He looked like all the other guys in old clothes delivering takeout on their twenty-five-year-old bikes."

Apax decided not to invest $5 million in a takeout delivery service. Kozmo eventually expanded to eighteen cities and made a deal with Starbucks to promote the service in its stores and serve as a collection point. Someone believed Kozmo would turn a profit, because the company raised $280 million in equity and filed to go public in 2000, but they aborted that plan when the internet "bubble" burst. In 2001, Kozmo filed for bankruptcy. The economics of the delivery business couldn't return the value it needed to justify all the money it raised. In that case and many others, a focus on the fundamentals coupled with hands-on due diligence saved me.

These themes, and others I accumulated, were like a roadmap for me when I walked through the doors to take my next job, at Central National Corporation, where I started to explore and make my own financial deals. But on the way I had already developed a taste for diversions beyond the business world.

POSTSCRIPT
Joyrides and Side Trips in Theater, Music, and Film

Not long after I returned to New York after college, I spent a great evening listening to Julie Andrews sing at the piano at a dinner party—she was in New York starring in *The Boy Friend* and happened to show up at a party hosted by the composer Leonard Bernstein, who I knew through friends of my parents. I serendipitously met a lot of people involved in the performing arts in those days. In 1958 I decided to make one of my first theatrical investments.

It was shortly after I was discharged from the Army, and I thought, before going back to Wall Street, I would try my hand at something new. I had always been a fan of folk singing and was a devotee of clubs like the Gaslight and Café Wha? on MacDougal Street in New York's Greenwich Village, where Bob Dylan got his start and I heard him play. Another leading folk singer named Oscar Brand also gave a performance at one of these venues, and I called him afterward to see if I could produce a concert for him. He agreed, and asked to include Jean Ritchie, another folk purist, on the program.

My mistake was not going to straight to Joan Baez or Bob Dylan, but Brand was willing to let a twenty-four-year-old kid try his hand at being an impresario. I booked a midtown Manhattan performing arts space called Town Hall for the event, hired a publicist, contracted with the performers, and printed posters to display around town advertising the February concert. All the plans were coming together...until fate played its hand and the International Typographical Union called a newspaper strike. For more than three months before the concert, there was a total print advertising blackout. Try as I did to use radio and promotions, I filled only half the house, lost money, and decided I needed a more stable income.

My interest in music never waned, though it transcended. After abandoning my efforts to get into the business of music, I became an unapologetic groupie. I'd attend concerts wherever and whenever I could. Given my passion, I absolutely intended to be at the Woodstock festival in 1969, but our car broke down on the New York State Thruway in a blinding rainstorm. While Joe Cocker was giving his rousing rendition of *With a Little Help from My Friends*, I was sitting on the bucket seat of a tow truck with my second wife, Susan, as it dragged our car back to the city.

Program for Town Hall Concert, Friday, December 12th. Produced by Alan Patricof.

Since then I've attended the Newport Jazz Festival, the New Orleans Jazz & Heritage Festival, and dozens of concerts at Jones Beach Theatre and Madison Square Garden. More than once I got to stand backstage with my close friend and neighbor Ron Delsener, the king of rock promoters. I've been most loyal to the Stephen Talkhouse in Amagansett, Long Island, near my summer home, where I'd go religiously—Ron as my wingman—to see some known and many unknown bands.

Once in a while, a surprise performer would step onto the stage: I've seen Paul McCartney, Jimmy Buffett, and Bon Jovi perform live just because I had the good fortune to be there on the right night. I even had President Clinton and Hillary with me the night Jimmy appeared—that gave me a bit of cachet. The lines to get into the Talkhouse often stretch to 100 people (it was 200 on the night when Mumford & Sons played), but I've been going so long

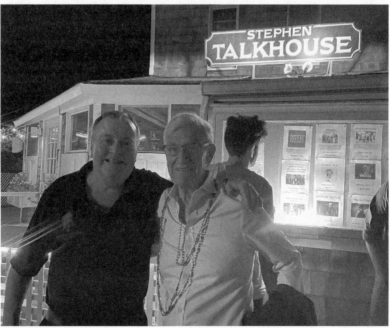

Outside of the Stephen Talkhouse with owner Peter Honerkamp and Alan Patricof in 2021.

that Peter Honerkamp, the owner, and his manager Nick part the waters for me.

This gets me a lot of brownie points with my grandchildren when they and their 10 friends cut the line with their grandfather in front of 200 of their peers. I think Peter and Nick like that someone my age would go there and then stand at the bar listening to a set and occasionally even dancing when the rhythm of the bands catches me. My presence helps to drive up the average age at the venue. Even now, you can often find me at the Talkhouse, glass of beer or ginger ale in hand, participating fully in the excitement of the evening. (I don't get on stage for Wednesday's Karaoke night, though!)

You would have thought after Oscar Brand, I'd just stick to enjoying the performing arts as an audience member, yet I jumped into the financial side again in 1960 when I met a twenty-year-old Peter Bogdanovich. He was a self-confident, arrogant guy even then. I was impressed and agreed to organize a backers' audition and reading of the Clifford Odets play *The Big Knife*, which Bogdanovich wanted to direct off-Broadway. My wife and I hosted the event in our brownstone, basement-garden duplex apartment. The event raised $15,000.

I jumped even higher in 1966 after I met Bobb Goldsteinn, a musician and songwriter who'd collaborated as a sketch writer with Woody Allen. Bobb was experimenting with a new audiovisual melding of music played to complement projected colors, photo slides, self-made video clips, and scenes from movies he flashed across the walls. Glittering lights rotated through the images, reflected off the mirrored balls he'd installed on the ceiling (I believe it was the first installation in North America of a disco ball). Bobb put on a performance of this new style at a Greenwich Village Christmas party I attended. Advertised as "Bobb Goldsteinn's LightWorks," it was a hit, the subject of multiple magazine profiles in the *New York Herald Tribune*, *The Saturday Evening Post*, and in an article by Albert Goldman in *New York Magazine* itself.

Bobb coined the term "multimedia" to describe his innovation, and it became all the rage. Henri Bendel commissioned Bobb to design a multimedia storefront and Helena Rubinstein asked him to create a commercial. I, too, was captivated, and agreed with two other Wall Street friends to raise money for Bobb and a theatrical artist, Josh White, to create a multimedia nightclub in Southampton, Long Island. (Josh went on to design light shows for major music acts like the Grateful Dead, Jefferson Airplane, Janis Joplin, Jimi Hendrix, The Doors, and others. He's still performing today.)

We found a sailing ship repair facility in Southampton that the owner, a guy named Maurice Uchitel, had renovated into a restaurant that failed. (Maurice also owned a successful restaurant called El Morocco in the city.) We convinced him to take a chance on a new idea—a summer season nightclub/restaurant. Jim McMullen, the owner and chef of a hip bar and restaurant on 3rd Avenue, agreed to join us and run the bar/kitchen.

L'Oursin, the sea urchin, opened for the summer seasons of 1966 and '67. Bobb Goldsteinn's LightWorks at L'Oursin would seem crude today given the advent of virtual reality, but back then it was an innovation, with images flashing across screens in all four corners of the room as people danced under the strobe lights. For two summers it was *the* place to be on Friday and Saturday nights from Memorial Day through Labor Day.

Did we have a great time! We were in the columns every week on account of our clientele, which included fashion designers, from Paco Rabanne and Giorgio di Sant'Angelo to Daniel Hechter, as well as the models that served as their muses. Regulars also included creative talent like Jean Shrimpton and leading Wall Street moguls, all filling the dance floor—if they could get in.

The gossip columnists of the day chronicled each weekend's events. Writers like Albert Goldman, Enid Haupt, Aileen Mehle (aka Suzy Knickerbocker), Walter Winchell, and Igor Cassini (brother to the fashion designer Oleg Cassini, and writing under the inherited pseudonym of Cholly Knickerbocker) all wrote about it. Even Daphne

Davis and Chauncey Howell of *Women's Wear Daily* (*WWD*), the bible of the jet set at the time, penned articles about L'Oursin.

I was there every weekend. Friday afternoons, I'd leave work and drive to Southampton, stopping at a gas station halfway to enter the men's room as Clark Kent in my grey flannel suit and emerge as Superman in my L'Oursin costume of bell bottoms, four button Mao jacket, and open shirt down to my mid-section.

Sadly, we couldn't find a way to make money. People only showed up en masse for a few hours every Friday and Saturday night. If you stopped by at eight or nine o'clock, the place would look empty, but by ten o'clock, you couldn't get in, and by two in the morning, it was empty again. We couldn't earn back the cost of running the restaurant and the show with such limited proceeds, and after the last weekend of the season in 1967, we closed down for good. Others tried in that location after us, and for a time there was a very popular disco called Conscience Point, but for me, L'Oursin topped it. Still, I ended the summer of 1967 on a high note, as I also successfully courted my wife Susan at that time.

Thrice bitten in the performing arts yet still not shy, I kept investing in the theater. I was a small investor in productions of Neil Simon's *Barefoot in the Park* and *Promises, Promises*. I also backed *Children of a Lesser God*. I flew down to Washington, D.C., to see a young James Earl Jones in *The Great White Hope* after reading a review in *The New York Times* of its dramatic opening night at the Arena Stage.

I was as thrilled as the reviewer, and participated in the financing as the troupe prepared the play for Broadway. I also backed *Ain't Misbehavin'* with André De Shields and Nell Carter when it opened in 1969 at the newly formed Manhattan Theater Club in the Old Bohemian Hall off-off-Broadway on West 74th Street. That show was a *big* success. It established a club *and* it launched at least two long careers. De Shields won the 2019 Tony Award for *Hadestown*, the same year that the Manhattan Theater Club celebrated its fifty-year anniversary.

There were also countless plays I backed that today remain unknown, like *Devour the Snow* (which I called *Devour the Investors*) and *Cry for Us All* (*Cry for the Investors*). By the early '00s, I was probably modestly ahead in my investments in the theatre industry when my friend Roy Furman asked me to partner with him on a new company to finance Broadway productions, since we were both phasing out of our first careers.

I was in the process of unwinding myself from Apax Partners and Roy was leaving his firm, Furman Selz. I was intrigued by the idea. Roy had been a well-known banker and was already making his name as a producer. We thought we could have a good time and forge a strong partnership, but when I went to see *Adult Entertainment*, the first show he was backing, I got cold feet. Despite the star power of Elaine May as the lead, I didn't think I wanted to be associated with a play about porn actors.

Over the years I've continued to support Broadway shows, including a number of Roy's productions. Right after I passed on *Adult Entertainment*, I made a small investment in *Tommy Tune* (which didn't do well), and subsequently *The Addams Family*. I would have done great just following Roy blindly, since he's had at least two major hits in recent years with *Book of Mormon* and *Dear Evan Hansen*. Sadly, I'm not an investor in either.

Separately from Roy, I invested in *On the Town* and *Tootsie*. My balance sheet record has turned positive due to a small investment in *Hamilton*, an opportunity that came to me after I saw Lin-Manuel Miranda sing and play on the piano some early snippets of his rap-musical at Roy's seventieth birthday party (Roy's daughter, Jill, is the producer). The original show became five subsequent spinoff companies playing around the US and the world. Every month I receive an envelope containing five checks with my share of the proceeds for each company.

In 2020, for the first time in several years, there was no envelope, given the COVID-darkened theaters on New York's Broadway, London's West End, and beyond. In 2021, *Hamilton* came back, launching the reopening of Broadway. Also returning to Broadway and a US tour is *Freestyle Love Supreme*, another Jill Furman–produced Miranda production that had a limited run in 2019 and was an instant success. (I followed Jill's lead and invested in that show for its 2019 run, and again in 2021.)

There had been a time when I imagined Broadway marquees might say "Alan Patricof Presents…" but my destiny was clearly elsewhere. Still, it's been fun, and I remain an avid and enthusiastic theatergoer, even if my returns come mostly in the form of positive experiences. One lesson I've learned from it all is that one should only invest in Broadway productions if you don't mind losing money and you like going to opening nights.

CHAPTER 3

Taking the Wheel

The first weeks and months in my new job at Central National Corporation (CNC) had the feel of a new romance. Everything was exciting and fresh, and my brain was on overdrive. I knew from experience that it could take half a year or more before the days settled into a routine. I'd barely reached that point at CNC when my Army reserve unit was called up for active duty. The plan I put into motion years before of serving six months active duty followed by eight years in the reserves to avoid two years of active service backfired when tensions rose again in Europe and the Berlin Wall went up between the East and West regions of the city. In response, President Kennedy activated 156,000 reservists, including my unit, the 411 Quartermaster Corps.

No president had called in the reserves since WWII. It was a huge deal and completely disruptive to the people involved. In thirty days, we were to report at Fort Lee, Virginia—just a month to give notice to our bosses and landlords, put our furniture in storage, and turn off the phone and utilities. I think of it every time I hear of servicemen and women being deployed today. I was anxious about my job, but Arthur Ross, my boss, assured me I'd have my position waiting for me and volunteered to pay my salary while I served—an act of generosity I never forgot.

Alan Patricof in 1961 driving a Jeep in Fort Lee, Virginia.

During this tangent, a pair of high-drama events took place that had nothing to do with the work of military service but taught me some lessons about the world and how I wanted to operate within it. The first drama began the day my unit arrived in Fort Lee. I'd been expecting to see the twenty-five or so men with whom I'd suffered countless Monday night reserve meetings for the past two years, as well as the annual two weeks of service we did during the summer at our Camp Drum training sessions in the Adirondacks.

We thought we were hard core, struggling to stay awake through the boring lectures and training films. Misery had made us close. It gave me a jolt when I joined my group in Fort Lee and saw that our numbers had ballooned to about a hundred—most of whom had never graced a single Monday night meeting or Camp Drum training session. Those of us who knew each other clustered together and asked where these guys had been for the last two years.

Eventually we got the story: the strangers in our midst had been making "gifts" to the chief warrant officer of the 411th. The officer was a short, portly guy with thick glasses who spent part of every Monday night meeting trying to get us to read his short stories. The absent reservists were rumored to have paid the warrant officer or the first sergeant between three hundred dollars and five hundred dollars to be checked in as present at the weekly meetings and the annual retreat at Camp Drum.

Over time it came out that the influence went even deeper: to get into the reserve program, we had to apply and hope we got accepted, since there were more applicants than spaces. Some people improved their chances by asking their congressman or some other power figure to recommend them to the draft board. When our unit was activated, the reservists who had friends in high places complained to their congressman. Only some of them were paying the warrant officer, but the complaints called attention to the 411th and the broader corruption within it. There was an FBI investigation.

That was all I knew of the event until forty years later when I ran into the short-story-writing warrant officer at a dinner party. His name was Mario Puzo, famous by then as the author of *The Godfather*. I asked him what ultimately happened with the investigation, and he told me the sergeant went to jail, but that he—Mario—had been released for "lack of evidence." We both knew that the two of them had organized the scheme together, but I didn't push it.

Later, after Mario's death, I was talking about the episode with my friend Mort Janklow—founder of a New York literary agency. Mort suggested I call Mario's widow, which I did. She told me Mario had used the episode of the payment to the warrant officer in the novel *Fools Die*. She even gave me the page number on which it appears. So in the end he didn't keep his involvement a secret. Life, I guess, *is* strange enough for fiction.

The responsibility of the 411th was to run the petroleum depots. For the previous two years, our Monday night meetings had taken place in one of dozens of nondescript industrial buildings owned by the government on 42nd Street between 10th and 11th Avenues. There we watched videos or listened to lectures about laying pipe.

At no point during our time in the reserves did any of us touch the materials needed to operate a pipeline.

In my case, I never remedied that deficit. Each of us got a job once we arrived in Fort Lee, and some members of my unit ultimately got to build an honest-to-god pipeline to ship fuel inland. I was given a classroom job teaching soldiers how to drive a two-and-a-half-ton transport truck. It was an odd assignment given that I had never driven one myself and wouldn't have known how but for the movies I was given to show my students. The one time I was given a truck to drive, I was petrified—the thing was huge, and I had no better idea how to control it than anyone in my class. There's definitely something to be said for learning by doing.

Nine, ten months passed like that, my days spent showing videos and my evenings killing time. Six months into my service a second drama occurred. The company commander (or CO) at Fort Lee was a tall and surly captain named Benjamin Ricketts, who went out of his way to make life difficult for a few of the members of our unit. During basic training at Fort Dix, it was Captain Ricketts's innovation to issue passes late in the day—often too late to get home and back in time for reveille.

At Fort Lee he had more opportunities for torment. In one instance, he ordered a group of his victims to go on a fifteen-mile walk in full fatigues and backpacks on a day so hot it was swamp-like. In another, he assigned a group to clean the grease trap for the base's kitchen from the *inside* of the trap. Why certain people were singled out was never clear to me. I wasn't one of them. I did know that the company commander was violating rules to punish people for no good reason I could see.

I was reminded powerfully of the film *The Caine Mutiny* and the unhinged behavior of the character Commander Queeg, played by Humphrey Bogart. Both actor and film won Academy Awards in 1954. Captain Ricketts, however, was real life, and I eventually got up the courage to report him to the inspector general—a colonel. It was a big deal for someone of my rank, a specialist fourth class (just above a private) to report a senior officer, but he was so abusive for no reason I could see. I think it helped that I was an observer and not a direct victim, because the inspector general immediately initiated an investigation. The CO was ultimately removed from command. Today, someplace in the archives of the US Army, there is probably a record of my report.

It was a relief, between the boredom and the conflict, when the time came for me to take my assigned two weeks of leave. With two friends from my unit, my wife and I (I was married to Bette at the time) decided to try for standby seats on a military troop transport plane out of South Carolina. The four of us waited on the tarmac for hours until the US Ambassador to Brazil arrived and we could take off for Rio, seated along the naked sidewalls of the plane, just like you see in the movies of troop transports. From there, we all toured Brazil, and then flew on a commercial plane to Cuzco, Peru, elevation eleven thousand feet. We suffered the ills of altitude sickness as we walked from the plane to our hotel, where we were confronted by a massive crowd carrying the bleeding body of Fernando Belaúnde Terry, the presidential candidate who would later win.

The next day we took an excursion to trek the ruins of Machu Picchu, which had not yet become the popular spot it is today. We were practically alone in the ruins. After Peru we went to Buenos Aires, Argentina, where we caught a transport plane back to South Carolina and on to Fort Lee with its endless truck-driving videos. I stayed there until August 1962, when President Kennedy decided to release the reservists. The Berlin airlift was in place, and he decided we were no longer needed. It was time to go back to New York and my job at CNC.

IN THE INVESTING BUSINESS, family offices like CNC are investment companies formed by the wealthy to manage and diversify their financial holdings. Rockefeller & Co, J.H. Whitney, the Bessemer

Trust, and a dozen other now–investment management firms started out as family offices. Their portfolios focused on public stocks, but they also invested in private companies, and some even dabbled in early-stage investments on a limited basis. Other than a few partners at a few key investment banking firms (like Lehman, Lazard, and Loeb, Rhoades & Co.) family offices were more or less the only source of investment capital for private companies in the 1960s.

When I walked in the doors of CNC in 1960, it had a reputation as a major investor in public stocks, with a portfolio valued at about a billion dollars. I was lucky to be there. The operating company had been founded in Hungary by Mendel Gottesman and then expanded radically under the leadership of Mendel's son Samuel, who made the family fortune in New York beginning in the 1920s, supplying raw materials like wood pulp to the paper industry. By 1960, the Gottesman Company had grown and diversified into newsprint distribution.

CNC, the family holding company, managed and reinvested the distributed profits with a strong bias for traditional industries. It had large ownership positions in International Paper and Container Corp. While I was there, we also bought a major interest in Rayonier Corporation, which made writing paper out of scrap wood that others would discard or burn. The company also had a hand in creating Southwest Forest Industries, a logging firm. CNC followed a value-investing philosophy. I felt right at home there given my time at Naess & Thomas, and from studying at Columbia Business School, the philosophical home of value investing.

My boss was Arthur Ross, who'd run the portfolio for more than twenty years and was very well connected in the investing world. Long before terms like "influencer" or "personal branding" became part of the lexicon, Arthur was cultivating his status as a person to know by attending social events, befriending local politicians and power brokers, and writing newspaper or magazine op-eds. He made it a point to know everyone of consequence in the investing world, politics, and beyond. He brought me into his circle and introduced me to many Wall Street luminaries. I met all the heads of the major Wall Street firms, such as Gus Levy of Goldman Sachs, André Meyer of Lazard Frères & Co., Joseph Klingenstein (J. K. as he was known) of Wertheim, John Loeb of Loeb Rhoades, and Robert (Bobby) Lehman of Lehman Brothers—they were the icons of that time.

I further benefited from Arthur's status by gaining access to the "Brimberg Lunches," a kind of Algonquin Round Table for the elite in the investment community. Described in the 1967 bestseller *The Money Game* by "Adam Smith" (a.k.a. George Goodman), the lunches were an invitation-only idea session for the investment community. Brimberg ran a brokerage firm and invited everyone from the prestigious buying firms. We'd all sit around in our folding chairs with plates in our laps eating corned beef sandwiches and exchanging ideas. I went whenever I could. It was years before I understood what a unique opportunity I had, given the caliber of the people I met there. They included Alfred Jones, founder of A.W. Jones, who created the concept (and in fact coined the name) of the "hedge fund"; Alan Greenspan, who became the head of the Federal Reserve; the economist Eliot Janeway; the billionaire investor Carl Icahn; and many others.

Another sign of Arthur's favor came in the form of a standing invitation—more like a requirement—to join him on his daily commute. The CNC officers were at 100 Park Avenue, at 41st Street, and Arthur and I lived a few buildings away from each other, thirty-six blocks uptown. He'd ring me in the morning and we'd walk the better part of an hour together, and at the end of the day we'd do the same route in reverse. Arthur liked to walk. Even in pouring rain he refused to get on a bus or take a subway if he couldn't get a cab. We used the time to talk stocks and the performance of this company or the challenges faced by that one.

The walks and the conversation had a familial feel. Arthur had two young sons and a daughter, and he tried to attract at least one of them into business, albeit prematurely. Clifford, Arthur's middle child, was about ten when I started, and came with us on a number of business visits. These field trips had the opposite effect of what Arthur intended—Clifford became a prominent artist and photographer. In the footsteps of his aunt, Helen Frankenthaler (another famous artist), Clifford is particularly famous for his photos of waves and of space, taken with a special camera he developed for the purpose. (His mother, Gloria Frankenthaler Ross, was also a well-known tapestry designer.) Arthur's other son Alfred and his daughter Beverly showed even less interest in the business than Clifford did.

Maybe Arthur saw that writing on the wall. It definitely felt from my perspective that he was helping me build my career and play a bigger role in the company's investment decisions. That impression solidified when I returned and life stabilized and I was able to see how formal Arthur could be with other people. He didn't cultivate the other employees the same way he cultivated me, and I learned from conversations with my colleagues that Arthur could be mean and self-serving. I never experienced that side of him.

I credit Arthur with giving me a broad perspective on life and the world. He was active in politics (most famously as a friend and supporter of New York senator Jacob Javits) and he would become well-known as a New York philanthropist. Today there is an Arthur Ross Book Award at the Council on Foreign Relations, the Arthur Ross Pinetum in the Central Park Conservancy, and the Arthur Ross Hall of Meteorites at the American Museum of Natural History. He didn't give much without getting his name on it, though he gave a lot to me in mentorship—and in support, while I was on active duty.

As an assistant vice president and subsequently vice president, I worked with Arthur and the two other VPs—Harold (Reg) Kingsberg and Don Peiser—to manage the investment portfolio. Arthur, Reg, and Don all had a strong bias for traditional commodities businesses: wood and wood pulp, metals, petroleum, as well as the adjacent manufacturing businesses that depended on these resources, all far afield from the avant-garde ideas that had attracted me to Lambert & Co.

I, on the other hand, had maintained my interest in new and innovative ideas. Though I spent most of my days researching traditional CNC investments, I stayed engaged through my friendships with up-and-coming Wall Street leaders, who told me about new companies and opportunities. Many were small-scale ventures—not anything CNC would be interested in. Now and again, I invested a little of my own money in them. One company I remember from that time bred mice to sell to research labs at private companies and universities. That seemed like a sure winner, until I learned that research mice needed to be pathogenically "pure" (not just clean), and these mice weren't pure. I also put some money in a small business producing the "Clive Entwistle Lamp." Clive was an industrial designer and engineer, a friend of a friend who designed a lamp revered for its modern, cage-like design and powerful light—so powerful that it burned everything in its glow and everyone who touched it.

Not everything that came my way was small, nor was I the first to nudge CNC to try a new idea. Arthur had always taken small stakes in private or new firms outside of the commodities sweet spot. Though he had little interest in high-risk, unproven sectors, he had enormous interest in his own status and liked being on the call list of the people who said they had him down for a half million dollars in this company, or a million dollars in that one. When considered in the context of the entire CNC portfolio, these investments were tiny, adding up to less than 1 percent of the total. Arthur kept the investment documents related to private companies in a file drawer that was seldom opened. Reg and Don didn't want to manage them. It was therefore natural, because of my interest, that when someone came to CNC with an opportunity to invest in a young, pre-public firm, I was assigned to investigate it.

In that way—gradually, organically—I began spending more of my time on private ventures. One of the first private deals I did was Susan Crane Packaging, in Dallas, Texas. Sam Ungerleider, one of the three Gottesman sons-in-law, introduced me to Ted Strauss, the company founder. I liked Ted and his business, which made decorative gift wrap and packaging. CNC made a small investment. (As an aside, Ted's brother, Bob Strauss, who I also got to know, subsequently became head of the Democratic Party and became known nationally as a political kingmaker.)

Later, when Ted told me he'd like to sell, I introduced him to Tommy Unterberg of Unterberg, Towbin & Co. (Tommy and I had met during my years at Naess & Thomas—he had been one of my guests in the white-glove dining room of Lambert & Co.) Tommy organized the 1966 acquisition of Susan Crane Packaging by the specialty retailer Cole National Corporation, another client of Unterberg Towbin.

Spencer Gifts—now Spencer's—was another investment from those early years. A chain retailer selling party favors and knick-knacks, Spencer's started as a mail-order catalog founded by Max "Spencer" Adler. Today there are more than six hundred Spencer's outlets, including the flagship location in the Cherry Hill Mall in New Jersey. Spencer Gifts went public in an IPO after I introduced the founder to their underwriter, Carter, Berlind, and Weill, Sandy Weill's firm at that time.

Not everything went well for Spencer's, however. In 1965, shortly after they went public, the company had a warehouse fire that wiped out its inventory. I still remember sitting down to watch the nightly news and seeing images of the building filled with smoke and flames on the screen. I got in my car and drove to Atlantic City, where the warehouse was located, to see the extent of the damage for myself. Max Adler was undeterred. He rebuilt and eventually sold his company to MCA, the entertainment conglomerate. Today, the private equity firm ACON Investments owns Spencer's.

Had I continued to focus on retail ventures like Susan Crane and Spencer's, my career might have followed a different path, but around that time I also got involved with LIN Broadcasting, my first media deal. LIN stood for Louisville, Indianapolis, and Nashville, cities where the company owned AM radio stations and some cable television licenses (a non-business at the time). Peter Solomon had the original idea of buying a stake in LIN. At the time, Peter was a partner at Lehman Brothers, though he later founded the financial advisory firm Peter J. Solomon and Company. Peter approached Tommy Unterberg to gauge his interest, and Tommy approached CNC via me. We each did our due diligence, and then came together with the joint conclusion that LIN was a good investment. Arthur approved and we did the deal in December 1964.

What did we all see in LIN that made us want to invest? Broadcast media in 1964 was clearly booming, with plenty of room to expand even further. Radio had dominated for decades and still played a major role, but beginning in 1948, TV began taking hold. Though a decade and a half had passed, and television had gone mainstream, the world didn't feel so far along from our first experiences with early black-and-white sets that looked like clunky pieces of furniture transmitting uneven, intermittent signals. The picture was so fuzzy someone needed to stand by at all times to endlessly fiddle with the elephant-ear antennas.

Parenthetically, when I was still in high school, only the richer kids in the neighborhood had a set. We'd gather on Saturday evenings in one of their living rooms to watch Lucky Strike's *Your Hit Parade*, a radio-cum-television program showcasing the top songs of the week, or one of the variety-comedy shows like *The Perry Como Show* or *The Milton Berle Show*. These were the standard attractions, particularly Milton Berle, who we watched like a ritual from week to week, just as TV watchers now wait each week for *Saturday Night Live* or, perhaps more intensely, *Game of Thrones*. When Berle was on, all other life stopped across the country. It was the original "Must-See TV" at the homes that had one—but not mine. By the early 1950s, Must See TV had expanded to include endless hours of Joseph McCarthy's "hearings" to expose communism in American society.

By the time Tommy, Peter, and I were looking at LIN, the post-war broadcast media industry—television and radio in particular—had expanded far from those early days of *Milton Berle*, but not to the point of full saturation. Time, Inc. was already a major, multiplatform owner of media outlets and content, but there was still plenty of room for regional players. The LIN investors ultimately included a group of clients brought together by Unterberg Towbin, a group of Lehman Brothers partners, and CNC. Collectively, we raised $525,000 for a 51 percent stake. I took a seat on the board to represent my firm's interest—one of my first board experiences. Fred Gregg, LIN's founder and CEO, held the remaining 49 percent.

Gregg used the money to buy cable and TV licenses throughout the southeast, which elevated the value of the firm and allowed us to raise another $3 million in 1968 based on a $12 million valuation. Gregg continued his buying spree. Among his purchases were a number of less obvious investments he did little to integrate, such as a billboard marketing company. Peter started to get concerned with how Gregg was running the company and spearheaded an effort to oust Gregg and replace him with Don Pels, a seasoned broadcast media executive.

Don took over, sold the cable licenses, and with the proceeds, bought a TV station in Houston, which had a bigger market than any of the others LIN occupied. It was a good choice. The company stabilized as Don built the radio and television businesses, and eventually participated in the first cellular lottery in 1981. LIN went on to become a major cellular company and was bought by AT&T in 1993 for $12 billion, though CNC was long gone as an investor by then.

Through my experiences with Susan Crane Packaging, Spencer Gifts, LIN Broadcasting, and a few others, I built my reputation. I also think I made Arthur more open to private investments in companies outside of the classic commodities and manufacturing sectors that dominated the stock market. That openness was perhaps on the mind of Armand Erpf of Loeb Rhoades when he approached Arthur in 1966 with an unusual idea.

Clay Felker was a famous and sometimes infamous editor who'd been ousted from *Esquire* before he was hired by the *Herald Tribune*—New York's number two daily at that time—to run a weekly magazine called *New York*. When the *Herald Tribune* folded, Clay purchased the name and rights to the magazine with $6,500 borrowed from the writer Barbara Goldsmith, a friend. He then set out to raise the capital to launch *New York* as an independent weekly and somehow connected with Armand, who was preparing to support him.

The audacity of trying to finance a magazine from scratch with no personal capital was classic Clay. (It wasn't so easy in those days to finance a venture deal, much less a magazine venture.) He was a man of contradictions: penniless, but an avid consumer of luxury; brilliant but touchy; aware of all the city's happenings but naïve about people and the ways of business. He was just right for the tone and energy and irreverence of *New York*, and Arthur agreed to do the deal. Together with Bob Towbin of Unterberg Towbin, Armand Erpf and Tom Kempner of Loeb Rhoades, and a few private investors including Edgar Bronfman, the CEO of Seagram's, we raised $1.1 million to launch the magazine in April 1968.

It's hard to overstate the sensation that was *New York*. Clay alternately courted or bullied some of the most talented writers of the time. Gloria Steinem, Jimmy Breslin, Tom Wolfe, Ken Auletta, Richard Reeves, Aaron Latham, Peter Maas—this was the caliber of writer handing their copy in to Clay on weekly deadline. The look of the magazine was just as groundbreaking. The now-renowned (though recently deceased) graphic artist Milton Glaser—famous for the I Love New York campaign—and Walter Bernard were behind the scripty *New York* masthead and stylish layout. That style and flair became hugely popular in the graphic world. Together, the writing and the visuals made *New York* the hottest magazine in town—if not in the country—from the very first issue. It set the standard that Los Angeles, Philadelphia, Washington, and subsequently even London, would try to meet with their own city magazines.

APRIL 6, 1968   40 CENTS

Jimmy Breslin on   Tom Wolfe   Gloria Steinem on   Clare Boothe Luce on
The Voices of   Tells If You're   Ho Chi Minh   Kenneth Galbraith's
A City in Trouble   Honk or Wonk   In New York   State Dept. Novel

New York *Magazine*'s
First Edition
© 1968 Jay Maisel.

Yet it almost didn't survive. Magazines live and die on advertising, and publications often rely on a handful of big names to buoy them along. In just its second issue, *New York* lost many of its leading sponsors, including the luxury retailers Bonwit Teller, Henri Bendel, and Saks Fifth Avenue. They abandoned the magazine when Clay published a scandalous piece by Barbara Goldsmith—the same writer who'd given him the money to buy the *New York* name. Barbara's article profiled Viva, one of Andy Warhol's muses. The article was edgy and the art shocking for the time, including nudes of Viva lounging on a chaise longue in Warhol's apartment. The advertisers had wanted *New York* to help it attract a young, hip clientele, but the potential scandal of the article was more than they had bargained for, and they backed out.

Clay had to scramble for new advertisers. It helped a little that he had a growing list of subscribers eager for the articles and tips that honed to the magazine's theme of "How to Survive in NY." Still, it wasn't enough. Saving the magazine required another full-fledged fundraise. I went to investors I knew to convince and cajole, and raised another $1.5 million for the magazine. That money carried us through until we went public in 1970. At an event celebrating the IPO, Clay and Milton Glaser, the designer, gave me a WWII-era poster of Uncle Sam saying, "We'll finish the job" in reference to my role in saving the magazine. It was a heady time. Sadly, it was also the pinnacle of my association with *New York*.

The problems began, as I experienced them, soon after the original round of financing. Armand from the outset put in writing the concept of "duality" between editor and publisher. He was concerned about Clay's history of getting involved in business matters, as well as his appetite for luxury and profligate spending habits. In an effort to keep a rein on the money and prevent such crossover, I was made president of the parent company and Armand took the role of chairman. Together, we ran the corporate entity, while Clay ran the editorial for the magazine, and George Hirsch, approved by Clay, served as publisher in charge of magazine operations and advertising. Therein lay the seeds of conflict.

From my perspective, Clay wasn't happy being "just" the editor. The fame and attention he received from sitting at the helm of the most-talked-about publication in the country wasn't enough. Despite his undisputed brilliance, despite the inside beat Clay had on nearly everything new and cool, and his access to events and to talent, it just wasn't enough. From day one Clay was in conflict with his board and everyone on the business side—me included.

I never experienced that kind of interpersonal conflict in a professional context before—or since. I made it a point to spend time with people, and was known—*am* known—for having good relationships, even with people others find difficult (case in point, Arthur Ross). Clay and I had intermittent periods of social friendship, and months or as much as a year would go by during which we had very little conflict. I remember a number of fun trips to London in the early 1970s when we were pitching a partnership to Tony Elliott, the founder and longtime editor of *Time Out London*. The partnership didn't come off, but Clay and I had a great time with our host David Frost, the UK journalist and TV personality of Frost/Nixon fame. On one memorable day, David, Clay, and I, along with fifty or so of David's friends, flew from New York to Bermuda for lunch to inaugurate the first purchase of a Boeing 747 by British Airways. The three of us enjoyed partying together when we met in New York, London, the Hamptons, or LA.

The iconic "21 Club" was one of my and Clay's regular lunch spots. Started by the Kriendler family back in the 1920s, it kept that "old days" vibe, with mementos hanging from the ceiling in the bar, along with a seedy, speakeasy atmosphere that made you feel like you'd stepped back into the past. I was usually happy to meet Clay at "21", except one day, when I balked at his choice of locale because of a scathing review of the restaurant that Clay had run earlier that week in *New York*.

"How can we possibly go there?" I asked Clay. "Jack will be fuming."

To which Clay said, "Don't worry, I'll take care of it."

Sure enough, Clay and I entered the restaurant as if nothing had happened. And sure enough, Jack Kriendler approached and started haranguing us. In the middle of his diatribe, a patron came up to Jack and said, "What a great article in *New York Magazine*."

On that cue, Clay said to Jack, "Can you show us to our table?"

That episode seemed to support the adage that all press is good press. Or more specifically, that when it comes to press, the details of the article are less important to readers than that they recognize your name—and it's spelled correctly. That rule clearly doesn't apply to truly serious issues, but for something like a review or an opinion piece, it pays to have a thick skin, because negative press hurts in the moment, but it does tend to fade. Later, people won't remember if the article was positive or negative, just that it appeared!

Life at CNC and with *New York* carried on. There was an evening in the 1970s that stayed in my mind when the entire *New York* board, Clay, and a few of the writers had dinner at Armand Erpf's home on Park Avenue. Armand had decorated his place with enough brocade and velvet to satisfy Louis XIV, and after dinner, served by butlers in livery, Armand suggested the men move to the library for cognac and cigars. Most of the women willingly moved to the living room for coffee and cake. Except for Gloria Steinem, who marched behind the men into the library before settling in with the guys. The few snickers passed quickly, deadened by the lack of encouragement, and there she stayed, exactly where she belonged.

Those bright periods became less frequent after the company went public in 1970, and they disappeared entirely after Armand died suddenly in 1971. In the void left by Armand, I became chairman and Clay rose into my former role of president. Over time, Clay grew more disenchanted with his role, with the very existence of an independent board and a chairman not named Felker. He was obsessed with running the business and the editorial side, and resented any and all controls placed on him in a business context.

He cultivated conflict with anyone he saw as a threat to his control, including the original publisher George Hirsch, who was forced out in 1972 after Clay gave the board an ultimatum: either George would have to go, or he would. Clay took the opportunity to consolidate his power and added the title of publisher to his editor moniker, then pushed Bill White and Gerry Goldsmith off the board, as well as Robert Schwartz, owner of the Tarrytown House Conference Center with which we'd merged. Clay filled their seats with his advocates to effect control, but the balance temporarily skewed back in the favor of the investors when we acquired *The Village Voice* from Carter Burden and Bartle Bull. Carter and Bartle became shareholders and board members through the exchange of stock, but soon enough, Bartle, publisher of *The Voice*, became the next target.

Meanwhile, the magazine continued to break editorial ground despite a degree of upheaval with the writers. Gloria left to launch *Ms.*—which had its debut as an insert in *New York*—and Jimmy Breslin left after a conflict over the direction of the magazine and a resulting writers' strike. Some who stayed continued to bristle at Clay's editorial style.

The hostility between Clay and the business side of the company continued until the board felt it could be resolved only by selling the property to a new owner. Even then, Clay's demands regarding salary, stock options, and a fifteen-year contract with no termination put off a lot of would-be buyers. I suggested to Clay he might want to find his own buyer given his requirements, but he took the suggestion only casually at first. Eventually, in the spring of 1976, Clay privately—and without informing the board—initiated discussions for a sale with the Pritzkers, who owned *McCall's*; Katharine Graham, owner of *The Washington Post*; Warner Brothers; Albrighton Publications; and Rupert Murdoch. None could come to his stringent terms.

Clay exhausted conversations with every potential buyer by the fall. A few months after talks fell apart, Rupert Murdoch approached me through my friend Stanley Shuman of Allen & Co. and restarted the conversation without Clay. Rupert already owned the *Star*, and was acquiring the *NY Post*. My dealings with Rupert were very straightforward and upfront. In 2021, when CNN decided to profile him, I spoke with them and recounted how the transaction had taken place step by step, with Rupert spending the holiday season of 1976 going from shareholder to shareholder collecting signed proxies. He even chartered a private plane to Sun Valley, Idaho, where Carter was spending the holidays, to have someone pick up his proxy. During the process, the price increased from $7 to the ultimate price of $8.25 per share, which was equivalent to approximately $15 million—not a lot given the assets in the business. On New Year's Day, Kathryn Graham called me and offered to reenter the bidding process, but I told her it was too late—Rupert already had proxies for 51 percent of the shares.

The sale was big news. As Stanley put it: "You would have thought we were selling General Motors," for the press it got. The story ran on the front page of *The New York Times* and garnered a second full story in *Newsweek*. Some of that attention was on the writers, who threatened to quit en masse in protest against Rupert's style and type of journalism. Many did end up quitting, though the board held a series of shadow board meetings to allow writer delegations to communicate their demands, and we tried to meet them. There were separate teams of lawyers representing the various parties, whose fees likely totaled more than the transaction value. I'm not sure how much they helped, given how many writers left anyway.

The exodus was well telegraphed, and Rupert was prepared for it. In fact, in my view, he was the successful bidder exactly because he was the only one with the chutzpah to step in on day one and take on all the editorial and publisher responsibilities in the event that there was a strike. When the walkout happened, Rupert immediately installed Jim Brady, the editor of the *Post* (which Rupert also owned at that time), as the editor of *New York*. Rupert had that ability with his editorial bench.

The departing *New York* staff was thought to have absconded in protest with the week's galleys. There was a minor panic to try to find them. When I discovered the CFO Ken Fadner standing with Binky Urban from the editorial department in the offices holding the galleys, I assumed they were with the protesters. I grabbed the galley from Binky's hands and rushed out to ship the pages to the printer in Buffalo in time to meet the deadline.

In one of life's odd codas, I sat next to Binky at a dinner party not long ago and we spoke about that night. It turned out that she'd always had the impression that I was a jerk for "trying to be the savior of the galleys." I learned from her that when I encountered them, she and Ken had also been trying to save the galleys and were preparing to take them to the typesetter themselves—not steal them, as I'd assumed. We'd had the same intent all along, and we could laugh about it forty years later.

As for the sale, it was a big disappointment for me. That may seem like an odd thing to say given that the business of investing is filled with sales, but I'd gotten involved with *New York* with an eye for the long term and was sad to see my association with the magazine come to an end. I was made by *New York* in a number of ways. To this day, in New York at least, it is probably the deal with which I am most strongly associated. The sale never had to happen, and none of us made very much money from it. I have often wistfully reflected on how satisfying it would be to still be chairman of *New York Magazine*. It's the one that got away.

Years later, Rupert sold the magazine to KKR, which sold it to the Wasserstein family, who sold it in 2019 to Vox Media. Clay went on to become editor of a group of shopper publications, then the *Daily News*, then (ironically) *Esquire*. Before he passed away from cancer in 2014, he worked as a distinguished professor teaching a much-sought-after publishing seminar at UCLA. He was a unique editorial talent, innovative and charismatic, and a great practitioner of his trade to the end.

By THE TIME *NEW YORK* was sold to Rupert Murdoch, I was long gone from CNC. During the eight years I spent with that firm, from 1960 to 1968, my responsibilities and experiences broadened, and I gained a reputation for doing my own deals. I even worked on private deals outside of the CNC orbit and found that I liked making decisions and being in charge. I had some skill in it. Before long it occurred to me, no matter how close Arthur and I were and how much he supported me, I would always be number two at CNC. Arthur was well into his fifties by 1968, but he showed no signs and gave no indications that he planned to step aside. I guessed—correctly as it turned out—that he would stay in the job until he died. (He passed away at the age of 96 in 2007.) If I wanted to lead, I would have to leave.

The opportunity came in 1968 to go work for Howard "Mickey" Newman, a respected financier and son of Jerome Newman, Benjamin Graham's business partner. To recap, Graham and Dodd coauthored *Security Analysis*, the value investor's bible. Mickey was chairman of the board and a major shareholder in Northwest Industries, a conglomerate engaging in active mergers and acquisitions. I saw an opportunity to learn about another side of the finance business from a legend, and I took it.

It felt like good timing given other changes going on in my personal life. As mentioned, my first marriage to Bette had come to an end in 1966. I moved out and got an apartment a few blocks away so I could stay actively involved in raising our son, Mark, who was born in 1964. I otherwise lived a bachelor's existence until I met Susan—my wife of fifty years, and mother to my second and third sons, Jonathan and Jamie.

When I met Susan, I was living in my bachelor apartment on the third floor of a brownstone "walk-up." Below me on the second floor lived a fellow who worked as a stage manager at a Broadway theatre. He had a lot of friends in the business, including an actress named Diane Scaravelli. My neighbor and the roommate conspired to host a small cocktail party at my neighbor's apartment to introduce me to Diane's roommate—Susan.

When I walked in and was introduced to her, I was transfixed. Susan worked as a casting agent at a well-known modeling agency, but she could have been the talent. She was so beautiful and had such presence, but she seemed shy to me that night and hardly spoke. I left without getting her number and didn't see her again until a chance meeting a couple of months later at Elaine's, the watering hole for many in the media and entertainment and finance business.

I was a regular at Elaine's back then because it was the place to be, a cross between the old Algonquin round table where Gertrude Stein held court and the velvet rope of Studio 54. "Elaine" was a rather stout lady with a brusque voice and a personality to match. She filtered the crowd, and you were either in or out. Believe me, you wanted in, because it was the place to see and be seen in the '60s and '70s, and still held cachet through the '00s despite its nondescript bar and average restaurant on 88th Street and Second Avenue.

The appeal of Elaine's lay in the fact that it attracted a large and familiar after-work or after-theater crowd from the downtown cultural and business elite—figures like Gay Talese, Woody Allen, Norman Mailer, Jimmy Breslin, Nick Pileggi, Pete Hammill, George Steinbrenner, and the list goes on. Everyone would try to make a stop at Elaine's if it would fit into an evening. When Elaine died in 2010, the energy left the place, and it closed in 2011.

Fortunately, Elaine was still alive and well in 1967, when I made it through her exacting filter to meet some close friends. At some point in the evening a fellow came to our table and handed me a twenty-dollar bill. I had apparently dropped it on the way in. I thanked him and pocketed the money. It was only when I was leaving that I passed the man's table and he pointed to his date, who'd found the bill—Susan. I wasn't going to let the chance pass a second time. I subsequently called her, and the rest is history.

I recently spoke with my longtime assistant and friend, Carolyn Hearn, and she reminded me that she had been in England when I met Susan. She says the first thing I said to her on her return was, "I've met the girl of my dreams." I don't remember saying that, but I remember how I felt. It's the same way that I felt throughout our marriage, which lasted until Susan's death in January of 2021. And I have continued the bad habit of carrying loose bills in my pocket and dropping them unintentionally behind me. I have probably enriched many others in the process. Susan is the only wife I ever met through that method, though.

Family is very important to me, and I did my best to be a full participant with Susan in bringing up our three sons. While I am sure there were times when I was negligent or missing in action, I tried to be present, attending parent-teacher conferences and performances and sports events. I still remember sitting on the bleachers at the baseball diamond waiting for one of the boys' games to start. Bob Meister, vice chairman of AON Insurance and a friend of mine, ribs me to this day for passing the time in the bleachers, between innings, reading *The Wall Street Journal.*

I vividly remember the fear I felt one summer afternoon in 1975 when Susan and I were visiting my friend Larry Saper at his home in Woodstock, NY. The house had a pool located about fifty yards down a hill from the house. My son Jon was about two-and-a-half years old at the time, and at one point, all the adults were talking when we realized he wasn't near us anymore. He normally liked to play near the car with the keys, so we ran in that direction, but he wasn't there. Susan then thought of the pool. We ran down the hill and I saw him in the shallow end under the water. I jumped in and pulled him out. Then I gave him mouth-to-mouth resuscitation while our friend ran inside to call 911. I was able to get him breathing by the time the paramedics took him to the hospital. It was the scariest event of my life and the price you pay for becoming a parent—part of your heart always belongs to your children.

Rules of the Road: Lessons in Early Leadership

CNC marked a turning point in my life and career. While there I transitioned from a junior member of a team to raising funds and leading my own deals. I went from exclusively taking advice and following guidance to giving both. I grew up at CNC.

One lesson that sticks with me from that time is "don't interfere with the entrepreneur's view of how to run the business." Remember, as the venture investor, you are the financial backer, not the operator of the business. The instinct is strong for many investors to get more involved than they should. More than once I have received a call from an entrepreneur frustrated because an investor was pushing some underinformed views about how they ran *their* business. In one notable example, the very prestigious CEO of a Fortune 500 company, who was on the board of a restaurant chain in which my first venture capital firm had invested, called me screaming, "Get that f____ partner of yours off this board! He's telling the CEO what temperature to cook the hamburgers and French fries." Do that often enough, and a good entrepreneur will hand you the keys to the front door and tell you to run the place yourself and see how you do.

A related maxim I've learned is that if the CEO wants to sell—follow his or her lead. Regardless of how diligent I am at following the progress of the company, the CEO has a 360-degree view and knows the state of product development, market dynamics, competition, and the environment of the internal organization. Admittedly, CEOs today in 2021 may be tempted to sell early if they've managed to hold on to a significant percentage of equity and believe they are personally better off selling now rather than going through more rounds of financing with consequent dilution. Overall, however, I have never found it wrong to follow the leader, even if it means selling too early. By the same token, I have never initiated a sale that wasn't supported by the founder or CEO, unless the company was at risk of running out of cash and the investors had said, "No more."

My time at CNC and my early activity with small, private companies also highlighted the importance of having a vision about what opportunities look like for you. Surprisingly, I learned that lesson from Clay Felker. When I was involved with *New York* I made it a personal policy to not get involved in anything to do with the editorial aspect of the magazine. I focused on the business. Yet it happened on a few occasions that a journalist friend would send me a piece and ask if I would vouch for them with Clay. Twice I thought the articles in question were terrific. Both times I sent him the pieces with a note. Both times Clay rejected the article (one of the pieces was by Daphne Merkin, who went on to great success as a writer). When I asked him why, he said, "Alan, I start every Monday morning with 128 blank pages, all white, and I have to fill them up. Don't you think I want to find the next great article by the next great writer?"

I thought about that statement many times in the following decades as I branched out to form my own business as an investor. Like Clay, every business has a proverbial 128 pages to fill every week, and just as Clay knew what "great" meant for the editorial side of *New York*, so does every entrepreneur need to know what great means for them. Investors also need that same strength of vision. I, too, start each week with a certain amount of capital available to invest, and I'm always hoping the next great entrepreneur is going to walk through my door. I regularly hear from friends who ask why I didn't finance this deal or that one. The only answer I can give is I am looking for the best as *I* define it—and as I understand it.

The deals I support have strong foundations in four fundamentals: a large market to serve, a product that addresses a clear problem or need, sound economics, and a management team in which I have confidence. I've developed my ideas about these fundamentals over years of value investing, and I held to those ideals through my time at CNC, even as I applied the concepts further afield from the traditional public companies of the CNC portfolio.

The elements I rely on to decide whether to make an investment have mostly served me well, even as I increasingly spent my time on early-stage venture investing, to which the foundations of value investing don't in all ways apply. I admit there are companies I have passed on because I didn't understand the market or the financial model, and they went on to do well, but overall, the discipline I developed of focusing on the fundamentals has framed my approach as an investor and helped me maintain longevity in this business and not to get carried away by the euphoric idea that value only goes up.

In today's environment, fundamentals seem to have gone out of fashion. Investors instead succumb to euphoria when extrapolating future value that the present performance often doesn't justify. Too many people making investment decisions today haven't lived through multiple business cycles and seen the inevitable ups and downs.

The near-decade I passed at CNC also taught me to try whenever possible to not end a negotiation with a "winner" and a "loser." Instead, try to make both parties feel like winners—and remember that the other side in any difficult negotiation, role change, or firing, has to continue to live in his or her family or community and explain what happened. Make sure you leave them with some self-respect. On a related note, try to avoid litigation if at all possible, and instead seek to part ways with the other party on amicable terms. I always opt for arbitration in any agreement I am party to if I have the opportunity. The only people who usually benefit from litigation are the legal counsels. Perhaps that is why, after sixty-five years in business, I have never sued or been sued by anybody.

More broadly, I also learned at that time of my life to deal with challenges that arise as obstacles to overcome, not as reasons for defeat. I had a number of formative experiences and career success during my years at CNC, but it was also a time of major change. The disruption of being called into active-duty service, the conflict with Captain Ricketts, my return to CNC and the range of start-up businesses I encountered, the volatile relationship I had with Clay Felker, and, on a personal note, the end of my first marriage to Bette—these were all major life events for me. Many others have suffered far greater difficulties, but these were mine, and they taught me some important lessons about challenges and how to deal with them. Life did not always unfold as I would have liked it to, and I decided to adapt to the new circumstances rather than retreat from them.

I also gained increased awareness that some challenges require a strong response—perhaps even one that forced me to take a risk. The behavior of the abusive Captain Ricketts, my commanding officer in Fort Lee, compelled me to speak up to the CO. What he did was wrong, and I didn't think I had an alternative choice.

I've continued to do that in my life. I always speak up, even when it means taking an unpopular position. It's worth it if I am standing up for something I believe in, or for a matter of personal integrity. It's hard for me to overstate the extent to which a strong reputation is gold for an investor—and for an entrepreneur. Your word matters, whatever form it comes in.

Captain Ricketts was not the only bully I have had to stand up to in my life. As it happened, when my army unit was called into active-duty service, I had a few investments I had to leave in mid-flight. In one case, I had invested in a small private company and introduced the CEO to a very prestigious duo (they became very famous by Wall Street terms). They were in the process of bringing the company public when I left for the army. The IPO happened while I was deployed, and the duo kept my profits from the arrangement for themselves. I did eventually get paid, but I had to fight for it over an extended period of time. The whole conflict was highly stressful and totally unnecessary—but there was no lawsuit.

I prefer to approach the world assuming it is filled with people intent on doing the right thing. While it may seem foolish, I trust the integrity of everyone around me. It relieves me of the burden of suspicion, which can absorb a lot of the energy. I prefer instead to think positively about how to make things better. Positive thinking doesn't mean that I ignore incorrect charges on bills, or that I don't carefully read documents for companies in which I am investing. Nor does it mean that everyone around me operates with the same integrity I take for granted. In fact, I still have the occasional experience that shocks me, but they are rare, and I continue to operate with an assumption of trust and optimism.

That approach served me as I left CNC to launch into a new phase of my career marked by increased responsibility, as well as increased financial risk.

CHAPTER 4

Steering My Own Route

Dave Packard and Bill Hewlett had their garage; Larry Saper had his kitchen table. I met Larry in 1962 after I returned from my time in the army at Fort Lee. My first wife, Bette, had a friend who was dating Larry, and the four of us would double date. Neither Larry's relationship nor my marriage to Bette lasted, but my friendship with him did. We'd often go to dinner or to a show. He played the piano and introduced me to the French-Roma guitarist Manitas de Plata, whose flamenco-style music was becoming popular and paved the way for groups like the Gypsy Kings.

Larry was full of ideas and palpable ambition. He'd graduated in 1949 with a degree in electrical engineering from City College, which had a reputation back then similar to MIT's today. Very smart people went there. When I met him, Larry had been out of college for more than a decade. He'd worked for Fairchild Recording, and then Bogue Electric before taking what ended up being an unsatisfying job with a Long Island start-up. When that company sold to a larger competitor, Larry saw his chance to strike out on his own.

It wasn't long before he invited me over to his house to see what he was working on. There at the kitchen table, with the Frigidaire humming in the background, Larry showed me his prototype: a small, lightweight cardioscope for producing a synchronized ECG to track a patient's heart rate. The medical monitoring devices that existed in those days had large and cumbersome screens and primitive mechanics. Larry's device used modern electronics and shrunk down the monitor size by using two overlapping traces. While one was fading, the other would appear. If the lines overlapped perfectly on the screen, the heart rhythm was normal. If there was an anomaly, it would show two different traces. Combine the ECG information with a heart rate monitor and an alarm to announce an abnormality, and Larry had something truly new and useful for the medical field.

But who would buy it? Back then, medical devices weren't regulated. If a doctor wanted something, he could have it. Larry had imagined the "Carditron" would be attractive for doctors making house calls. The original advertising specs touted the device as the "smallest, lightest scope on the market." It weighed less than seven pounds and could easily fit into a physician's bag. Unfortunately, the era of house calls was coming to an end, and the remaining stalwarts didn't think they needed anything more than a stethoscope. No family physician would pay close to $500 for an untested device.

Undeterred, Larry attended a trade show sponsored by the Medical Society of the State of New York to see if he could find his market. An anesthesiologist at the show observed that the Carditron was the perfect size for him to use in the operating room. If the device could be made with flame-retardant materials, mounted on a five-foot tripod and grounded, it would serve as a tool for the anesthesiologist to monitor his patient from the head of the operating table. At that same show, Larry met the director of medicine from Binghamton General Hospital in New York, who put in an order for two Carditron 650 units. Today we'd call Larry's embrace of anesthesiologists a key "pivot" that shifted him away from the family physician market and toward hospitals. A less talented entrepreneur might have found it difficult to make that shift, and he or she would have failed. Larry's ability to adapt based on feedback from the market proved transformational.

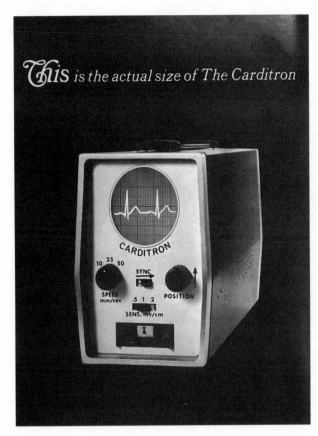

This is the actual size of The Carditron

The original Datascope Carditron monitor in 1965.

With his first orders in hand and a go-to-market strategy ready, Larry agreed to have me raise $50,000 to officially launch his business, which he named Datascope. It was the summer of 1964, the same year I worked on LIN Broadcasting. I took on Datascope as a side project, ex officio, completely separate from my day job. Hindsight makes it seem that investing in a medical device company at the dawn of cardiac innovation was an obvious bet, but back then no one wanted to take a chance on an untested technology without seeing it in operation. I barely managed to scrape together the money from ten people willing to put in about $5,000 each, and I put in a little myself. I am amazed today by the caliber of investors I was able to convince, including some prominent players like

Larry Tisch of Loews hotels; Edgar Bronfman, whose family owned Seagram's; and Sandy Gottesman, who founded First Manhattan Corporation and was also one of the first people to back Warren Buffett in Berkshire Hathaway.

Larry formed a board, of which I was the first member, and Dr. Joe Grayzel—a cardiologist—was the second. (As a coincidental side note, Joe's uncle had been a famous obstetrician, and had attended my birth thirty years before, a testament to how small the world can be.) To run sales, Larry hired George Heller, who had been working for Cordis, a pacemaker manufacturer, and agreed with the anesthesiologist that Datascope's market was in the hospitals. With Larry's innovation, George's selling skill, and me acting as free labor—brainstorming with Larry on strategy and advising on selecting legal counsel, banking, and accounting—the company gained momentum.

In 1966, its first full year of operations, Datascope did $80,000 of sales. In 1967—just before I got involved with *New York Magazine*—I put together the second round of $147,000 in financing. By the time Datascope needed a third round of $110,000 in 1969, I was doing the groundwork to launch my own venture investment firm.

Datascope played an important role in my decision to go into business for myself. It was the first significant private investment I made, and one of the first companies with which I became intimately involved. I drank and ate Datascope with Larry in the early days—on the phone, in his kitchen, and at his first office in an abandoned dental practice on Grand Concourse in the Bronx. Larry's first employee was the building janitor. Datascope gave me a taste for the excitement and challenges of standing as close to the front-lines as an investor can get.

The relationship went both ways. Larry Saper invested in my first fund in 1970, contributing $100,000 worth of pre-public Datascope shares. Datascope actually ended up being one of the most successful investments in that fund. The company was on a roll by then. It introduced a series of successful cardiology products, including one of the earliest defibrillators on the market, the "Resuscitron," followed by the intra-aortic double balloon pumping system (IABP), which would quickly become the most effective means for preventing patients from going into shock during heart surgery. By 1972, Datascope revenue topped $2.2 million. The company also went public that year, selling 20 percent—100,000 shares—at $10 per share. Yes, only $1 million for the IPO of an eight-year-old company, but that's the way the new issue, over-the-counter market was then.

I served on the board of Datascope for thirty years. I stepped down in 1994 because the medical industry had grown so complex I could no longer dedicate the time I needed to stay informed, especially given that Datascope was no longer in my fund's portfolio by then (we'd distributed the stock to our investors in the 1980s). In 2018, the patient monitoring business sold to Chinese company Mindray Medical International for $240 million. Later that same year, the cardiac assist business (which included the intra-aortic balloon technology and newer collagen products for halting bleeding) sold for $875 million to Getinge, AB of Sweden. Datascope was a true success story and a definite turning point for my venture career.

FROM MY TIME AT Central National Corporation, I knew that family offices had no way to manage investments in private companies. The staff had enough to do managing the portfolio of public company stocks. I wondered even then if companies like CNC might pay an investment advisor to alert them about new opportunities, but I didn't act on it right away.

Instead, I left CNC to work for Mickey Newman at Northwest Industries. As I noted in the previous chapter, Northwest was a conglomerate, and I thought the company and Mickey would offer some corporate industrial experience I wasn't going to get serving as number two behind Arthur Ross. It did, but not the way I had intended. Mickey was Northwest's chairman of the board, the largest shareholder, and was based in New York, but the president and CEO was Ben Heineman in Chicago.

Mickey and Ben had opposing views about how to run Northwest, and each held fast to his position. It was like watching two tennis masters engaged in an endless volley, and I was the net. My presence in New York made me Mickey's man in Ben's eyes, and I was cut out of the loop. I learned a very important lesson there: CEO means boss. As an aside, Northwest shared an office at that time with Mickey's father, Jerry Newman, who had been Ben Graham's partner (of Security Analysis fame) in an investment firm named Graham Newman. Jerry was from the old school in every way, carefully taking off his suit jacket every morning when he came into the office and putting on a grey cotton jacket like they wore at that time on the floor of the New York Stock Exchange. Mickey followed with the same habit, so I was the only one in the office wearing a traditional suit and tie during the day.

I tried to cultivate relationships with Chicago, and for a while I felt like I was making progress. Northwest attempted to take over Goodrich in 1968 and I traveled to Akron carrying the physical proxies for Northwest's voting shares. I vividly remember driving down the main street of Akron feeling like Gary Cooper in *High Noon*: outlined in every doorway and window I imagined Ohio's sharpshooters cocking their pistols to stop me from taking over the most prominent business in town. No one knew why I was there, of course, and in any event, we lost the proxy fight.

I also lost the bigger battle to broker peace between Mickey and Ben, and by 1969, I had enough of my de facto role as peacemaker. It was time to break out on my own and become an advisor to high-net-worth individuals on their investments in private companies. With the help of my assistant Carolyn Hearn, I sent letters to my contacts at family offices asking them to retain me as their advisor. Carolyn sent out the letters proposing my idea on thick brown paper skimmed from Northwest's office supplies and embossed with a logo designed by Milton Glaser, the graphic designer I knew from *New York Magazine*. The name, Alan Patricof Associates, ran around the edge of the paper like a modern-day stock ticker. It was literally one of a kind.

Nine family offices responded to my letter, among them CNC. All nine retained me for two years at $25,000 per year, plus a 10 percent carried interest in whatever investments they made, so I was fully funded before I opened the door. In parallel, I raised the first Alan Patricof Associates, Inc. fund of $2.5 million from another fifteen or so friends, many of whom still invest with me today, fifty years later. Carolyn came up with the name Decahedron for the fund—the tenth side.

We opened the doors of Alan Patricof Associates (APA) on January 1, 1970, at One East 53rd Street in a building owned by Bill Paley, the CBS chairman.

With me from day one were Carolyn, Patricia Cloherty, and Leonard Vignola—I'd met the latter two at meetings of the Society for International Development, where Pat was president. (I'd maintained my interest and engagement with international development that had begun for me in college. Remember that I had considered, but ultimately rejected, a post-college stint with USAID.)

Leonard left APA within six months, but Pat became a full partner within a year and built the business with me for the better part of thirty years. She's known today as the first woman venture capitalist, former president and chairman of the National Venture Capital Association (NVCA), and manager of the US Russia Investment Fund and the Delta Investment Fund, which invested more than $500 million in Russian businesses. Back then I knew her as a very smart Californian and fellow Columbia graduate who'd come to New York after three years with the Peace Corps in Brazil. She had no background in investing, but she was so smart I figured she would learn this new venture capital business fast, and she did.

In many ways, I established a habit, beginning with Pat, of hiring people who were intellectually talented but didn't necessarily have

Alan Patricof at the start of his first firm, Alan Patricof and Associates, in 1970. Located at 1 East 53rd Street in Manhattan.

experience in finance (let alone this new area of venture capital), and taking the time to teach them everything I knew. I hear from many of the investment professionals I have developed in this way that the energy and interest I put into them—all of it willingly given and totally sincere—is unique in our field. I'm not sure why. I do it because it pleases me to see someone develop into their potential, but even assuming I was purely motivated by self-interest, I can't think of a more efficient way of building a reputation for my firm than by populating it with very smart people who feel connected to its success. Ed Goodman, of Bergdorf Goodman lineage, was another such person I recruited early on from the nonprofit Bedford Stuyvesant Restoration Corporation. He stayed with us for six years before moving on to start his own venture capital corporation.

I'm not the easiest teacher, nor the most structured, though I believe in exposure. I bring junior investment professionals to meetings my peers might reserve only for more established guests. They also come to board meetings, lunches with partner investors, and pitch meetings with entrepreneurs. They sit in on my calls and accompany me on field visits. I have a wingman or woman almost everywhere I go. I don't view the world as having meetings that are "too important" for a more junior investor to attend. They come and they learn, or they leave.

Patricia immediately showed herself to be an immensely talented investor, but she joined me at a time in history when not everyone shared my views on merit over gender. Early on, an entrepreneur came in to pitch his business, and when he saw Patricia at the other end of the table—all fiery red hair and Katharine Hepburn style— he recoiled. "I don't want to work with a woman," he said to me. And I answered, "Then this meeting is over."

The 1970's were an exciting, if difficult, time for APA. Today it feels like new start-ups and growth companies beat a path to our door for capital, but back then it was catch-as-catch-can. "Venture capital" was not an industry yet. It was better described as an activity. Though Harvard professor General Georges Doriot had founded the bell cow of public VCs just after WWII, venturing was still rare. General Doriot himself retired from the pioneering American Research and Development Corporation (ARDC) in 1971, six years after his most famous deal financing Digital Equipment Corporation. In his wake we all swam, sometimes upstream. Tech-focused small businesses were beginning to school around Stanford and UC in Southern California, but here on the East Coast we didn't have anything like that kind of concentration. We had to take what was available.

Our first investment at APA out of the box was pretty non-tech. A "scrappy" twenty-something named Howard Meyers wanted to buy a lead smelting plant in the port of Newark, New Jersey. Howard had worked at the plant to pay his way through NYU's undergraduate business program. He'd been an hourly worker on the plant's blast furnace, and later a junior salesman until his path was changed for him by the draft for the Vietnam war. When he returned from the Navy, he went to work for American Metals Climax, a large metals trading and production firm. His old employer became one of his biggest customers. When he later told Howard of his plans to retire, Howard offered to buy the business.

APA agreed to raise $235,000 for Howard to purchase the lead smelting company. Some of the money came from our fund, Decahedron Partners, and the rest from a few of the clients. Together with a loan of $300,000 from the Bank of Commerce for working capital, we did the deal, and Revere Smelting and Refining (RSR) was born.

RSR sticks in my memory not only because it was our first from APA, but because of the way it reflects a few of the success elements I was learning to recognize in a venture—namely, starting a business in an area the entrepreneur knew well and attracting former associates to join. RSR appealed to me, like Datascope did, because the concept was clear and it served a large, well-defined market. As important, however, was the faith I had in Howard. He was tough and smart and had a deep understanding of the metals business and a clear vision for where it was heading. Howard saw the long-term market for recycled metals, which his refinery sourced by taking old batteries, mechanically breaking them, and separating the materials. Rubber casings went to the landfill, and the metals—mostly lead, with some antimony and copper—were extracted, melted down, and sold back to the battery manufacturers.

The industry still operates that way today, though with more automation and robotics. A key difference between now and when Howard started is that environmental controls came through the emerging Environmental Protection Agency (EPA), converting an industry once dominated by dirty, soot-covered smelters with furnaces spewing dark smoke into one with pristine plants, scrubbers on the smokestacks, and employees in white uniforms. Howard understood the implications of the new regulations well before they were in place, and he understood the economics of running scrap and recycling businesses profitably within them. With one plant or twenty, Howard knew how to make money.

That knowledge served him, and us, as RSR expanded. The year after we financed RSR it acquired a plant in Dallas, Texas. Eighteen months after that it acquired a company with multiple plants around the US, resulting in an anti-trust lawsuit by the government—for a company that was barely two years old! RSR went public in 1973 and subsequently went private ten years later, but it did not stop expanding. In the 1990s, long after APA distributed returns from the original investment, Howard acquired multiple plants in the UK, Germany, and Italy, and bought Metallgesellschaft, a large German conglomerate.

Today Howard's company operates as Quexco Corp in the US, and as Eco-Bat Technologies in Europe, and operates dozens of plants and collection facilities around the world, all of which are surrounded by green fields (or near to it) with nothing coming out of their smokestacks. It is believed to be the largest producer of refined lead in the world, and the only closed-loop recycling operation capable of collecting, refining, and storing. Revenues for 2017 exceeded $2.5 billion.

Howard Meyers is still a close friend and has invested in every one of my funds over the past forty years. He often gives parties to celebrate one event or another. At some point in the evening, he usually gets up to give a toast and says, "Without Alan Patricof, there would be no Quexco and no Howard Meyers." And my favorite retort is, "That's great for Howard. He travels around the world in his Challenger jet and his 180-foot yacht, and I'm still in coach!"

All true!

BOTH DATASCOPE AND RSR WENT public after just a few years in business. Datascope sold 20 percent of the firm on the public market for $1 million; RSR sold 33 percent for $5 million. Those are tiny numbers by today's standards, and they reflect the IPO environment of the time for everyone. I didn't have the privilege of investing in Intel in 1971 when it went public, raising just over $8 million at a $40 million pre-money valuation, but that tiny valuation by today's standard was typical at the time. As I observed about my time at CNC, the majority of investors in private start-up companies were private individuals, including family offices like Central National for the Gottesman family, the Bessemer Trust of the Phipps family (partners in Carnegie Steel), Venrock for the Rockefellers, and the Whitney family's J.H. Whitney & Company. Institutional money was not yet involved in IPOs for a number of reasons, and the private investors were satisfied investing as little as a few thousand or as much as a few hundred thousand dollars.

The bankers and brokerage firms making markets also looked different then and worked together more extensively. Dozens or sometimes scores of underwriters would come together to underwrite a stock offering, or as members of a "selling group." Likewise, small investment banks formed to take advantage of high commission rates and wide spreads between bids and asks for the secondary sale of stock. These firms made the aftermarkets, and developed research reports on companies and industries. Together they created a robust public market for young high-growth companies. I created a small M&A and private placement boutique myself during this period, Patricof & Co., as a way to generate fee income during slow times in the '70s—that company will become more relevant later in my story.

Yet the days of small offerings underwritten by small companies did not last long. The stock market crashed in the early 1970s, as interest rates ran up to over 20 percent, making investors skittish for most of the decade. While the market slumped, the US Congress passed the Employee Retirement Income Security Act (ERISA) of 1974. That paved the way a few years later for adoption of the Plan Asset Regulations by the Department of Labor, which allowed institutional money to move into venture capital funds and IPOs. As a result, institutions began to take part as investors in venture funds and in IPOs. Their participation surged in the 1980s and investment banks gradually began to cater to them, sidelining the private investors that had previously been the primary participants in new issues. Since institutions also had so much more money to invest, the size of the average IPO grew to accommodate the demand.

To illustrate the change, consider that Intel went public in February 1971 with an IPO of 350,000 shares at $25 per share, an $8.75 million offering. Fifteen years later, in March 1986, Microsoft went public with an offering of $58 million. But another twenty-five years passed, and in May 2011, LinkedIn went public and raised $358 million. As the IPO size grew, the number of underwriters supporting each one went in the opposite direction: Intel had more than sixty underwriters and Microsoft had more than a hundred. LinkedIn had just six.

From the early 1970s to the late 1980s, the hundreds of small firms underwriting IPOs were subsumed by a few large banks. Robertson Stephens, Hambrecht & Quist, Montgomery Securities, and Alex Brown were known as the "four horsemen" and dominated new tech company issues through the '80s and '90s. Yet even they over time closed, were acquired, or were absorbed by larger parents. Today Goldman Sachs, Morgan Stanley, Credit Suisse First Boston, and JPMorgan Chase are the in-demand underwriters for brand-name tech companies, who wait to go public until they can support

Red Herring and Prospecti, 1980–1996.

an IPO big enough to accommodate institutional buyers, each with orders of $10 million, $50 million, or $100 million of stock.

The decline in the number of banks that served as underwriters, employed brokers selling the stock, or hired research analysts to provide coverage for what would now be described as "small-cap IPOs" was also unintentionally facilitated by a handful of SEC rulings, one of which reduced decimalizing (the spread referred to commonly as tick sizes) from 25 cents per share to 1 cent per share. This, along with the removal of fixed commissions, took away the incentive for traders and market makers. With fewer banks underwriting small IPOs, fewer brokers selling the stocks, and fewer research analysts providing coverage, fewer small companies could find underwriters willing to work with them to go public. From 70 percent of the IPO market in 1991, small-cap IPOs raising less than $50 million shrunk down to 10 percent or less of all new issues. Many of the SEC rulings were intended to protect investors and reduce costs, but they had the opposite effect, in many instances raising the cost of capital for most small companies in their growth phase. The changes also perhaps had the incidental impact of shifting funding for young companies to the venture capital industry, since they couldn't go public and raise small amounts of money anymore.

It's hard to convey the new issue frenzy of the 1970s, when all new issues went immediately to a premium, mostly fueled by public market investors searching for the next "hot deal." Offerings were mostly small in size, and brokers could use a small number of shares—fifty, one hundred, or two hundred—to make their customers feel like they had gotten a windfall. The private market was populated by a few high-net-worth individuals who wanted to diversify, the private accounts of the partners of the investment banks, and the aforementioned family offices like J.H. Whitney, Venrock, and Bessemer Securities. As time passed, these family-connected firms would evolve into venture capital firms, joining APA, Warburg Pincus, and TA Associates on the East Coast, and

Kleiner Perkins, Davis and Rock, Sequoia, IVP, and a few other young firms on the West Coast.

We're seeing that level of market euphoria again in today's market, especially during the COVID crisis, with underwritings that leave a lot on the table as the institutional buyers purchase the new issues, which seem to capture quick immediate premiums. A company sells for $20 in an IPO, the institutions buy it, and when it goes to $40, the company doesn't get the value, the IPO buyer does. The world is circular.

My involvement in the Apple IPO in 1980 offers a personal illustration of an offering that took place on the cusp of the change toward institutional influence. Whenever I give a speech or appear on television, I am introduced as an early investor in Apple Computer, which is true as it stands, though APA's role was very modest. The truth is that I got a lucky telephone call from Tommy Unterberg, my friend from those long-distant Lambert & Co. lunches. Tommy's business had risen in prestige, and by 1979, he and his partner Bob Towbin were considered among the leading tech bankers in the country (they were among the underwriters of Intel). Tommy had been contacted by Peter Crisp, a partner at Venrock, who wanted co-investors to acquire a secondary block in Apple Computer.

I knew from reading newspapers and staying informed of the breakout growth expected in the new personal computer market. Texas Instruments, Commodore Business Machines, Atari, and Apple Computer, which was only two years old, were the names discussed in the press. Sequoia Capital was selling the block on behalf of some of the Apple founders and I jumped at the opportunity to take a share. We did the deal and bought what was available: 30,000 shares at $10.50 per share for a total $315,000 investment. At the time there were 5.5 million shares outstanding, which translated into a total valuation for the company of $60 million. Today Apple earns that much in about one hour, but at that time, $60 million represented less than one-and-a-half times revenues and twelve

Stock certificate for the partial sale in the IPO of holdings by 53rd Street Ventures, managed by Alan Patricof and Associates.

times profit off of Apple's 1979 revenues of $47 million and profits of $5 million.

In 1980 Apple went public. Its revenues had increased to $117 million and its profits to $11 million. The public offering was at $22 per share after a ten-to-one split, raising $90 million at a valuation of $1 billion. Our shares in Apple Computer at the time of the public offering were worth $6 million, twenty times more than we paid for them. We took a small amount off the table to recover double our cost and rode the remainder for several years before making a pro-rata distribution of the shares to our investors.

I have often wondered whether anyone has continued to hold the stock consciously or unconsciously. Recently for fun, and to cry in my beer, I calculated that at the current share price, and reflecting several splits and dividends, our original investment of $315,000 would today be worth around $7.5 billion. There is no point in looking back and saying "what if." It was the beginning of a completely different environment for IPOs. All venture capitalists have at least one story like this to tell. This experience and many others have made me more committed to finding venture investments I believe have long-term potential. I never want to make an investment for a fast exit. Venturing shouldn't be thought of as a short-term, quick-turn business, but as a longer game of investing in the future of an idea. Remember that an investor makes the most money on the last double—in other words, the last time the stock doubles in price before you sell. I wish I'd held that view about APA's Apple shares.

FROM LEAD SMELTING TO AN early investment in Apple, how did a small company on the "wrong" coast touch such diverse investments in less than a decade? Our New York location forced us to be diverse at the beginning, and over time, helped us stay that way. My association with *New York* made us the first call for almost every media-related project. We saw a lot of magazine pitches and financed a few of them, including *Scientific American* and *American Photographer*, and in the 1980s we launched *Details*. We got into another area of media with an investment in E.P. Dutton, a book publisher now part of Penguin Random House.

We also saw Federal Express as early as 1972. I met with Fred Smith to talk about the idea. We were excited about the concept, but we realized it was going to take an enormous amount of capital.

APA had such a small fund at that time, we could envision our investment being severely diluted if the company needed a second or a third round, so we decided to pass. As it turned out, FedEx had three or four private rounds before it went public, which severely diluted or wiped out those first-round investors, so our instincts were right. When it did finally go public, to capitalize on our prior due diligence, we took the exceptional step of participating in the IPO as a public investor and very quickly made five times our investment with no lock-up.

APA's first deals in more typical venture territory came back-to-back in 1971 and '72. The first came to us through Dr. Howard Frank. A professor at Berkeley, Frank had taken what was supposed to be a one-year leave of absence to work at the White House in the Office of Emergency Preparedness. While at the OEP, Frank and his team came up with a computer program to analyze natural gas pipelines. His work reportedly saved the government $100 million in 1969 alone. It occurred to Frank that he would have received a percentage of those gains if he'd done the project as a private business, so he started a company, Network Analysis Corporation (NAC), to do just that.

In that intermission between finishing at the OEP and going full-time to NAC, Frank met with Larry Roberts, a scientist at the Advanced Research Projects Agency (ARPA), now known as DARPA. Roberts was the true technological father of the internet (not Al Gore!), due to his work at ARPA applying packet-switching technology to build the ARPAnet. Roberts asked Frank for a proposal from NAC to analyze how the nascent ARPAnet would perform if it grew from the four nodes it had at the time to fifteen, thirty-five, or hundreds. NAC won the contract. Other contracts followed with companies like NASDAQ and a cable television network.

APA financed NAC in 1971 with a few hundred thousand dollars. I still remember NAC's offices in Glen Cove, Long Island. The company had set up in an old twenty-bedroom mansion that had been owned by the Russian government, which used it to house their employees working at the UN—at that time, Russian nationals weren't allowed to live in the New York city limits. We held our board meetings in the dining room and each employee was given an empty bedroom to work out of. NAC was probably one of the first companies to provide free food for employees, but they had to prepare it themselves in the kitchen since the nearest restaurant was five miles away and there was no takeout or delivery. Long before Silicon Valley made it de rigueur for start-ups, NAC kept a ping-pong table in the living room with plenty of room to play, since the Russians had taken all the furniture.

NAC did groundbreaking work, including ongoing projects to design the expanding ARPAnet, but the company stayed small, never passing $4 million in revenues. We ultimately sold it to Continental Telephone in 1980.

Shortly after NAC we financed Periphonics Corp., a company in Bohemia, New York, maker of some of the earliest human-simulated voice software for call centers. I remember vividly one day I was demonstrating the system to one of our clients in England, and a live AT&T operator interrupted the call. Our English friend said, "Get off the phone, I am talking to a computer." To which the operator responded, "Not on this line you're not!" That pretty much sums up the familiarity and use of voice response at that time. If someone had told me we'd all be dictating our grocery lists to Siri and Alexa fifty years hence, even I would have raised an eyebrow. Periphonics got through some early challenges, went public in the 1980s, and in 1999 was acquired by Nortel Networks in a negotiated transaction for $360 million in stock.

Periphonics was also noteworthy because our co-investor was Exxon Enterprises, the arm of the oil and gas giant tasked with exploring new technologies and businesses for the parent. Many large companies in traditional industries were launching similar divisions to scout talent and identify acquisition opportunities. Most of Exxon's portfolio was in the energy sector, but three or four were in new technologies. The experience was not easy. Exxon was just learning how to do small investments and took a long time to make decisions—in one instance, Exxon took six months to make an investment. Whenever the board had a big decision, the Exxon representative would have to go back to his bosses to get a yes or no. It was an exhaustive process. I learned then to beware of corporate strategic investors that don't give their board representatives local decision-making authority and are motivated to access new innovations for the operating company, not by investment profit.

THE FACT THAT WE HAD so many deals at APA during our first years may give the impression that everything was smooth sailing. In fact, the first five years of any business are uncertain, but venture investing brings particular challenges of timing, since we don't control when a portfolio business goes public or sells, or whether it will need another round of cash that dilutes our position, or whether the idea will fail entirely.

In general, I like to focus on the positive, but venture capital is a high-risk business. Even as we saw early wins at APA, there were investments that went badly wrong. For example, we formed an investor group with the precursor to Citicorp Ventures to invest in a smart married couple named Willy and Cathy Buchera, who'd come over to New York City from France. The Bucheras copied an idea from Decoux to build glass-enclosed bus shelters on city sidewalks to protect passengers from weather and provide a source of ad revenue for the city.

The Bucheras pioneered the idea in New York, and signed a three-year trial contract with the city, the execution of which required them to invest their own savings on top of our investment. When it came time to award the permanent contract, however, New York politics set in, and a committee of city representatives awarded the permanent contract to the lowest bidder—not the Bucheras. It spelled the end of their American dream—and their marriage. An obviously useful concept turned into a case study in the challenges of partnering with city governments—especially New York City.

Failure offers useful lessons about the multiple ways in which good ideas sometimes fail due to bad timing, an inability to execute, or the wrong partners. I learned firsthand the dangers of bad timing in the 1980s when we invested in Kingston Quality Meats, a meat distributor that had a virtual monopoly over the territory, ranging from fifty to two hundred and fifty miles around New York City. With its fleet of around twenty-five trucks, the company served most of the supermarkets and butchers in the region until a freak collapse in the price of beef parts left Kingston selling inventory for pennies to the dollar spent. Overnight, a company with fifty years of profit went bankrupt.

The Kingston management team approached us, minus the owners, to secure the funding they needed to revive the company. Everything was still intact: the same meat processing facility in perfect condition, the same managers, the same drivers, the same trucks and route structure, and presumably the same customers. It sounded like very attractive financial opportunity and we agreed to do the deal. Sixty days later, when Kingston Quality Meats emerged from bankruptcy court, we financed the revived entity. Thirty days after that, it was again out of business. Why? We'd failed to consider the customers. What were the butchers and supermarkets going to do without their meat supplier? Did we think they would stop selling meat? Sixty days is a long time, and they did what anyone else would have done: they found alternative sources. New local firms popped up, and by the time Kingston was back in business, only a small fraction of their previous customers were open to changing back.

Dislocations like this are common in business, and they often serve to show entrepreneurs and investors that nothing is forever. Give them a reason, and customers will change their habits, and once changed, they aren't likely to change back. We've seen this happen during the pandemic, when people have changed all sorts of behaviors, such as how they buy groceries, support local restaurants, or watch movies. The past is not a prologue to the future.

Another noteworthy example of failure during the early years of APA is Adams Laboratories, an example of inability to execute. Founded by Dr. Roger Garrett, a PhD biochemist, Adams Labs was making chicken feed supplements out of fats rendered from restaurant scraps when the company came to Alan Patricof Associates with an idea. Dr. Garrett had purportedly developed a process to extract and concentrate key components in animal fats that were known to improve the feed-to-weight-gain ratio. Each individual part of the process had been widely used in isolation in various industries, but not in sequence, as Dr. Garrett proposed. He could charge more for the resulting product, and it would have a larger market beyond chicken producers, but he needed funding to build the manufacturing plant.

Adams Labs probably wouldn't get a penny of financing today, but back then, an APA partner named Jack Prizzi did the deal with Adams Laboratories for an initial round of money to pilot the plant and prove the concept. The plant worked beautifully in the pilot stage, and we put in more money with a group of investing partners to construct a full-scale plant. Unfortunately, after that first pilot batch, Adams Laboratories never again produced a product with the appropriate yield. We added another round of financing to allow the company to troubleshoot the process, and another when the team seemed close to a breakthrough. In the end we had to conclude that the process didn't work. Dr. Garrett believed that the engineering firm that designed and built the plant introduced a flaw but could never prove it. We closed down Adams Laboratories and sold what we could of the plant equipment.

Deals like Adams Labs helps illustrate why APA in those days engaged in a number of parallel activities. My original idea of boosting cash flow with advisory fees from family offices didn't survive the second year, so I sought out other ways. I formed the Patricof & Co. investment bank to take advantage of fee opportunities. To access a more permanent pool of capital, I also created a Small Business Investment Company (SBIC) fund, 53rd Street Ventures, which tapped into an Eisenhower administration program that allowed SBICs to access government loans in a one-to-three capital ratio to invest in small business.

Another non-venture business opportunity came to us through the Ford Foundation, where Sol Chafkin and Talton Ray were running one of the first Program Related Investment (PRI) programs. PRIs use nonprofit program funds to invest in private enterprises whose commercial activities fulfill the program's goals. PRIs were the precursors to what today are known as "social impact investments." They are now a standard part of a large foundation's portfolio, but they were rare then. Ford was a pioneer, and they asked us to advise them about how to do it.

Patricia—who majored in Spanish literature as an undergrad and spoke Spanish and Portuguese—travelled with me to the Dominican Republic. We met the heads of two of the wealthiest families in the country at that time: Jimmy Pastoriza and Carlos de Bonetti. With them we set up the Small Business Investment Fund of the DR. We later went to Mexico City and partnered with the Mexican government to promote small businesses in that country.

In this way we made it through our first years in business, marrying major and minor successes with some failures, as well as short-term, fee-based efforts that we enjoyed and that gave us a way to keep the lights on.

As the '70s progressed, our firm grew by adding partners and finding new small businesses to support. The number of deals grew, and more of them were in new and innovative technology.

In the early '80s, I took a meeting with a pair of fellows out of GE Research in Schenectady (yes, GE used to be based in Schenectady!). Their company, PlayNET, had developed a gaming graphical user interface (GUI) that could connect multiple games and allow players to enter the "lobby" and navigate to different game rooms. No one had seen anything like it at the time. APA put some money in PlayNET, but I believed the product wasn't big enough to survive on its own, so I brought the idea to Jim Kimsey, the acting CEO of a nascent gaming company called Control Video Corporation (CVC), in which APA was an investor.

Kimsey had been a former Army special forces commander during Vietnam and a successful restauranteur. He was also a West Point friend of Frank Caufield of Kleiner, Perkins, Caufield, and Beyers, the preeminent West Coast venture capital firm, and an early CVC investor. Because Kimsey was based in D.C., Caufield installed him at CVC to bring management discipline to the start-up and nudge out the brilliant founder, Bill von Meister, who couldn't execute. Kimsey promoted a young marketing executive named Steve Case, and together with the product lead, Marc Seriff, was trying to work a deal with Commodore as part of a last effort to save CVC from bankruptcy. Commodore coincidentally also knew about PlayNET and preferred its interface for the solution CVC was pitching. Kimsey executed some asset transfers to set CVC adrift toward the sunset and re-emerge as a new entity named Quantum Computer. At this point APA invested $1 million in Quantum. We were joined by Citicorp, Inco, and Allstate Insurance. Commodore added a $1 million loan.

In addition to our investment, I helped Jim effectuate a license and ultimately an acquisition of PlayNET. A little while later, Quantum launched the Q-Link online community for Commodore users. If Kimsey thought the Commodore deal was the end of his problems, he was wrong. Commodore was facing its own market challenges due to the launch of the Apple II and put little into promoting Q-Link. Quantum needed another source of traffic and actively courted Apple. I did what I could through my relationship with Apple CFO Al "Pepsi" Eisenstadt, an acquaintance of mine, to bring about a deal for Quantum to create the AppleLink online service.

Neither Q-Link nor AppleLink made Quantum, and in time, both relationships deteriorated. They bought the company time, however, for the home PC and networked services markets to grow to the point that the world was ready when Quantum again recreated itself as America Online (AOL). Twenty years later, before he passed away, Jim Kimsey said to me, "Believe it or not, the original PlayNET technology is the key underlying foundation for the AOL we know today."

AOL went public in March 1992, offering two million shares at $11.50 per share, raising $22 million on a market valuation of $62 million. APA exited a few years later at a multiple of over ten times our investment. But we were gone long before the big payout in 2000 when, under the leadership of Steve Case, the company was sold to Time Warner for $165 billion, in what is now considered one of the worst corporate mergers in US history. In 2015, the same AOL was sold again to Verizon for $4.4 billion.

Rules of the Road: Driving Lessons from Starting a Business

In the previous chapter, I drew a distinction between the role of the investor and the role of the early-stage entrepreneur building a business. In the context of APA, however, I was both. The experience of running my own company forced me to develop a point of view about the practices that make a successful investor and those that make a successful business owner. I probably learned much of this before, and I definitely continue to operate this way today. Starting APA solidified a number of truisms for me as I worked to operate under my own steam and build an independent reputation for my firm.

The first is that curiosity is the keystone for succeeding in business. Start by reading, reading, and more reading. I read about general business and economic trends. I read about specific sectors in which I have an investment. I read about subjects that have caught my attention, whether because they seem interesting or because a company building a product in that field came to talk to me. Good investors check out new developments and seek out ideas that are just germinating. Keeping knowledge fresh and ahead of the market has helped me be aware of opportunities before they become mainstream, from solar fusion to artificial intelligence, space travel to nanotechnology, maglev trains and, yes, personal computers. The PC seems mundane today, but when I took Tommy Unterberg's call about Apple in 1978, the company was far from a guaranteed success. I made the investment because I had heard of the company, knew it was among the up-and-coming names on the lips of the cognoscenti, and I believed the market for personal computers was about to emerge.

Such basic, foundational interest provides a simple critical test for anyone who thinks they are interested in either the investing business or in running a start-up. Do you have the curiosity to follow up on an article you read or a conversation you had to learn more about a subject? At the bottom of that rabbit hole may rest a compelling venture. If you'd rather not chase white rabbits, the start-up world is not for you.

Nor should you get involved in venture if you're unwilling for some of those rabbits to lead you down paths that are simply too early to accept what you have to offer. Though curiosity is key to venture investing, a corollary lesson I have learned is to be careful about committing too much of a portfolio to companies that have to educate their market about their new-to-the-world product.

I often think about Jaron Lanier in this context, now considered the founding father of virtual reality. I had read about virtual reality in a newspaper or trade magazine, and sought out Lanier and his company, Virtual Reality, Inc., at the CES show in Las Vegas in 1984. After searching through the directory and asking everyone I ran into, I finally found the company's display and Jaron himself in the corner of the basement of the vendor expo. He had a large screen set up and a large pair of gloves which allowed the wearer to simulate playing various games or other activities that appeared on the screen. It was primitive compared to what is available now, but exciting for the time. Jaron was non-conventional and living totally off the grid, but I decided to take a chance on Virtual Reality, Inc. with a small seed investment. The company never found a killer product or market and eventually disappeared.

Only now, thirty-five years later, is VR gaining momentum in markets like education, defense, medicine, and entertainment— gaming in particular. Instead of gloves, virtual reality hardware more often relies on headsets and goggles, with and without control. The technology still has not lived up to its original hype, but it is a real business today compared to its mostly conceptual status in 1984— the advances in processing power have made much more possible than could be done back then. Jaron himself continues to serve as a speaker and advocate for the technology, both on conference stages and through his multiple books, including *Dawn of the New Everything: Encounters with Reality and Virtual Reality* (in which he mentions our first meeting).

Jaron might be gratified to see how right he was about the power of his creation, but it took a very long time. It's a classic example of the painful exercise of educating a market. It's tough enough to sell a product or service to someone who has an immediate need. Selling a future need usually causes the early pioneers to get a lot of arrows shot at them. The battlefield of business is filled with the dead bodies of first movers.

A related lesson for both investors and entrepreneurs is that not every new business is right for venture investing. Throughout my career as a venture capitalist, I have from time to time met a talented founder with a reasonably good concept and a plan to execute on it—yet the market was too small to warrant venture investment. The idea may be too parochial, or relevant only to a small geographic area—for example, a local chain of family-owned hardware stores or a home decorating business. It may present as a high-quality small business, but without the potential to grow large enough to make it worth the requirements that an outside investor will impose, such as audited statements, legal papers, reports to outside shareholders, and so on. In general, venture capitalists are looking at companies with a large total addressable market (TAM), and with the potential to double their revenues annually over an extended period of time—around ten years—potentially reaching at least $100 million in revenue. Founders that don't obviously have that potential are better off financing with their own capital, combined with capital from a small group of private investors culled from their personal contacts.

It might be easier to self-finance than you think. In the current environment, many successful businesspeople want to diversify their investment portfolios with an opportunity to own a piece of the next Uber, Airbnb, Instacart, DoorDash, or for that matter, the next Salesforce. If you're a founder with a strong idea, start by going through your existing contact list and select those who know you well and who know you and your skill set. You may be surprised to discover how many of these people are capable of investing between $25,000 and $100,000 and are just waiting to be part of something exciting and new with which they can identify. Crowdfunding also plays a stronger emerging role in financing today.

It can benefit both the founder and the investors: Section 1202 of the tax code, also called QSBS—qualified small business stock—allows a company to raise up to $50 million from individuals who are not taxed on the gains so long as they hold the investment for five years (consult your tax counsel to make sure your project applies to receive this benefit). If your contact list has names with greater capabilities, you can probably find sources of capital with ten times the number I have stated. Walking this path doesn't prevent you from seeking venture capital later, should the idea prove to have bigger potential than it seems at the outset.

Talent is a third key lesson I learned to heed in the first years of APA, one I have seen reinforced time and again over the decades. Bet on the jockey, not the horse, became a mantra I live by. Ideas are without a doubt the foundation of a high-potential growth business, but ideas aren't worth the paper they're printed on without a skilled founder making the day-to-day decisions that convert ideas into jobs, customer benefits, and profit. Larry Saper had a powerful idea for Datascope, but he also had the mental agility to pivot his original concept to a better market than he had originally designed the product for, and to build an experienced board from the outset with people who had skills and knowledge he needed to grow the company. Howard Meyers similarly impressed me with his knowledge of lead smelting and how to make money with it—it's a basically boring business that he knew how to turn into a gold. mine. This pattern will appear time and again throughout the following chapters in companies that have a chemically active combination of a great idea, a large market, and skilled management.

The importance of talent reinforced a habit I solidified while building my own firm—namely, to be responsive to people. Whether they're reaching out for advice or to gauge my interest in specific investments, I like to respond as quickly as possible. I have always practiced a policy of returning phone calls the same day I receive them. If a friend or business acquaintance asks me for something, I deliver it as soon as I can, sometimes before they've had time to return to their office. Operating in this way has helped me build a reputation as someone my clients, colleagues, partners, and friends can rely on. I can't overstate how important this is.

A wide network of people consult with me, not only because they respect my opinion, but also because they know I am accessible. Friends, former colleagues, mentees, and many others know they can call and ask for advice or shop a deal, and I will get back to them with a response in a timely fashion. Through this practice, I have developed a strong array of relationships, including some with an impressive list of investors who have stayed with me for decades and through successive fund-raises, not to mention entrepreneurs who've come back a second or third time for financing of subsequent businesses.

Anyone who has visited me in my office has seen me pick up the phone to make an introduction or get the answer to a question when it comes up. I avoid "putting off till tomorrow what I can do today." If you actually mean to follow up, why not do it now? Opportunities don't wait until you are ready to receive them. By the time it crosses your mind again it may have gone to a more responsive firm.

"Responsive" does not necessarily mean I always say yes. It means that I won't keep you guessing. The next best thing to yes is a quick no. And the best no is direct and honest, yet respectful. Remember, the company I'm rejecting was important enough to someone that they staked their career on it. Saying no is tantamount to telling them their baby is ugly. There's no need to be unkind about it, but nor is there any reason to show more enthusiasm than I feel. I am known for my candor, even *admired* for the fact that I ask questions that cut to the heart of a venture and say exactly what I think about it. Honesty and directness delivered in a timely way can be a kindness.

The alternative is either misguided hope, or simple confusion. I'm not immune to it myself, especially when meetings end without a clear directive from both sides. Over the years I have learned to listen at the end of a meeting, when your host escorts you to the door or the elevator, for the last thing they say as a clear indicator of whether they want to proceed. I first learned that lesson on a visit to Japan, where I would go regularly as APA evolved and grew. My Japanese partner coached me on how to greet people at the elevator and how to say goodbye, which is somewhat of a ritual involving bowing, and in some cases, placing your hands in a specific position. Most importantly, my partner told me to listen closely for the last thing said as the elevator doors close—that was the key takeaway from the meeting. It could range from "Nice to meet you" (a noncommittal closure), to "Hope to meet again sometime" (more promising), to "We will be in touch for a follow-up" (even better), to We will get back to you within a week after we have time to review" (very positive). I carried that practice around the world and use it to try to clearly understand what the next steps are at the close of a meeting (assuming I want one). It helps keep potential deals moving and allows you to move on in a timely way from those that don't interest you.

Timeliness has an analog in the fact that it is important to communicate news in a timely way, especially financial news, and even when the news is bad. No one likes unpleasant surprises. If some issue has the potential to derail one of my portfolio companies, I would much rather hear about it when it's still a possible disruption, and not get blindsided later when the full damage is done. I don't know anyone in my world who'd rather be kept in the dark.

I have a theory that I can often predict how well the quarter went for one of my firm's portfolio companies based on when the email arrives with the financial results. If the month ends on a Monday and an email arrives on that day, I don't need to open it because I can assume the news is good. If the email instead arrives on the weekend before the Monday, I can assume the news is *very* good, and if it arrives on the previous Friday before the month even ends, it was probably a fabulous month. Conversely, if the news hasn't arrived by the end of the following month, or if the company has gone radio silent, I can (not always, but often) assume it's been a so-so or negative period, and I have to call them to find out. Humans can't wait to share great news and they can't bear to share bad. The news is the news, though, and it should always come on a timely basis—don't force people to drag it out of you.

I've had my fair share of good news to share as my business grew, and my life has also diversified beyond my business activities.

POSTSCRIPT:
Joy Rides and Side Trips in Art

I made my first art purchases by chance through a young dealer named Thomas Gibson, who I got to know socially. Thomas was a temporarily transplanted Englishman working at Marlborough

Gallery, one of the leading galleries in the world at the time. (In 2020, after five decades in business, the gallery closed its marquis gallery in midtown Manhattan. It happened concurrently with the coronavirus pandemic, but the closing was as much related to competition from the auction houses. People just don't go to galleries as much anymore.) I credit Thomas for my initial foray into collecting.

First let me clarify that I am a total amateur at collecting art, and I haven't amassed a major collection. My estate might sell some of it when I die, and give some of it away, or to the trash collector. I won't be offended. I didn't buy the pieces I own for their future value. I bought them because I liked them and because art came to play a meaningful, peripheral role in my life.

When I started collecting in the late '60s, one of the activities I most enjoyed at the time was to attend gallery openings, where the gallerists served wine and cheese at regular Thursday-night openings. It was a great chance to mingle with other collectors, young and old. Once I got hooked, I started to visit other galleries and openings and I spent my Saturdays making the rounds. Many name-brand galleries were on 57th Street. They moved to Soho in the 1980s, and then to the East Village, and ultimately to where they all are now, in Chelsea.

Through Thomas I purchased over a number of years three paintings by a young, London-based American painter named Ronnie Kitaj. Each piece I bought cost less than $2,500. Ronnie eventually achieved much fame and fortune, which resulted in a dramatic rise in the prices of his paintings. Over the years I got to know Ronnie and his wife Sandra and visited with them in London and New York. At one point his work was the subject of a one-man exhibition at The Tate Gallery in London, which is about as high as you can get for a modern artist. Unfortunately, the critics reviewed the Tate show badly; they thought it pretentious due to the long monologues he wrote about each painting, which were posted next to the canvas.

Ronnie was very badly affected by the notices and by the subsequent death of his wife—he believed her death had been precipitated by stress. He then moved to LA, but he never recovered his momentum. He committed suicide in 2007, but his reputation has been subsequently resurrected in multiple recent gallery shows and exhibitions. Published posthumously, his autobiography *Confessions of an Old Jewish Painter* was heralded by the writer Philip Roth, in a *New York Review of Books* interview published shortly before Roth's death, as one of his favorite books.

I had three Kitaj paintings and loved all of them. One hung next to my desk for a few years. The title was *Aurelian*, and I looked at it every day until 1974, when Thomas called me several times over several months to indicate he had a buyer who was desperate to own a Kitaj—and particularly mine. I repeatedly said no, until the day Thomas called for a fourth time. I had been to lunch at the NY Hilton for The Economics Club, and the main speaker had been Pierre Rinfret, a well-known and well-respected economist.

Rinfret said that day, "The world is coming to an end; prices are going to collapse; I'm selling all my stocks, buying gold, and moving to Paris." I came back to my office from lunch and looked at *Aurelian*, and said to myself, "What if he's right? What use is this painting?" That's when Thomas called and I said I would sell. I have regretted it ever since, as I truly loved that painting. I hope the buyer loves it as much as I did—if he still owns it. I still own a Kitaj called *The Nice Old Man and the Pretty Girl (with Huskies)* that hangs proudly in my dining room in Manhattan; the third one I gave to the Metropolitan Museum of Art.

I have stayed friends with Thomas, who has guided me a bit through the art world. I subsequently bought a painting (again under $2,500) through Marlborough by Frank Auerbach, another Englishman who is now considered one of the great living English artists. I never got to meet Frank like I did Ronnie, but I still have the original Auerbach painting I purchased.

I also bought a painting in the 1970s by Larry Rivers from his *Dreyfus* series. I was very fond of this painting, hung it in my home, and pointed to it often with pride. But some years after I bought the Dreyfus painting, Larry went to Japan and began to pursue a different style and subject matter featuring Japanese prostitutes, which veered toward the pornographic. I began to second-guess owning a Rivers painting and approached the dealer I bought it from to ask if he would be interested in buying it back. He did. I regretted selling it many times. Then, twenty years later, I had another opportunity to buy a Rivers painting, this time from a new series that was closer to his earlier style. I bought it and eventually met Rivers and became friendly with him. While visiting him at his home, I told him about my experience with his *Dreyfus* painting and my dislike of the Japanese series. He said, in jest, "Some friend you are. I make one mistake and you sell me down the river!"

Over time I got to know other gallerists. I developed a friendship with Terry Dintenfass, who I met through my first wife Bette. Both Bette and Terry had worked for Edith Halpert, the world-famous art dealer and famed gallerist for Georgia O'Keeffe, John Marin, and Abraham Walkowitz. Terry eventually left Edith Halpert to open her own gallery, and when Edith died, Terry and I collaborated to buy Edith's famous folk art collection from the Edith Halpert estate.

I also was fortunate in the 1970s to become friendly with a neighbor in my apartment building who owned one of the up-and-coming—and now leading—galleries in the world, Pace Gallery. Arne Glimcher and his wife Milly became good personal friends. Over time I bought some great paintings and sculptures from Pace, including Lucas Samaras, Elizabeth Murray. Much later in the '80s and '90s, when I could afford to spend more, I added small works by Picasso, Léger, and Dubuffet, and several sculptures from Mark di Suvero, Noguchi, and Joel Shapiro.

Gallery visits became a ritual in my early life. As with every form of investing, some of the artists whose work I bought did better than others, and some disappeared entirely. Art, unlike business, is very hard to evaluate in any quantitative way, so I've had to focus on buying works that appeal to my own personal taste, which is eclectic. I approach collecting in a similar vein to how I approach venture capital. I've tried to research the artist and the gallery representing the artist, and where possible, to meet the artist in person and sometimes visit their studios. In most instances, especially in the early days, I was collecting unknown artists whose works were available in the price range I could afford—a few hundred dollars or up to a few thousand dollars. That low entry point hardly exists today.

Over the years I bought pieces by Alex Katz, Janet Fish, Joan Nelson, Jack Beal, Mary Frank, and Jim Dine, all of which went on to become relatively well known. Others like Stephen Edlich, Ken Bowman, Tony Frank, Paul Kane—the list goes on—have faded from the art scene. These artists can't be found in any directories today. Several of the galleries are also remnants of the past, like Terry Dintenfass, Waddell, Emmerich, and Alan Frumkin, among others. As in any other field, some survive, and the others pass into history, if not the history books. Along the way, for lack of money, I made the shortsighted decision to pass up Francis Bacon, Frank Stella, Lucian Freud, and Philip Guston, among other artists that are well-known today.

I also went to galleries whenever I could when I was in London. While there, I got to know Waddington Gallery, Bernard Jacobson Gallery, and Angela Flowers, and started buying young English artists like Tillyer, Howson, and others. I also became friendly with a poster gallery in NYC run by Susan Reinhold and Bob Brown, and through my friendship with the two of them over the years, put together an extensive poster collection.

Traditional visual media aren't my only passion, either. Among my prized aesthetic possessions is an original chair designed by the architect Thomas Heatherwick and given to me by him as a gift. Though Thomas is an architect, he is also a three-dimensional artist—one of his sculptures is in the Royal Academy, and he's had a number of one-man shows, including one at the Cooper Hewitt in New York. For that reason, I often think about him in the context of my activities in art.

How I met Thomas is an interesting story in itself. In 2016, at the TED conference in Vancouver, Canada, I got to hear Thomas speak. He was at that time known for his design of the British Pavilion at the World's Fair in China, which won first prize in 2010, as well as a bridge in the UK which looked like a Ferris wheel when open, but folded and unfolded across a stream. After the talk, I approached Thomas to ask what he'd done in New York City. In a very self-effacing manner, he indicated that no one had approached him. I suggested that if he came to the city, I would set up a lunch for him to meet some developer friends of mine. He sheepishly, in wonderment, said that would be so nice, and about two months later, a dozen or so real estate developers came to my office for lunch to meet and hear Thomas present. Everyone walked away impressed, but it didn't come to anything at first.

The one person who couldn't make the lunch was Steve Ross, CEO of The Related Group. Steve reached out with his apologies, which started a conversation that ultimately (and unrelated to my introduction) resulted in Steve hiring Thomas to design the *Vessel*, the centerpiece of the Hudson Yards, a massive new real estate development in Manhattan. Barry Diller, CEO of IAC, shortly thereafter hired Thomas to create a new park on an island pier on the Hudson River off the west side of Manhattan, now a major tourist destination site known as the "Little Island." Within just a few years, Thomas's work now appears all over New York and other cities around the globe. I don't claim credit—that goes to Thomas's talent, which I did try to introduce to people who he could help and who could help him. He seems to appreciate it, as the chair was a generous thank-you gift for arranging that first lunch. Herman Miller is now manufacturing the design en masse, but I got a first edition!

Over the years of collecting various art forms, I have learned how important a gallery is to building a budding artist's career. Galleries show artists' work, publish catalogues, get them into museum shows, and support their prices at auction. Most importantly, galleries promote artists and build their careers. Galleries also play an important role for the buyer—I have learned the hard way that galleries come and go. I am not averse to buying a sculpture or painting from a young gallery, but if the gallery fails (and most fail), the young artists they support can quickly disappear from public view. In some ways it's almost as important to pick a strong gallery as it is to pick a work of art. I think about that model in relation to the entrepreneurs in my firms' venture capital portfolio.

Beyond galleries, anyone interested in art has to become a frequent visitor at auctions, the most famous of which are run by Sotheby's and Christie's. I have bought many paintings in this way, but I always follow the practice of submitting a written bid beforehand and not attending in person so I don't get carried away by the euphoria and heightened excitement of the auction floor.

I accidentally deviated from that rule once in the 1990s. I was spending a leisurely Saturday strolling in Bridgehampton, Long Island. The local community house was having an auction, and when I looked at the catalog, I saw an array of furniture and a few paintings. Among the paintings was a Milton Avery. Avery is a well-known painter, but the provenance was not authenticated, so there was some risk that it was a fake. The price estimate was $19,000–$22,000. I placed a written bid of $21,500 and left to walk around town. Susan and I went for lunch and finished just as the auction began. Because we were nearby, I thought it would be fun to break my rule and watch the auction unfold, so we went back to the community house. The Avery was number four on the docket, and was up as we walked in. The bidding went $19,000; 20; 22–24; 28; 30; 32. The auctioneer said, "Going once at thirty-two, twice at thirty-two—sold to the woman in the front row for thirty-two thousand dollars," as he banged down his gavel. At which point the woman shrieked and jumped up and said, "Thirty-two thousand dollars?" She clearly had thought it was $3,200!

This kind of mistake doesn't happen too often—in fact, almost never—but the auctioneer realized he had a problem and decided to start the bidding all over again. Now I was in the middle of the battle. Captured by the drama, I couldn't resist participating and ended up far above my written bid. Today I have my Milton Avery proudly displayed in my home over the fireplace, authenticated by the Avery estate—a happy buyer despite paying 50 percent more than my original bid!

When it comes to buying art, I have learned over the years, first and foremost, to only buy pieces that resonate with my aesthetic sensibilities and not to be swayed by others who may or may not agree with my taste. Before I buy, I try to read articles about the artist and look at previous show catalogues or reviews to get a fuller sense of their style. I also attempt to assess whether a piece I'm considering buying is consistent with the artists' past work or represents a segue into another style. Whenever possible, I attend gallery and museum openings, where I can hopefully meet the artist. Occasionally I have been able to visit an artist in their studio, which allows for an even better understanding of their style, past and present, and their ability to convey the thought process behind their works.

I have a large collection today after nearly sixty years of collecting. Some of the pieces in my collection are by unknown artists that have since built major careers; others I couldn't find today, even with the help of Google. I am nonetheless a happy collector. Over the years, I have sold only one or two paintings out of more than a hundred in my collection. Art is for looking at, and I hang my pieces around my office, my city home, and my weekend home. I always think I'm out of wall space, but I somehow manage to find room for one more, as I am against both storing work and buying art simply to make money on the purchase. Collecting has continued to be an important part of my life, and to this day I still try to visit galleries looking for new artists.

I expanded my impulses over the years, as I started collecting old cars, bought for how they look and for nostalgic value—not in expectation of earning a profit on resale. I bought my first old car in 1980, after attending a house sale in East Hampton for the estate of Jerry Wexler, who'd been one the leading music producers of that

Alan Patricof in his father's 1939 Lincoln Zephyr.

era. In the driveway sat his weathered 1942 Buick two-door coupe. It was old, gray, and in poor condition. It wasn't part of the sale, but on a crazy lark I offered to buy it and threw out a price of $2,500, with no idea what it was worth. Two days later, the estate called and said the car was mine if I wanted it.

This purchase launched me into the world of "old" cars—as distinct from "classic" cars, which must be in pristine condition. It also led me to the only repair shop at the time in East Hampton capable of caring for our old car, and to a repairman by the name of John Johnston. I think I spent more time with John and the '42 Buick over the next decade than I did with my family, as it was almost a ritual every weekend to visit his hospital for sick cars, as mine was a constant patient. While with John one day, I saw on a rotating display at a nearby Buick dealership a 1939 four-door Buick Phaeton convertible, massive and gorgeous with its "suicide" doors. I bought that one, too, and kept it for decades until I sold it in 2019 to my current car doctor, Jim Shelly, who everyone in the Hamptons knows as the antique car specialist. Once in a while over the past two years I have had reason to visit Jim's garage, and I'd see the Buick with its in-process face-lift and I'd get wistful. I'd feel like I'd lost an old friend. Jim finished restoring the car early in 2021 and took it on a thousand-mile cross-country rally called the Great Race. He came in 10th place in my old Buick out of 110 cars in the rally!

After I bought my second Buick, I started attending the annual Hershey Classic Auto Show in Hershey, Pennsylvania, in the same way I frequent New York art galleries. Every year I would bring my sons and put Mark, Jon, and Jamie up to making the rounds of all the parts dealers to ask if they had any parts for a '39 or a '42 Buick. At Hershey, I eventually bought a bright yellow 1927 Franklin convertible with a rumble seat—not the same make, but the same type of car my father drove when I was a kid. In a different year I bought a 1953 MG, because every young man who came of age in the 1950s dreamed of driving one—and now I can.

Alan Patricof at the starting line of the Bridgehampton Road Rally in his 1927 Franklin Boat Tail.

CHAPTER 5

Driving on the Left Side of the Road

In 1981 I took a lunch meeting with a pair of aspiring business partners who wanted financial support to apply for a cellular license. The US government had scheduled a lottery to distribute cellular service licenses in each of the thirty cellular markets defined by the FCC. Each market would get two licenses, but the first license went automatically to the incumbent telephone service provider. The second would go to the winning applicant. Lifelong friends from Cleveland, George Blumenthal, who ran a small stock brokerage firm, and Bill Ginsberg, a former Deputy Chief of Policy for the FCC (they met in grade school), wanted to form a company to apply in Ohio, their home state.

It's hard to get across in today's mobile phone–driven market how speculative George and Bill's idea was. At the time there were over seven hundred radio paging companies, many of them public. Everyone expected them to compete and assumed they would have an advantage as known entities. Then there were AT&T and Motorola, who had partnered with the FCC in Chicago in a cellular experiment that resulted in only modest market projections: AT&T thought the ten largest markets would end up with one million cellular devices total; Motorola—the leading provider of radio and mobile technology—estimated three hundred thousand. That works out to market penetration of 1–2 percent.

George and Bill believed the market would be bigger than that. They didn't know *how* big, but they believed new technology would improve cellular service to the point that mobile phone sound quality would be as good as what you got from a landline. Improved usability would then lead to increased demand, and eventually, lower prices for the customer.

The economics of building the business were also appealing. George argued that the radio towers needed to send the signals wouldn't experience physical depreciation—they'd go up once and stay up, allowing any business that built them to break even with relatively few subscribers. The initial projection called for subscriber revenue of $70 per month and total growth in subscribers over five years to eight thousand users for a four-cell system. (To put that into context, the state of Ohio today has more than eleven million cell phone users.)

Despite their only modest credentials, George and Bill had enormous enthusiasm and had done an impressive amount of preparation. They also had a number of financial commitments from creditable individuals who were familiar with the application process. Based on that, APA decided to support them. I brought in Venrock, the investing firm for the Rockefeller family, as an investing partner. Ted McCourtney represented the firm. Sidney Knafel also joined us as a private investor—he was a former partner of Loeb, Rhoades & Co.

When the lottery took place, Cellular Communications Inc. (CCI), as George and Bill named their firm, was one of twenty-five applicants; LIN Broadcasting was another. The low market projections had scared people off, to CCI's benefit. The company won licenses for six contiguous Ohio markets. Through partnerships and trading, CCI ended up with different levels of ownership in Cleveland, Akron, Canton, Cincinnati, Dayton, and Columbus, Ohio, and a small ownership stake in Dallas. In March 1985, CCI went live in Ohio with 6,750 subscribers—84 percent of its projected five-year market penetration. In July 1986 it went public, raising $25 million by selling 20 percent of the company.

CCI grew and expanded far past the Ohio market to become, for a time, the third largest carrier in the US. It also formed an international company with licenses in Italy and India, which held similar lotteries to the one that took place in the United States. A third CCI-owned company operated cellular networks in Puerto Rico. In 1996, AirTouch (PacTel) acquired CCI for $2.5 billion; in 1999 Cellular of Puerto Rico was acquired for $800 million by Southwest Bell and Cellular International by Olivetti for $2.2 billion.

CCI is among the great successes of APA. The story, however, would not be completely honest without including the final chapter. During its fast-growth period, CCI bought a stake in International Cabletel (renamed NTL), a player in the UK cable television market. Unique for the time, the UK allowed a cable company to also offer telephone service, and CCI jumped on the opportunity. NTL was on a roll, raising equity and substantial debt through the 1990s and early 2000s—in fact, too *much* debt. We sold bonds as easily as the Good Humor truck sells ice cream cones on a hot day. If we announced a plan to sell $200 million in bonds at a 2 percent interest rate, by the time the sale opened, we had demand for $300 million at a 1 percent interest rate.

We ultimately became victims of our own debt-selling success. There's an important lesson in that for today's investor and entrepreneur—don't get carried away by your own ability to raise capital and lose sight of the true economics of the business. NTL became overleveraged and couldn't then raise equity to pay down the debt and get the company back on track. It was forced to engage with a workout group, which forced out the existing shareholders and successfully restructured the organization. NTL survived under new ownership and merged into Virgin Media in 2006, which was acquired by Liberty Global in 2013 for $23 billion. If we could have held on and financed the company, NTL would have been worth more than all George and Bill's previous companies we had sold.

Given the ubiquity of mobile telecommunications now, I am often surprised that there are still places with spotty cell coverage—most notably East Hampton, where I own a home, and where influential denizens have objected to the aesthetics of cell towers and kept one from going up in the town. The consequence is poor call coverage and regularly dropped calls. I got so sick of it, I recently sponsored a full-page ad in our local newspaper encouraging readers to write to the head of the town planning board and express support for another tower. The copy of the ad read, "We've had it up to here with horrible, non-existent cell phone service in Wainscott/ Sagaponack and on 114 from East Hampton to Sag Harbor," and followed with descriptions of scenarios where people needed help and couldn't get it because they had no cell coverage. The most recent vote approved a new tower. George Blumenthal would be pleased.

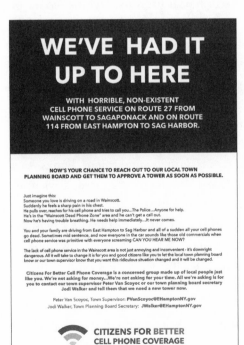

Full-page newspaper ad encouraging readers to write to the local planning board to express support for a new cell tower in East Hampton.

CCI REPRESENTED A GREAT FINANCIAL success for APA, and it marked a symbolic transition for the company from the catch-as-catch-can environment of the 1970s to more abundant, bigger, and more ambitious opportunities beginning in the 1980s and extending into the '90s.

I mentioned in the previous chapter how the liberalization of the SEC's rules for how pension funds could allocate capital, captured in the Plan Asset Allocation rules passed in the late 1970s as part of ERISA, served as a major catalyst for change. By the early 1980s, institutional investors began to make investments in venture capital funds. This meant more than just a new source of capital. Previous ERISA rules required regulators to go a layer down to approve each individual investment in a fund—not worth it for the institutional investor. The changes did away with that granular level of scrutiny. After the rules changed, only the fund as a whole would be evaluated.

The changes completely altered the private investment business. The high-net-worth individual investors of the 1970s and early 1980s were happy investing a relatively small sum of money for a relatively small share in a firm. Institutional investors, in contrast, wanted to invest larger amounts of capital. Concomitantly, the investment banks that had been taking smaller companies public started seeing competition from larger investment banks that wanted a piece of the expanding IPO market. The deal sizes grew over the subsequent decades to accommodate the investors' appetite, and the banks grew to handle the volume. By the late 1990s, the small investment banking firms and aftermarket brokerage houses that made the market for new issues in the 1970s could no longer compete. Eventually they sold themselves or went out of business.

Amidst these changes, APA also had to grow and adapt. One of the earliest signs of the changing times came in the early 1980s when I got a call from Tom Judge, a legend in institutional private equity and the head of AT&T's pension fund. AT&T was a pioneer in pension fund investing at that time. Signing Tom Judge and AT&T would be a major coup, and I eagerly arranged a meeting between me, Pat Cloherty, and Ed Goodman on our side, and Tom and his deputy Russ Steenberg for AT&T.

Now, I was and always am very careful with my clients' money. The decadence associated with the Wall Street of the 1980s was in full swing and gave a bad reputation to many of us in the investing world. I went out of my way to distance myself from the excess. When Tom and Russ asked about APA's management fees, I explained what they paid for and how careful I was about expenses. "I count everything, right down to the pencils and paperclips," I told them.

My answers seemed to satisfy them, and at the end of the meeting we shook hands and promised we'd speak again the following week. As soon as they left, I rushed to my office to gather my things. I had to give a speech in New Haven that evening and needed to leave. Harried, I made my way to the street, where I found a huge white stretch limousine in front of our building, the name Alan Patricof in a sign pressed into the window. I groaned. The service I used usually sent a simple black sedan, but the driver said they had a number of fares that evening, and the limo was the only car available. Having no choice, I got in. On the opposite side of the sign I found a note left for me by Tom and Russ:

Dear Alan,

Wonderful meeting. We were delighted to hear how cost conscious you are. This white stretch limousine is a perfect demonstration.
   Break a leg in New Haven.

Tom and Russ

I called Tom the next morning to explain that the car was not my doing, but he was laughing while I sputtered an apology. My reputation had preceded me. They invested in the Excelsior Fund we were raising at the time, starting a long relationship with APA.

Tom Judge is widely considered a pioneer among pension fund managers. As the chief investment officer of AT&T's pension fund, he was one of the first to put a share of a pension fund's assets into alternative investment vehicles like venture capital or private equity. Where he went, others followed. The pension funds of Conoco, DuPont, Manufacturers Hanover Bank, Mobil Oil, National Lead, and others became APA investors, leading to growth in the size of our funds.

There's a funny story connected with how we convinced Conoco to invest in our Excelsior I fund, the first to include pension investors. My brother-in-law Craig Hatkoff, Susan's brother, was at Columbia Business School at the time. He had been a computer science minor in college and learned to program in BASIC and FORTRAN. Craig used those skills in his job at Chemical Bank, where he commandeered a Hazeltine 1000 portable computer that weighed around thirty-five pounds, and which he lugged home nights and weekends to write BASIC programs to automatically calculate things like the interest reserve rate for each loan in the Chemical Bank portfolio—a standard metric that involved a lot of tedious, manual calculations. Craig's program allowed the bank to run scenarios more quickly and easily in that pre-spreadsheet era.

Intrigued, I asked Craig to create a program to simulate a venture capital portfolio performance based on various assumptions. He created a Monte Carlo simulation for the purpose, and at my request came with me to a meeting with representatives from the Conoco pension fund, his computer in tow (he'd named the Hazeltine HAL in homage to *2001: A Space Odyssey*). Craig's program showed that Conoco could expect between 20 percent and 30 percent annual returns on its investment, based on assumptions about how many companies were in the portfolio and what proportion would fail, break even, succeed modestly, or succeed wildly. Based on that presentation, Conoco invested $3 million in the Excelsior I fund. Craig's predictions turned out to be more optimistic than reality, but our performance was still good enough that Conoco invested again in the next fund.

As APA RESPONDED TO THE changing environment of the 1980s, it became more important to establish a presence on the West Coast. Through a recruiter we found and hired Bill Bottoms as a partner in 1984 to run the Palo Alto office. Bill was a technology expert and an executive with Varian Semiconductor Equipment, a supplier to chip manufacturers. We hired him in part because we saw the need for a technology specialist in the heart of Silicon Valley, though his interests ranged widely.

Bill brought Tessera Technologies to the portfolio. Through connections at Stanford, Bill had met a trio of IBM engineers with innovative ideas about semiconductor packaging that could enable chip manufacturers to make semiconductors lighter and smaller. The semiconductor industry was focused on fulfilling "Moore's Law," the prediction made in 1965 by Intel CEO Gordon Moore that computer processing capacity would double every twelve to eighteen months. Light and small chips were key to realizing Moore's Law, and the Tessera founders left Big Blue to develop their ideas independently.

For their first six months, they occupied the office next to mine at APA's Park Avenue location. The close quarters, coupled with the uncertainty of getting the company financed, were too much for one of the founders, and he went back to IBM. The two that remained, Igor Khandros and Thomas DiStefano, relocated to Tarrytown, just north of New York City on the Hudson River, and subsequently to Silicon Valley in pursuit of the technology crowd. Though it took more than ten years, the company became a big success. The partners, however, had a falling out, and Igor left to form a competing business in the semiconductor space called FormFactor. Thomas also eventually left Tessera (now called Xperi) after a merger, and founded Centipede Systems, a company that provides semiconductor technology for microelectronics. Xperi continues still, and recently acquired TiVO to expand into audio and television.

Bill also brought Chevys Fresh Mex to APA when it was a small outfit with a few locations. As Bill tells it, he'd eaten in the first Chevys in Alameda and enjoyed it, then discovered another while on a day trip with his wife a few months later. Bill approached the owner and explained how a small-and-growing company could meet its goals faster with venture capital. The owner demurred but reached out months later. The Chevys ethos of fresh food and custom décor scaled to thirty-seven stores before it was acquired in 1993 by the Taco Bell subsidiary of PepsiCo.

APA also invested in the hamburger chain Johnny Rockets under Bill's watch. I can't help but share the following interaction, which happened while APA was an investor. Mike Shumsky, the president and CEO, called me one day about a letter he'd received from Warren Buffett—I've included the letter on the next page, along with the rest of the correspondence.

The day after Mike's phone call by a strange coincidence I saw Warren at Michael's having lunch with a young couple who had contributed $250,000 to a charity in exchange for the right to dine with the Oracle. On the way out, he and I greeted each other. "I really do love those strawberry milkshakes," he said. "By the way, when is Johnny Rockets coming to Omaha?"

Three months later, Johnny Rockets not only gave Warren a VIP pass but posted on one of the signs in both the Palos Verde and San Francisco restaurants saying, "Warren eats here."

George Jenkins was another APA partner who joined in the mid-1980s. George had been a banker with Midlantic National Bank and had lived in London and Hong Kong, building branch networks and establishing relationships with aspiring multinational companies. I met him after he returned to the US to manage Midlantic's investments in venture capital funds. We got to know

BERKSHIRE HATHAWAY INC.
1440 KIEWIT PLAZA
OMAHA, NEBRASKA 68131
TELEPHONE (402) 346-1400
FAX (402) 346-3375

WARREN E. BUFFETT, CHAIRMAN

April 26, 2004

Mr. Mike Shumsky
Chairman and CEO
The Johnny Rockets Group, Inc.
26970 Aliso Viejo Parkway, Suite 100
Aliso Viejo, CA 92656-2621

Dear Mr. Shumsky:

Bill Gates has sent me a copy of your March 31 letter making him a VIP.

For years it has been gnawing at him that I have a VIP card from Hooters and that he doesn't. Now he has attained this advantage over me, since obviously Johnny Rockets carries much more prestige than Hooters.

It's an unquestioned fact that I eat at Johnny Rockets – both in San Francisco and Laguna – far more often than Bill frequents your establishments. I am a *huge* fan. If you see fit to send me a VIP card, I promise not to use it in order to save money, but simply to once again regain my rightful position in the pecking order vis-à-vis Bill.

Please correct this injustice.

Sincerely,

Warren E. Buffett

Warren E. Buffett

WEB/db

each other through mutual interest in a New Jersey wireless equipment company called Anadigics, another APA investment.

When George left Midlantic in the mid-1980s I invited him to lunch. While walking to the restaurant I asked about his plans. He said he intended to raise a venture fund and I literally stopped in the middle of the street. "Don't do that," I said. He joined APA instead.

THE JOHNNY ROCKETS GROUP, INC.
26970 ALISO VIEJO PARKWAY • SUITE 100 • ALISO VIEJO, CA 92656 • (949) 643-6100 • FAX:(949) 643-6200   johnnyrockets.com

June 2, 2004

Warren E. Buffett
Chairman
Berkshire Hathaway Inc.
1440 Kiewit Plaza
Omaha, NE 68131

Dear Warren:

We were delighted to receive your letter detailing the "injustice" you feel now exists as a result of our newest VIP, Bill Gates. We at Johnny Rockets realize that we have disturbed the vital "pecking order" that you have enjoyed for so long and would like to remedy this situation that could, if unchecked, alienate one of our favorite and influential customers!

It is in this spirit of executive recognition that we extend to you all benefits and bragging rights associated with being an official Johnny Rockets VIP! This VIP card entitles you and your guests to a free hamburger, starter and drink every time you visit. Just show your VIP card to the manager and he/she will be happy to take care of you.

In addition, per the attached photo, we are changing the décor of our Laguna Beach restaurant to include a permanent sign that reads "Warren Eats Here." We reserve this rite of passage for those who are our most loyal customers!

Please accept this gesture as a symbol of our unyielding commitment to our prominent clientele. We are honored that Mr. Gates and yourself are such strong fans of Johnny Rockets and are proud to play a small role in your competitive yet loyal friendship. We hope you stop by soon to enjoy some fresh American fries, one of our Original hamburgers and hand-dipped shakes while our servers dance up a storm to great jukebox music!

As always, it's a great day at Johnny Rockets!

Mike Shumsky

Mike Shumsky
Chairman and CEO
The Johnny Rockets Group, Inc.
26970 Aliso Viejo Parkway, Suite 100
Aliso Viejo, CA 92656-2621
(949) 643-6100
mshumsky@johnnyrockets.com

George made an early mark by establishing an APA fund in Pennsylvania, part of an effort by the Pennsylvania government to stimulate small business investing. Between 1988 and 1995, we raised three Pennsylvania funds totaling $200 million. One of our early investments was a chain of physical therapy and rehabilitation centers called Rehab Systems Corp., which sold to NovaCare just before going public. Another was Fore Systems, a Pittsburgh-based maker of network switches. Marconi purchased it in the late 1990s for $4.5 billion.

An amusing coda: years after Fore Systems sold and APA cashed in its shares, I received a call from the company's CEO and co-founder, Eric Cooper. He wanted me to speak at a high-tech conference in Pittsburgh. Flattered, I accepted the invitation, but when I arrived for the event, I received a lesson in English phonetics. The high-tech conference was really the Chai-Tech Conference—an annual meeting of Pittsburgh's Jewish entrepreneurs in technology. Chai—pronounced "high"—means alive or living in the Hebrew language. It also refers to the number eighteen, which has sacred meaning in Judaism, and is one reason why invitees to a bar or bat mitzvah give cash gifts in multiples of eighteen. Eric had assumed that since I was Jewish I'd know he meant *chai* and not *high*, but I missed it. Thankfully, my speech on the trends in tech was still relevant and went off well, but I made a note to ask more questions next time so I didn't get caught unprepared.

As APA GREW ITS PRESENCE in the US, the firm also reached further afield to explore opportunities in Europe. That effort began as early as 1975, when I first met Ronald Cohen through my friend Stanley Shuman, a partner at Allen & Co. (the same Stanley Shuman who connected me and Rupert Murdoch to restart negotiations to sell *New York Magazine*). An Egyptian-born, UK-raised polyglot of uncommon intellect and energy, Ronald attended Oxford and the Harvard Business School before co-founding a boutique investment firm called Multinational Management Group, or MMG (Ronald joked the acronym really meant "make money grow"). MMG had an office in London, which Ronald ran, and a legally separate office of the same name in Paris run by a fellow HBS graduate, Maurice Tchenio. MMG's Chicago office had closed when a third classmate from Harvard decided the business wasn't for him.

Ronald referred to MMG as a merchant bank—as distinct from an investment bank—to make clear the company intended to eventually raise a fund, though at that time MMG was a fee-based business focused on negotiating mergers and buyouts. It was not lost on us that what Ronald and Maurice were doing in Europe was similar to what I was building with the combined activities of APA and the Patricof & Co. Capital investment bank I'd formed to do fee business.

Needless to say, Ronald and I hit it off. On the basis of personality alone, we were both ambitious and high energy and shared the view that good people at the helm of start-ups and growth firms were key to good investment deals. In our first meeting we passed a few animated hours discussing the potential we both saw for venture investing in Europe.

It was fortuitous for both of us to find another person who shared that view. There was little appetite among talented Europeans of the 1970s for the risks involved in launching a startup. Senior-level business professionals in London and Paris had long-term financial security, a thirty-five-hour work week, and contract terms that included a personal car and driver. Why give that up for the uncertain salary and long hours of the start-up entrepreneur, especially in a country that offered no payback? Going public with an IPO in the UK in 1976 was virtually impossible. Add in the fact that failure carried a stigma for Europeans (as opposed to Americans, who've self-selected for risk since the *Mayflower*), and it's clear why our views were generously labeled iconoclastic—and less generously, foolish. Without start-up entrepreneurs to back, there would be little point in raising a fund. That was the received wisdom, but sooner or later this would change and both Ronald and I knew someone had to go first. We were both confident enough to believe it could be us. And so it ultimately was. (Peter Brooke didn't open Advent Ltd. in the UK until 1978.)

Months after our first meeting, Ronald and I came to terms over dinner at a restaurant in Chicago. He says we were at an Italian restaurant called Zorians; I remember us eating Chinese food. Undisputed is the fact that APA was a little more than six years old. The portfolio was growing with companies like Datascope, RSR, NAC, and Periphonics, but the venture environment was still tough after the stock market crash in 1973. Ronald and I agreed that I would rebrand the investment banking business, Patricof & Co. Capital, to MMG/Patricof. I would also place a plaque on the door next to the APA venture capital firm logo. Ronald and Maurice would, in turn, put up an Alan Patricof Associates plaque on the doors to the UK and Paris offices next to the MMG/Patricof logo.

Ronald, Maurice, and I agreed that each office would carry its own costs and have exclusive rights on deals in its local market. For international investment banking transactions, however, the firm operating as MMGPatricof would split the fees fifty-fifty between Europe and the US after assigning a 20 percent fee to the originating office. We would also eventually form venture funds in Europe under the name APA, for which the US would receive 33 percent of the management fees and carried interest of the first fund; 25 percent of the second fund; 20 percent of the third fund; and 10 percent thereafter.

At the end of our meal, the deal worked out, the waitress brought our check. Ronald and I agree fully on the fact that she also brought orange slices and fortune cookies—how could we have been at an Italian place that served fortune cookies? Ronald has many times recalled that one of the cookies held the message, "You will make money with your friend."

Every deal brings some uncertainty, but I didn't hesitate to make this one. It excited me to see my young financial firm become an international entity overnight with offices in New York, London, and Paris. I was very much carried away by the vision of my nameplate in the lobby in these world cities. Ronald, Maurice, and I commemorated the launch of our partnership by holding a mini-conference in London at the Grosvenor House Hotel. We invited local bankers, lawyers, and accountants to attend. Bill Casey, then head of the US

SEC, agreed on my urging to be our keynote speaker, a real coup for a new firm with no recognizable clients.

Shortly thereafter Ronald sold Lawry's Foods—maker of the seasoned salts and sauces originally used in Lawry's Restaurant in Los Angeles, California. The buyer was the Thomas J. Lipton Company, a subsidiary of Unilever. The US office played no part in the transaction, but since buyer and seller were US-based, Ronald sent the appropriate share of the fee anyway. "That was the agreement," he said when I called him to protest. That act of partnership set the tone for the next twenty-five years.

At around that same time, the US investment banking operation had an assignment with a retailer in Texas called Solo Serve. We worked together with the MMGPatricof UK office to organize an investment in Solo Serve by General Atlantic Partners, a holding company founded by a gentleman named Chuck Feeney, who had already made his fortune with Duty Free Shop. General Atlantic Partners was also just beginning to make its own investments. The company would evolve to become one of the largest and most active private equity firms in the US, but back then it was early days, and General Atlantic Partners became one of the first limited partners in APA's Excelsior Funds—the series of funds that came after our inaugural Decahedron Fund. Chuck Feeney is also well-known today as a pioneer philanthropist and social investor.

These early transcontinental successes predicted a long, fruitful partnership for MMG and APA. Almost twenty years later, after significant growth and international expansion, we merged each of the investment banking and each of the venture capital operations and rebranded them as divisions of Apax Partners. It was a necessary step in an increasingly populous field of investors. We debated what to name the merged entity for a long time, and even hired a brand consulting firm to launch an elaborate effort. In the end, one of the firm's partners came up with a simple solution: Add an *X* to APA (Alan Patricof Associates) for "cross border." That settled the matter, though Ronald likes to tell people the name "Apax" derives from the Greek word for "once and once only."

FROM THE OUTSET, RONALD and I planned to work on investment banking deals in the mold of MMGPatricof & Co. and over time introduce venture capital to the European market through APA. As it happened, four years passed before we raised the first venture funds: a £10 million fund in 1981 in the UK and a 100 million-franc fund in France in 1982—about $17 million each in 1981 currency rates. It took over a year to raise the capital for each fund. Such was the attitude toward early-stage investing. In the end, the investors were a fifty-fifty mix of US private sector investment funds and UK county councils making modest investments from their pension funds. Both the US and the UK investors were pioneers seeking new opportunities for their capital. It was a leap of faith.

Finding viable startups was a different challenge. Ronald and I and Peter Englander, who we hired to lead the venture team in London, along with an early hire named Adrian Beecroft, scoured the business pages and made calls, just as Pat and I had done in the US a decade before. I went to London and Paris almost every month to work with Peter, Adrian, Ronald, and, later, Maurice, and to train them in conducting due diligence on new companies with no financial track record.

The pickings were even slimmer than they had been in the US, and we were desperate for projects. One of the first investments we made in the UK was Motomop. A self-propelled vehicle with a sponge roller at its base to absorb liquid from flat surfaces, the Motomop could quickly clear cricket fields and golf courses to keep tournaments running (it rains a lot in England!). I was optimistic when the company won a contract in 1984 with the US arm of the Professional Golfers' Association (PGA), but a year later, Motomop was in liquidation.

Another early investment, in which Patricia was involved, was in PPL Therapeutics in Scotland, the company that cloned Dolly the sheep. PPL also bred genetically modified cows and pigs. In each case, its purpose was to more efficiently produce a protein, enzyme or other therapeutic agent for pharmaceutical purposes—essentially use animals as pharmaceutical factories. It was a big idea, but PPL Therapeutics never managed to earn revenues despite plenty of press and attention. The company ultimately failed, though Dolly made the front page of every newspaper in the world—part of scientific history.

The promise of using animals for advanced medical purposes continues today. Just last week, doctors at the University of Maryland Medical Center in Baltimore successfully transplanted a pig's heart into a human, a technology that Patricia explored from a team at Princeton close to thirty years ago. Their demonstration pig was named Wilhelmina. We ultimately didn't invest because we knew it would take a long time to commercialize, but it's interesting to see the long arc of innovation from Dolly to Wilhelmina in the 1980s to a man with a new heart in Baltimore in 2022.

PPL Therapeutics in Scotland successfully cloned Dolly the sheep.

Gradually the environment improved, and the European offices made some hugely successful venture investments. Among them was Computacenter, an early B2B provider of PC systems, and later, managed networks for UK businesses. We also invested in Ginger Media (Sir Richard Branson was a co-investor) and Esprit Telecom, which was later bought by George Soros's Global TeleSystems Group. Our French firm was a founding investor with Rothschild & Co. of the cosmetic retailer Sephora.

The most famous and lucrative venture investment for the UK branch of the business was in an enterprise software provider specializing in big data. Eventually branded as Autonomy, it would become the UK's largest enterprise software firm and first £1 billion stock issue. (HP bought Autonomy in 2011, a decade after Apax UK sold its 7 percent stake in the company for £700 million. The HP/ Autonomy acquisition is now the subject of a major lawsuit—Apax is not involved).

In this way Europe broke through the lack of start-up culture to build a venture capital industry. Ronald was eventually knighted by the Queen of England for his role in establishing the venture industry in the UK. Maurice led the French business according to his style and sensibility and was awarded the Légion d'Honneur by the president of France for his contribution to France start-up culture.

For decades, I have had to accept the ignominious unofficial title in the US of "legend" due to my age and longevity in the venture industry—not quite the same. I had long accepted that fate when I received a letter in late September 2020, in the midst of the COVID-19 crisis, informing me that I had been awarded the French Légion d'Honneur by President Macron.

Years earlier, a friend in Paris, Vivien de Gunzburg, had suggested that I receive the Légion, and enlisted Marcel Wormser (along with Maurice Tchenio), who had originally guided us in obtaining license number one. I had completely forgotten! So now I get to be legend and a Légion for my role in starting the first venture

Alan and Susan Patricof visiting Tokyo in 1998 to establish Apax Globis Japan Fund's first investment in 1999.

fund in France nearly forty years ago and working to pass enabling legislation.

In 1989, we merged the investment banking business with that of a very similar Swiss firm called Corporate Finance Partners (CFP), led by Michael Hinderer and Max Berger. I had first met Michael in 1988 when he approached me after I gave a keynote at a venture capital conference in Düsseldorf, Germany, hosted by the German newspaper, *Handelsblatt.* CFP had only been in business for a year or so by then, yet it was in the running for a deal involving a Swiss cosmetics company called La Prairie, which was owned by Sanofi in France. The French arm of MMGPatricof was also pitching the deal, but CFP won it—and that got my attention. I was further convinced they would make good partners after Max came to meet me in New York during a layover between Zurich and Bogotá, where he was going for the holidays. After several round-robin negotiations across multiple countries, CFP changed the name of their corporate finance business to MMGPatricof and they opened a venture business they named Alan Patricof Associates. Thus, they became the third leg of the European stool.

Almost immediately after the ink was dry, APA's institutional investors in the US began asking about investment opportunities in the German market. Reunification of the east and west parts of the country into a single German Democratic Republic was underway. On the urging of our investors, Michael and Max established a second office in Munich, Germany, and raised a 90-million deutschmark investment fund (about $40 million at the time). We eventually opened offices in Madrid, Spain and Milan, Italy, and formed a Japanese joint venture, Apax/Globis, where I personally spent a year training investors and establishing the business.

In spite of some major successes, however, early-stage investing was never the primary activity anywhere in Europe. Try as they may, none of the European offices could find an adequate number of start-ups. The failure rates were high, and entrepreneurs were few. Germany's *Mittelstand* ethos of family-owned businesses with slow-but-steady growth is just one example of the cultural challenges we continued to face with a financing model dedicated to helping early-stage-growth companies. Instead, the German operation found significant buyout and merger opportunities. One transatlantic deal involved the purchase of a large US commercial printer, W.A. Krueger, by a Swiss printer called Ringier. More commonly, the German partners were busy consolidating large and disjointed markets inside Europe. In another notable deal, Michael and Max consolidated a number of bread and bakery businesses under the brand name Kamps—a known retail brand in Germany—and sold the combined entity to the Italian food producer, Barilla.

These examples were typical of the deals that were available at the time—larger-scale buyouts of established firms. Eventually the partners in Europe stopped looking for venture deals and fully embraced a private equity model of finance.

Ronald and I had, and continue to have, a very close relationship based on a range of mutual interests and shared sensibility, but we ultimately dealt with different markets and pursued different goals for the firm's capital. Ronald reminded me recently when we were speaking of the past that gradually he and the other European partners came to believe that the best goal for the European funds was to seek the best return possible for investments of large amounts of capital. They lost any appetite for investing early-stage growth capital, and instead gravitated to later-stage, larger investments with less downside risk. Private equity, in other words, presented a more comfortable and profitable way to deploy larger amounts of capital in their markets.

The US partnership, in contrast, continued much longer to try to achieve the highest return on, by comparison, smaller investments—venture. Even so, the US took the opportunities we saw to do later-stage deals, and over time the balance of our business began to shift as well.

THROUGHOUT THE 1980S IN THE US, we brought on more people focused on larger and later-stage investments. Robert Chefitz joined APA in 1987 from Golder Thoma, where he'd focused on consolidating fragmented service industries like funeral homes and pager companies. At APA, Robert funded Office Depot before it had its first store. John Megrue, a leveraged buyout specialist, also joined for a few years to lead deals like one we did with Sunglass Hut, which went public under our watch, as well as Dr. Leonards, a healthcare equipment supplier.

Alongside these leveraged buyouts and late-stage investments, our ventures continued. Tech opportunities exploded by the early '90s, and the venture capital industry had expanded in kind. Dozens of funds were now competing with ours for the same pool of promising start-ups. The challenge shifted from finding great companies to convincing the ones we found that APA was the right partner.

We also saw a lot of media deals and did a few of them. As the media industry began to embrace digital publishing formats in the 1990s, APA invested in a few specialty publications, most notably MedScape, a company founded by Peter Frishauf to provide the most current medical research for medical professionals and informed citizens (a radical idea for the time). I became chairman and brought in CBS as a partner and eventually took the company public before it was ultimately sold to WebMD. MedScape is now a major content component of that company, something Peter reminisces about every day.

Another digital media investment came my way via the journalist and writer Don Katz, who asked to meet me in 1996 to share his idea for distributing audiobooks. Audible emerged from Don's obsession with listening to books and music on a Sony Walkman while he jogged. The Walkman was cumbersome and inefficient, especially when it came time to turn the tape. Helped by some geniuses from Bell Labs, Don built and patented a design for a solid-state cassette device. He reached out to me while raising his first post-angel round. Together with Kleiner Perkins, APA invested $1,250,000, for which each investor acquired 10 percent of the company.

Audible needed several more rounds of financing in 1997 and 1998, which brought in $3 million from AT&T Ventures, an investment from an affiliate of Compaq, and $5 million from Microsoft Corp. APA and Kleiner also contributed another $2 million each, to reach a total of $27 million raised pre-IPO for almost 50 percent of the company. Audible sold another 16 percent for $36 million through its IPO. The company then went public with a valuation of $225 million based on quarterly revenues in 1Q99 of $315,000— clearly, we were in the midst of the tech bubble.

A major inflection point for Audible occurred in 2001, when Steve Jobs invited Don Katz to Cupertino to get a firsthand look at an early version of the iPod. Don realized that handheld MP3 players would entirely change the trajectory of Audible. The device's functionality, ease of use, and form factor would make audio content ubiquitous and easily accessible for millions. Katz stopped making Audible's proprietary hardware and formed a partnership with Apple, but not before Microsoft invested another $10 million in the company.

In spite of these business wins, Audible's stock price suffered during the dot-com crash, and by December 2002, it had fallen to $.30 per share—one of "the living dead" public companies that could only be found on the Pink Sheets. By 2003 Amazon had become involved as a distributor of Audible books, and by the end of that year the stock had gotten back to $4 per share, still less than half the IPO price. APA, together with a few of the other investors, bought the shares Microsoft owned, which set us up nicely for the 2008 purchase of Audible by Amazon for $300 million. Today, Audible is purportedly a $1 billion-plus business. While we can contemplate "what if," such massive growth was likely only possible because of Amazon's capital, its massive content distribution platform, and its powerful negotiating power in book publishing.

Biopharmaceutical companies also became a larger part of the portfolio, initially through Patricia's foresight. Among her most successful investments was Agouron, a developer of one of the first antiretroviral treatments for HIV/AIDS (Agouron is now a division of Pfizer). Due to the complex and specialized nature of the healthcare industry, APA ultimately formed a dedicated healthcare practice, which came to include investors like Adele Oliva, who joined in the late 1990s. She worked on a number of high-profile deals, including Alliance Medical, a third-party re-processor of single-use medical devices for hospitals, and Prometheus, which focused on diagnostic technologies and therapies for gastroenterology.

In the mid-1990s we hired Paul Vais, a technologist-cum-marketer who'd worked for NeXT, the company Steve Jobs founded in the interregnum after leaving and before returning to Apple. Paul was an energetic presence in the tech halls of Silicon Valley during the internet boom. As a result of his influence, we backed Cadence Design Systems, a Silicon Valley company with products used to design computer chips and circuit boards, and mobile media and gaming company Jamdat Mobile, now part of Electronic Arts.

Jamdat, as Paul opined to me recently, was the last pure early-stage tech venture deal APA did in the US. There were other early-stage investments in companies like Life Time Fitness, one of the first public company gym chains, but the balance had shifted. In 2000 the US raised its first $1 billion fund. It was a major event, but less significant in the international context of Apax Partners. The UK business, once so modest, had already surpassed the $1 billion mark to become much larger than the US operation. The new generation of talent joining APA in the US were leveraged buyout experts or late-stage investors. One representative example is Jackie Reses, who'd spent seven years at Goldman Sachs before joining APA as a media specialist. She immediately wrote a business plan for APA to execute multinational leveraged buyouts in media. In that role she worked on a successful international deal with the London office to acquire the Yellow Pages company. (Until recently, Jackie ran Square Capital, the small-business finance arm of the digital payments company, Square. She was recently profiled in *Forbes* as a newly-minted billionaire due to the stock-market success of Square).

Jason Wright, an investor who was new to APA at that time, likes to tell a story about me related to Yellow Pages. It was Jackie's deal, but it was also a media company, so I took a special interest in it. By "special" I actually mean skeptical. The deal involved the market leader in the UK, called Yell, acquiring Yellow Pages in the US, where Yell already owned a non-leading competitor called Yellow Book. It seemed to me to be a low-margin advertising business with a lot of competition. My views were confirmed one evening (I thought) as I stepped into the kitchen of a friend of mine during a dinner party and saw Yellow Pages competitors stacked on the table under the telephone. There must have been three or four of them. I brought them to Jason the next day and threw them down on the desk and told him to look into them.

Jason likes this story because he says it's very "Alan", by which he means that I was hyper-focused and curious about the details. My primary concern is always how the company makes money, and whether the investment valuation matches the reality of the business. When I have a real-world experience with a company, as I did by seeing all those competing yellow books piled on top of each other and probably opened by no one, I learn as much, if not more, than the numbers an entrepreneur presents in their pitch. It's human nature to sugarcoat, and the only way an investor can learn the truth is by looking for it outside the list of references provided by the start-up.

Though I remained skeptical about investing in the Yellow Pages acquisition, I was ultimately overruled and the deal went forward, and it turned out to be successful for Apax. It's hard to believe, given our present-day environment, in which "search" is synonymous with Google and yellow-page directories are a near-extinct memory of days gone by. Acquisitions and takeovers were the core of Apax by then. The internet bubble and then the bust that transpired from 1999 through 2001 put the final nail in the venture coffin at APA.

The minority of deals we still had in the portfolio that were pure venture in nature struggled to make payroll, while on the other side of the house, we were providing lower-risk capital for deals like Phillips-Van Heusen's (PVH) purchase of Calvin Klein, and shortly thereafter, Tommy Hilfiger. Private equity had become more important in the structure of the firm. APA in the US eventually merged with a private equity firm called Saunders, Karp & Megrue (John Megrue had been an APA associate in the 1980s), and all of the separate country entities except for France merged into one legal entity known as Apax Partners. (You know how independent the French are.) Jason Wright, the young associate conducting due diligence on Yellow Pages and a close personal friend, now runs the Apax Partners Global Tech and Telecom division.

By all reasonable measures, APA/Apax Partners was and is a huge success. As I write this, the company has more than $60 billion under management. Even in 2001 it was thriving despite the general economic malaise. I, on the other hand, felt unmoored. The firm had announced it wouldn't raise another venture fund and would instead focus exclusively on private equity. That wasn't for me. I like building things, and I like variety in my life. I was experiencing less and less of both at Apax. On the contrary, I was spending the majority of my time dealing with small matters, such as hiring and firing staff, reviewing documentation, attending internal offsites, and otherwise dealing with the operational minutiae that exist in every large business.

I was bored.

I remember calling Susan from the office one hot summer Friday in 2001. I was feeling very low about something—probably another of our venture investments spiraling down—and I said we should go to a funny movie. We ended up seeing *Rat Race* with John Cleese and Whoopi Goldberg. To this day, after multiple viewings, I think of it as one of the funniest movies I've ever seen. More relevantly, that night marked something of a turning point for me. The venture business had changed. The company I founded had changed. I wasn't enjoying what I was doing anymore. After thirty years, the time had come to try something new. My sons have pointed out that the decision I made, shortly thereafter, to transition from Apax, left a lot of money on the table. Money alone, however, wasn't enough to keep me. I was ready to try a new route.

Rules of the Road: Driving Lessons from Mid-Career

The period of the 1980s through 2000 presented new challenges for APA/Apax as a company—and as an investor. Larger, more diverse deals gave us more opportunities to solidify our reputation.

As the heat went up on the start-up and venture capital market in the '80s and '90s, I saw scores of companies grapple with the challenge of how to finance growth in a way that limits dilution. Do you seek outside finance in exchange for selling a share of the business, or do you try to limit how much of the company you need to give up?

I recall many years ago my friend Thomas Gibson—the former head salesman at the Marlborough Gallery—came to see me to ask if I would finance a new art gallery he was planning in London. I didn't believe that an art gallery was a good candidate for venture investment and suggested instead that he get several clients to consign their collection for sale to the gallery in advance of the opening. Then he could use the profits to capitalize the new endeavor. That way he would keep 100 percent ownership while doing what galleries do—sell art. He followed my advice and maintained full ownership until 2019, when he transferred ownership of the gallery to his son.

On reflection, the model I suggested to Thomas of using customer prepayments to fund the business is the one I myself had followed when starting APA in 1970. I continue to encourage entrepreneurs to consider ways to reduce their need for outside capital. Some options include capturing "free" inventory like Thomas did, signing customers to a fee-in-advance-based model as I did in the first years of APA, or negotiating with suppliers for extended payment terms, among others—anything to reduce capital needs and thereby reduce the need for equity, which dilutes the founder's ownership. Of course, capital-intensive businesses that need huge inflows of capital early on can't grow in this way, but they are seldom financed by venture capitalists unless they have large upfront development costs.

My time at APA/Apax clearly coincided with a major period of innovation in the tech space, and thus with a wave of patent-seeking by certain growth businesses. Many entrepreneurs believe patents (which are usually pending at the venture stage) are compelling assets in the minds of investors. I am here to tell you that the only way a patent has value is when the entrepreneur has the time and money to defend it and go after violators.

I speak from experience. My first serious encounter with patents was when we backed Tessera (now Xperi), the semiconductor packaging technology firm started by the former IBM engineers. For thirty years, Xperi has filed patents for multiple semiconductor packaging technologies, and spent many years in the courts full time defending its intellectual property. According to its annual report, the company has employed at one time or another as many as twenty-four in-house lawyers to defend its ten thousand patents. Every so often Xperi wins a suit and collects prior royalties, but it takes years of litigation, only to have it appealed, which puts the company back in the courts for another five years of litigation and motions. These experiences have taught me (and Xperi's shareholders) the hard way that even with patents in their portfolio, they still have to build manufacturing activities, diversify, and build solid operating businesses.

Other storied companies have had similar experiences, including Rambus and Qualcomm. These firms had unique and extensive patent portfolios that, in the end, the market made clear were not valuable in and of themselves, and did not determine market success. A further point of reference, Kodak and Polaroid—giants in the photography market—had thousands of patents that became less valuable due to changes in technology. When the companies went into bankruptcy, the existence of those patents added limited amounts to their respective valuations.

It's the rare start-up company that has patented a fundamental process in a sufficiently narrow way as to create a true differentiating element. More often than not, any violators are larger companies with more resources, including lawyers on staff solely to prosecute or defend patents. They can delay you with so many appeals that years can pass without resolution. In the meantime, the market continues to move, and the patent becomes less valuable. In the end, winning in the marketplace is what counts, both in the short and long run. Patents are almost never a winning strategy.

Winning in the market requires patience while the firm executes its strategy over stages. One of my key principles of venture investing is that you should wipe out the biggest amount of risk with the least amount of capital. In practice, this means giving founders sufficient capital to reach the next inflection point of their business—whether that is to prove the concept or the business model or reach a certain level of scale—but not so much that they scale or expand before they've mastered the fundamentals of their market. In the case of a deal like Office Depot or Life Time Fitness, for example, I wanted to invest so that the founders could stand up a limited number of locations and prove their market value before scaling to five or ten or a hundred locations.

This idea of proving the business model and squeezing out the risk with a limited amount of capital is in direct contrast to the prevailing approach to start-up financing today, which is for investors to give, and for start-ups to take, as much money as they can get. Today's investors and entrepreneurs are more likely to embrace the ethos promoted by Reid Hoffman and Chris Yeh in *Blitzscaling: The Lightning-Fast Path to Building Massively Valuable Companies*— which asks investors to "throw money at" a promising early-stage venture so it can fully occupy a market before competitors can come in and get traction. In my view, this rapid-scale approach downplays some of the problems companies confront when they raise huge amounts of capital without a proven economic model to justify it. It also creates a bigger hurdle that the start-up needs to overcome to justify its valuation and pay back the investors. A solid business idea that is ultimately only relevant for a moderate market could still be successful on its own terms and earn a reasonable return for investors that put in a small amount of capital. Furthermore, why sell 25 percent of your life's passion if you can grow to critical mass selling only 10 percent?

Another key lesson that became painfully apparent toward the end of the dot-com boom is best summed up in the words of a great, now deceased, CEO, Monty Shapiro of General Instrument, who always said, "Don't count on a cascade of miracles." There is a tendency among enthusiastic entrepreneurs and investors to make predictions for the future that depend on a set of variables aligning in perfect timing. Reality never works like that, however, and therefore entrepreneurs shouldn't build budgets or growth projections based on the compounding of positive assumptions. Revenues do not automatically go up while gross margins also increase, and overhead drops and efficiencies increase. Account for the fact that some things won't go your way.

One area where it's important to maintain a sense of realism is around growth. Every once in a while, an early-stage entrepreneur will come in and present an idea that has achieved impressive early results. One of the investors might say, "It looks too good, it can't be true." More often than not, the issue isn't that the business didn't achieve those results, but that the results can't be sustained. We saw that with CareSync, a company that served Medicare recipients using nurses operating out of call centers. For months, the numbers only went up, and then attrition set in. But for a while it *was* too good to be true...and then it wasn't true at all. We also saw it with Viddy, a video-focused social media platform that for a few months everyone thought would be the next Twitter, right up until it tanked. The lesson is, don't get carried away when results seem fantastic to the point that it defies logic. The business needs to sustain those results before you can count on them. If something seems too good to be true, it probably isn't sustainable.

There is a corollary point for both investors and entrepreneurs on the importance of paying meticulous attention to details. Looking up all the competing Yellow Pages is an example of the kind of attention I mean. Having a detailed understanding of the customer, a relentless willingness to confirm facts, the discipline to control costs, and a head for reading contracts can often mean the difference between failure and survival. Meticulous attention to detail is a quality I look for in every entrepreneur who's walked through the doors of Apax, and now through the doors of Greycroft. I want people for whom nothing is too small to ignore when it comes to their business and how they manage talent, customers, product development, expenditures—everything.

Another lesson learned by long experience is to avoid thinking in parochial terms. What works or doesn't work in New York City, or any other place, is not necessarily applicable to the rest of the country...but it could be. Case in point: in 1984 one of the young associates at APA on the West Coast was an outdoor aficionado and into health foods and nutrition and counter-culture experiences. One day he brought up a possible investment in a new coffee shop chain which had four or five stores in Seattle, his hometown. I automatically thought this was just another flaky counter-culture idea of his. Anyone from the Big Apple knew that we had an overabundance of coffee shops, one or two on every block. The world didn't need more of them.

Well, the company he introduced to us so many years ago, as you may have guessed, was Starbucks. Clearly, I was wrong. I was burdened by my own local thinking and didn't latch on to the broader concept of a new type of coffee shop designed for socializing. It was a new lifestyle concept of people not just going to get coffee, but hanging out, which I didn't catch because of my local prejudice. I imagine Howard Schultz laughing at me as Starbucks opens store number fifteen thousand.

Though not literally, *Rat Race* marked the end of my time at the company I started in 1970. In 2001 I announced I would transfer my ownership from Apax Partners to the other partners, and I began the process of unwinding my relationship with the firm. It would take almost four years for all the companies in which the firm had active venture investments to fully gain liquidity. We had a responsibility to our investors to unwind our existing portfolio, even as the firm expanded towards later-stage investments. In the meantime, I took some time to figure out where I wanted to travel to next in my life. At the time I had no idea what I was going to do, but I knew there was another venture in my future.

CHAPTER 6

Road Trips in Politics and Volunteering

To understand how I decided to spend my time as I was withdrawing from Apax, I need to pan back in time to when I first became involved in Democratic politics. Everyone who experiences a modicum of business success will at some point start to get calls from politicians asking for support. I am no exception, though it didn't happen early in my career. I only had one small experience in 1960 when I ran a fundraiser for the city council campaign of Ronnie Eldridge, a New York television personality and activist. Ronnie lost, and no one asked me to raise money for them again, nor did I volunteer, until I met Bill Clinton in 1988, notwithstanding a brief flirtation with Jimmy Carter's presidential campaign in 1978.

Bill and I were introduced by Liz Robbins, a Washington lobbyist who has a house near mine in East Hampton. Every summer in August, Liz hosts a weekend-long soirée at the shore to introduce friends to up-and-coming politicians. She calls this annual event "summer camp." She, ahead of others, felt that Bill had presidential potential and wanted to help expand his network and introduce him in a more intimate forum. (Many years later, at another "summer camp", the Robbins

142

home was overbooked, and a then-young senator Joe Biden was left without a room. Susan and I invited him to stay at our home, thus marking the Blue Room bedroom in our East Hampton house for posterity as having hosted two presidents and one almost-president of the United States, since Bill and Hillary had also each by then stayed with us.)

In that summer of 1988 Bill had some ground to cover, after giving a speech earlier that summer at the Democratic Convention. He was supposed to speak for fifteen minutes on policy and then announce the nomination of Michael Dukakis. Instead, he spoke for a boring thirty-three minutes, dragging on for so long that the audience cheered when he said, "In conclusion..."

People thought at the time that he'd killed his future prospects, but Lizzie came up with a great way to loosen any tension. At the Saturday night dinner she hosted during her summer camp, all twenty guests asked Clinton to speak. On her coaching, he got up, said, "Thank you all for coming," and then sat down. That got a big laugh and a lot of applause. Everyone got the message that Bill got the message. The next day he umpired the annual East Hampton Artists and Writers Charity Softball Game, which brings out all the leading media and politicos who summer in East Hampton. He followed that up a day or two later with an appearance on *The Tonight Show Starring Johnny Carson*, where he played the saxophone. Those events returned him to grace.

My personal connection with him began at Liz's Saturday night dinner celebration, when Bill mentioned his plan to jog on Sunday morning. I was the only other runner in the group—a veteran of five prior marathons—and I volunteered to join him as a running companion. Our running conversation ultimately landed on the topic of the South Shore Bank in Chicago and the work it had been doing to alleviate poverty and stimulate small business development on the south side. The governor expressed an interest in bringing a similar operation to Arkansas.

One of us later sent the other a book about the South Shore Bank and we agreed to discuss it further, which we did. We continued to have intermittent contact, such that it was natural when he reached out to me in 1991 to invite me to a small group meeting about his plans to run for president. I was supportive, and my wife Susan and I gave a dinner party at our home in Manhattan to introduce him to some of our friends and acquaintances. Attendees included George Soros, Leonard Lauder, Bernard Schwartz, and many others who met him for the first time that night and stayed supporters through the primary, the election, and through Bill's two terms in office.

That small dinner party also goes down in Patricof personal history for what happened after the guests left. My teenaged son, Jamie, had arranged to go to a prominent jazz club called Tattoo with his friend Gus Ornstein, whose father owned it. Bill went too, and again played his famous saxophone. The star notched a bit higher.

A few months later, in February 1992, Susan and I organized the first major "Clinton for President" fundraiser in New York City at the Sheraton Hotel Ballroom on 53rd Street and 7th Avenue. We collaborated with Bill's NY staff finance chair, Paul Carey, the son of the New York governor Hugh Carey. The event was an immediate sellout. We were grappling with how to accommodate the all-star crowd of close to one thousand people when word of Bill's relationship with Gennifer Flowers hit the front page. The sellout devolved so fast and far that we had to move from the full ballroom to a smaller space, and then smaller again. We eventually had to fill even the smallest event room with huge plants surrounding the seating area in order to make it look more crowded than it was.

The evening went well despite the bad buzz and the crass shouts about infidelity from Stuttering John of *The Howard Stern Show*, a familiar gadfly at these events, which he attended to feed the radio program. The support we got from the Sheraton Hotel and Ed Kane, its manager, has made it the location of choice for virtually every Democratic Party event in New York City since that day, as well as every Clinton Foundation dinner or event. Loyalty runs deep.

I continued to support Bill by taking a lead role in New York fundraising, along with Ken Brody from Goldman Sachs and Stanley Shuman from Allen & Co. New York usually represents over 70 percent of Democratic fund raising in the US. The three of us also participated in the financial issues group and spent considerable time giving input to the paid staff led by Paul Carey. Paul served as Special Assistant to the President after Bill became president, and later served as commissioner of the SEC. He and Susan and I were close friends until he died at the age of thirty-eight of a rare cancer. Susan helped his family form the Paul Robert Carey Foundation in his honor and sat on its board—the foundation provides funds to people and their families suffering from the same disease to help with non-medical costs, such as travel to the few hospitals that offer treatment, accommodation, and so forth. Our relationship with the Carey family—all eleven of them—continues to this day.

At the same time that I worked on fundraising, I came up with an idea to get the small-business venture community behind Clinton. To that end, I formed a group called "Entrepreneurs for Clinton-Gore". with Glenn Hutchins and Nancy Rubin, two political junkies I met on the campaign trail. We sent out waves of mail and made phone calls to enlist entrepreneurs who identified as democrats and were willing to put their names down as supporters of the Clinton-Gore campaign. There was no financial commitment required, and we gathered about a thousand names from business owners in this way, since everyone likes to be identified as an entrepreneur no matter how big their business may be.

Under that same umbrella, Glenn, Nancy, and I, with an ad hoc committee we formed, developed a number of small-business-friendly policy recommendations that Clinton could incorporate into his campaign platform. They included lower capital gains tax rates, R&D tax credit regulations, and incentives to encourage the formation and growth of young companies, all of which became part of the successful Deficit Reduction Act (DRA).

I am particularly proud of what became Section 1202 of the tax code to establish "Qualified Small Business Stock," (QSBS) which was, and continues to be, very helpful to new business formation. In its original form, the QSBS clause states that investors holding stock in a qualified company that raised less than $50 million in equity pay only half of the capital gains tax when they sell, so long as they held the stock for five years or more. This clause became even more favorable when President Obama increased the exclusion to 75 percent and subsequently removed all taxes after the financial crisis of 2008. The clause also gives a strong incentive to invest in and form young businesses. The Build Back Better Act, under consideration as I write, proposes to take away a chunk of that benefit.

Election night on the lawn at the governor's mansion in Arkansas was truly a memorable experience. I was as happy to be there as I was to stand on the lawn near the Lincoln Memorial on inauguration eve, and then sit on the podium at the Capitol during the swearing in. On his first day in office, President Clinton invited me to the Oval Office, where he thanked me profusely for supporting and sticking with him. He looked at me at one moment and said, "Can you believe we're here!" I proudly display a photo of that visit behind my desk in my office.

Many people who do the kind of work I did for the president might after the fact have their name come up as a candidate for some government role or post. "She'd be good as a board member on the National Endowment for the Arts" or "he'd make a great ambassador to Israel" kind of thing. It's not enough for your name to come up, though. There are hundreds if not thousands of presidential-appointed government posts, all listed every four years in a document known as the "Plum Book" (officially, the *United States Government Policy and Supporting Positions*), which gets released in the month or so after a presidential election. *The Plum Book* lists all the four thousand available politically appointed positions and ambassadorships, each of which has scores of people vying for them. For most people who come into politics through fundraising, if you really

President Bill Clinton with Alan Patricof in the Oval Office on the morning after the President's first inauguration.

want a role in the government, you need to actively campaign for it. I wasn't interested in a government post, didn't encourage people to name me for them, and asked for nothing, and thus got nothing, other than a few opportunities to contribute a degree of expertise.

For example, early on I was invited to speak on behalf of small businesses at the Clinton Economic Summit in Little Rock, Arkansas, a consensus-building event hosted by the president-elect in December right after the election. I was petrified because the caliber of attendees was so high, including people like John Sculley, the CEO at the time of Apple Computer, Harold Poling, chairman of the Ford Motor Company, Hugh McColl, chairman of Nations Bank, Robert Allen, chairman of AT&T, as well as known academics and economists, like Michael Porter of Harvard Business School,

Alan Blinder of Princeton, Alicia Munnell from the Federal Reserve Bank of Boston, and so on.

A year into Bill's first term, Erskine Bowles, head of the Small Business Administration, implored me to serve as chairman of the White House Commission on Small Business. There are a number of prestigious commissions in the federal government, but this was not one of them. The commission had existed in name for decades, but no president had operated it for about twenty years. The neglect stems from the fact that small businesses are such a volatile and variable group—some survive and grow into large businesses, but the ones that don't aren't around to support policies or candidates. Nonetheless, George H. W. Bush had promised to resuscitate the commission late in his term. When he was voted out of office, he left Clinton with this albatross around his neck.

I took on the challenge, and the commission lasted for two years. We held a hundred local meetings around the country to get input and ideas. We followed those meetings with twelve regional sessions that culminated in a national meeting in Washington. More than 25,000 people across the country attended the local and regional meetings and contributed to the platform we ultimately published at the 1,200-strong event in Washington. It was a true effort to consider local and regional issues from across the country. Many of the ideas turned into implemented policies.

Due to my work with the White House Commission on Small Business and my personal connection to Bill and Hillary, I spent a lot of time traveling back and forth to Washington. Susan and I were also invited to the White House numerous times over the eight years they were in office. We attended state dinners and at least one Christmas party, slept in the famous Lincoln bedroom, and spent a wonderful Easter weekend at Camp David close to the end of Bill's second term, where I played a typically (for me) miserable round of golf.

One memorable event from that era took place in 199 on the steps of the Corcoran Museum, where we went to see Yitzhak Rabin,

Christmas at the White House with the entire Patricof family in 2000; (front)
Alan Patricof, Jonathan Patricof, Victoria Patricof, Kelly Sawyer, President
Bill Clinton, Secretary Hillary Clinton, Susan Patricof, Martha Patricof
(back) Jamie Patricof, Mark Patricof.

King Hussein, Yasser Arafat, and President Clinton after they signed
the Israel-Palestinian Peace Accord. Coincidentally, I was standing
next to Ron Brown, former head of the Democratic National
Committee and then Secretary of Commerce, who lamented that
he was depressed and under enormous pressure due to an investigation underway against him for corruption. He remarked to me at
the time that he was finding the atmosphere in Washington hostile,
and he wasn't enjoying his work as much as he used to. Ron died in
a tragic plane crash not long after, and that conversation stuck with
me. He was truly one of the nicest people I met in the Clinton years
and his loss affected me, as it did others who worked with him.

On the night of the signing of the peace treaty, Daniel Abraham,
the CEO and founder of SlimFast and a major Democratic supporter,
as well as strong supporter of Israel, gave a party at the Hay-Adams

Hotel. The thirty or forty attendees waited for about an hour for Arafat to arrive. When he walked in and passed me, I reached out to shake his hand, but ended up with a kiss from him on each cheek. A photographer captured the moment, and I kept the picture on my desk for years as a memento of what was, at that point, a proud moment in history. Subsequent events shattered that idea, and I eventually took down the picture and put it in a drawer—somewhat analogous to the end of the peace process.

Once on the radar due to my participation in the Clinton campaign, I started getting calls for support from other Democratic candidates. Chuck Schumer called me, for instance, in 1992, when he was still in the House of Representatives and up for reelection. He came to see me at my office, but we hadn't finished our conversation by the time I had to leave. My son Jamie—a senior in high school at the time—was competing in a basketball game in Brooklyn, and I didn't want to miss the tip-off. Unwilling to miss the opportunity, Schumer followed me in his car and continued the conversation in the bleachers between quarters. Chuck was then, and is to this day, a determined vote getter and fund raiser.

Hillary also started thinking about running for Senate in New York while Bill was still in the White House. She asked me to come to Washington to talk to her about it. We met for breakfast on the terrace of the presidential quarters. I subsequently agreed to head up the finance committee for her Senate run, and later for her two runs for president. In that capacity, I met Bill de Blasio, who later served as mayor of New York City; at that point he was Hillary's Senate campaign manager. During her time as a senator, she made a Herculean effort to visit every county in New York state to listen to local problems and do something about them. She formed a task force led by Roger Altman, an investment banker, called "New Jobs for New York," of which I was a member. We travelled with her around the state to encourage and support economic development. One idea was to resurrect some of the dying industries of upstate New York. Our group visited cities like Buffalo, Utica, Albany, and

Poughkeepsie to host organized gatherings focused on economic development.

One of the more exciting experiences I had with the president took place after his term in office, in 2002, when he was invited to the Jeddah Economic Forum, fashioned after the Davos World Economic Forum and scheduled to take place a few days before. The Saudi crown prince, Abdullah bin Abdul-Aziz Al Saud, sent his 727, outfitted for royalty, to bring Bill and forty "of his closest friends" to Saudi Arabia. Susan and I went, as did Stanley Shuman, of Allen & Company and his wife Sydney, a board member of the Rockefeller Foundation; Sergey Brin and Larry Page, founders of Google; Ron Burkle, a Democratic fundraiser and investor best known for deals involving grocers like Safeway and Kroger. We flew to Jeddah, where Bill made a speech, after which we attended a buffet dinner and party under the stars. The next day we flew to Riyadh to ride camels in the desert and attended an audience with King Fahd, half-brother to the crown prince, in the throne room.

A striking moment occurred when Brooke Shearer, an investigative journalist and the wife of Strobe Talbott, Clinton's deputy secretary of state, stood up in her abaya to her full height of barely 5'1" and asked the king, "Why isn't your country more open to minorities and women?" He responded without pause, "Why isn't *your* country more open to minorities and women?" That was the end of our audience with the king, though we were still invited to a lavish dinner party in a private home that night. Almost all the local guests, contrary to public protocol, were dressed to the nines in luxury Western style, while the forty of us were in the traditional Arabic abayas and *thobes* that were given to us by the crowned prince.

We left the next morning for Davos, where Bill delivered a major address to the World Economic Forum, and then, without stopping for sleep, to Baden-Baden, Germany, where he addressed another assembled crowd. Around midnight some of us, including the president, walked over to an adjoining casino and gambled at the tables for an hour. It was a very sleepy, well-travelled group that returned to Teterboro, New Jersey, the next morning.

I've been invited to join Bill in a golf game many times since I've known him. I never took much to golf, and I'm not very good at it, but Bill is a decent golfer with a strong shot that occasionally goes off course. When it does, the other members of his foursome urge him to take a mulligan; or if his ball goes into the brush and a good-will search effort turns up nothing—even with participation by the Secret Service—we'll encourage him to give up and drop another; or if he chips and the ball rests two feet from the hole, everyone will call it a "gimme"; and so on. In short, people tend to be deferential with the president, which makes it difficult to keep accurate score— although I have never seen his scorecard. Anyone who's played golf with Bill also knows that he is also a generous golf teacher, quick to offer coaching on stance and swing or give one of his clubs as a gift to someone if they are a particularly good student. The time spent on instruction and do-overs can stretch eighteen holes out to five or more hours, making the mulligans and gimmes and golf lessons a necessary part of the game if you ever want to get to drinks in the clubhouse.

My friendship and support of the Clintons served as my entrance into the world of Democratic politics, which I have continued to inhabit with the same hands-on approach I like to take to everything. I don't just sit in my office and make phone calls on behalf of the candidates I support. I get involved. I canvassed for John Kerry in Philadelphia during his run for president, walking the streets and going door-to-door to talk to voters (I had originally supported Wes Clark in 2004 and canvassed for him in New Hampshire before he dropped out). In 2008, I canvassed for Hillary in seven-degree cold in Davenport, Iowa. I didn't walk for Barack Obama after he won the Democratic presidential nomination, since I hadn't been involved with his campaign, but I did host an event for him at my home on behalf of his campaign.

After informal conversations with many of the Democratic potentials in late 2018 and early 2019, I decided to throw my support fully behind Joe Biden. Our conversations began in March of 2019, when I got a call out of the blue from Katie Petrelius, who had been the finance director of the Democratic Congressional Campaign Committee (DCCC). Katie asked to set up a meeting between me and Joe. He was still just considering a run for the presidency at that point. After some back-and-forth on location, I eventually met him at his New York City hotel. I share that to make clear how early it was in the campaign—there wasn't even an office or an organization yet.

The meeting was very cordial, and we exchanged reintroductions, as I had not seen him in a few years. Weeks later, Katie called me again to ask if I would put together a meeting of a few prospective supporters. I agreed and made a list of a dozen people who had been active in previous financial presidential efforts, but Joe ultimately asked that we keep it to a limited group, as he didn't want too many people involved at that stage. At the meeting, he told those who attended that he planned to run and would announce in April.

After the meeting, three of the attendees said they were leaning towards supporting other candidates. I was supportive of Joe's candidacy but started to get concerned when I didn't hear back from Katie for many weeks. I was going to just leave it be until I got a call from Heather Murren, who I did not know—she had signed on to be the National Finance Chairperson for Joe's campaign. She came to visit me and strongly encouraged me to get involved early to send the message that Joe had strong support in NY, a critical source of funds for any political campaign. Heather was persuasive and her plans impressed me. I agreed to both publicly support Joe and put together an initial group of supporters, which I did at a lunch meeting at Maialino restaurant in November 2019. The lunch attendees were given an outline of the campaign plans as they stood, and the group agreed to put together an initial fundraiser in New

York City. It took place a short time later at the home of Arne and Milly Glimcher, who own the Pace Gallery.

The rest is history. Over the subsequent year, I mobilized people, hosted events, went to Nevada for one of the Democratic debates, and canvassed in Des Moines, Iowa, before the caucuses—again in freezing conditions—and more pleasantly in Orlando, Florida, the weekend before the election.

As the response to that first meeting makes clear, Joe Biden was not the favorite Democratic candidate for the regulars among New York's active presidential campaign contributors. My peers have commented on my prescience as one of the only people who believed in Joe Biden from the beginning. People assume that makes me a candidate for a role as secretary of the Treasury or some other prestigious position, and I have to remind them that there is an Alan Patricof equivalent in every city in the country, and their local friends all think he or she is going to be the next secretary of the Treasury or ambassador to France. I still have no aspirations for a position in government, and I am staying in New York. What counted to me was getting Joe elected, along with a wave of Democratic candidates.

Beyond the work I have done to support candidates and small-business policies, I have also done my best to support the Democratic party as a whole. In the mid-1990s, for example, I met Erica Payne at a Clinton event in New York, and got to know her when she stayed at my house for a month while working on Clinton's reelection—Susan and I had taken to opening our home to many of the out-of-town campaign workers. Our connection made Erica reach out years later when she and Rob Stein, an attorney and Clinton administration veteran, were trying to gain support for a new organization. Rob was traveling the country presenting a PowerPoint he had developed that laid out the tactics used by the Republican party, beginning in the 1970s, to communicate a message and galvanize the voting public behind it (the presentation argued that this movement by the right began with a note penned by the future Supreme Court justice Lewis Powell to a friend at the US Chamber of Commerce). Rob and Erica believed the Democratic party needed to initiate a similar rebirth. They eventually founded The Democratic Alliance, which was their method to achieve those goals.

As I believed in the idea, I worked with Erica over multiple years, first by hosting small gatherings where Rob gave his presentation, and later to establish the organization, which remains one of the leading influencers of financial contributions in the Democratic political field. Erica left after a few years to form another nonprofit called Patriotic Millionaires, which represents successful individuals who share the feeling that those who've been more successful should accept higher taxes and support issues that affect lower-income individuals. I support Patriotic Millionaires through vocal advocacy and by writing op-eds on key topics, though I never liked the name.

My connection to politics has likewise opened regular opportunities for me to advocate for small businesses at both the federal and international level. When President George W. Bush launched The Millennium Challenge Corporation (MCC), I was nominated by Representative Nancy Pelosi to serve on its board. The MCC is considered, along with the President's Emergency Plan for AIDS Relief (PEPFAR), one of the lasting, positive legacies of the George W. Bush presidency.

The MCC board includes the secretary of State, the secretary of the Treasury, the US trade representative, the head of the National Security Council, the head of USAID, and four private sector representatives—two nominated by the Democratic members of congress and two nominated by Republicans. During my tenure, I served with Kenneth Hackett, president of the nonprofit Catholic Relief Services; Bill Frist, a former transplant surgeon, senator, and part-owner of the Hospital Corporation of America; and Ambassador Mark Green, a former congressman from Wisconsin, ambassador to Tanzania, and former head of USAID. Each of the private sector board members could bring a "plus one" with them to board meetings. I brought Julie Sunderland, who I met through the pro bono work I was doing in Ghana (I'll describe that later). Julie is another example of a very smart young person doing interesting things that I met serendipitously. Over the course of a decade, we traveled around Africa together and wrote articles and white papers about the need for capital for small businesses in developing countries. She went on to run program-related investments for the Bill & Melinda Gates Foundation and created a new model for philanthropic impact. She recently left that position to start her own venture capital fund, Biomatics Capital, to focus on bio-tech companies.

As for the MCC itself, it is a federal agency that provides foreign aid to developing countries based on requests for specific initiatives. The kinds of projects the MCC would support include health infrastructure initiatives, education programs for girls, support for country-level small- and medium-sized business development, and other similar programs. MCC staff mostly come from the

Alan Patricof representing the MCC at the Ghana highway opening in 1994.

private sector and spend considerable time and effort vetting each proposal. This model is closer to that of a for-profit fund than to the approach typically taken by the Agency for International Development (USAID), which gives aid to countries that are friendly to the US and limits how they can spend it (for example, by requiring that the countries buy US-made products). The initial MCC allocation by Congress was $1 billion. Allocations have fluctuated, but mostly stay at about $1 billion—the original intent had been to allocate $3 billion a year.

I served on the board of the MCC as a Democratic nominee for five years, two terms—the maximum period allowed for any individual to serve. I was nominated by George W. Bush, and Condoleezza Rice, President Bush's secretary of State, served as the board chair. After President Obama re-nominated me, I served under Secretary Hillary Clinton, who was very active and engaged—I don't think she missed a single board meeting during that time, and neither did I (I rarely miss board meetings; it's a point of pride for me). During that period, the MCC made grants and commitments to more than thirty countries defined as "substantially poor" based on the World Bank's definition.

After the end of my term on the MCC, President Obama nominated me for his President's Council on Global Development. I'd been recommended for the role by Rajiv Shah, then head of USAID, and now head of the Rockefeller Foundation. I spent two and a half years on that council under the chairmanship of Mohamed El-Erian, the former CEO of Pimco. The ten council members recommended development policy to the president. Only a few of our proposals were implemented before President Obama left office. All the members submitted their resignations when Donald Trump took office, and he abandoned the council and the ideas generated from it.

As these things go, my involvement in Democratic politics is on a very minor scale, but the fact that someone somewhere was monitoring it came to my attention a few years ago. I opened

The Guardian on June 28, 2010, and read a headline stating, "Ten 'Russian Spies' Arrested in US." It seemed that the FBI had been monitoring ten spies for more than a decade in one of the most important US counterintelligence victories against Russia. Among them was the now-famous spy-turned-model Anna Chapman, as well as a Russian woman posing as a mundane New Jersey accountant and mother of two named Cynthia Murphy—*Cindy* to me in her capacity as the excellent bookkeeper with fine attention to detail assigned to me from the third-party accounting company I used for my personal financial management.

Cindy, whose real name was Lydia Guryeva, had been part of a sleeper cell that had been in the US for thirteen years to collect information and pass it along to their Russian handler. Sometime in 2009, the FBI, according to the record of the case, had recorded Murphy speaking to her handler about her firm's new client, Alan Patricof (me!), an "active fundraiser and personal friend of Hillary Clinton." The handler says, "Keep close to him." Apparently, Cindy was supposed to solicit "remarks regarding US Foreign policy, rumors or invitations to major venues."

The arrests happened when they did because the FBI was concerned that Chapman might leave the US and/or that Cindy would get too close to me. The idea is absurd, as we never discussed politics, Hillary Clinton, or the Democratic Party, though it is true that when we were in a fundraising mode for Hillary, I probably would have invited Cindy to a fundraiser unwittingly if she had asked, and probably offered her a chance to take a picture with the candidate—but she never asked! Two episodes of the Smithsonian Channel series *Spy Wars with Damian Lewis* entitled *The Spies Next Door*, recounts the events leading to the spy exchange.

Cindy, her husband Richard (Vladimir), and eight others were exchanged for four Americans accused by Moscow as spying for the West on the tarmac of an airport in Vienna. Cindy and Richard had two children, who were deported a few days after their parents. The postscript to the story comes in the form of the television series *The*

Americans on FX, which I could swear is based on the events (but fictionalized to create more drama).

SINCE I NEVER WANTED TO take a full-time position in government, all of the political activity I've described took place at the same time as I was growing—and then withdrawing from—Apax Partners. In 2001, when I decided it was time to step back from the partnership, George W. Bush was in the White House, Hillary Clinton was the junior senator from New York, and I was not yet a sitting board member of the MCC. In other words, it was a time of relatively low extracurricular activity.

There were a handful of organizations with which Susan and I had become deeply involved by that point. One I must note was the Northside Center for Child Development, which had been serving learning-disadvantaged children and their families in Harlem since 1946 with mental health services, a critical resource for the four thousand families Northside serves in this particular area of New York City. Northside was founded by Kenneth and Mamie Clark almost a decade before the landmark 1954 Brown v. the Board of Education Supreme Court case concluded that the country's "separate but equal" education policy was unconstitutional. (Kenneth testified before the court about his and Mamie's infamous Black doll vs. white doll experiments, which demonstrated the ways in which racial segregation negatively affected the self-esteem of Black children.)

Susan and I both got involved with Northside in 1975 and I am still involved today. Susan was chairman of the board for more than forty years, and I was a member of the Finance Committee. We worked tirelessly to assure the survival of the organization. Northside's new, permanent home just opened—a testament to how the organization has prepared to serve its community long into the future. As a permanent tribute to Susan, Northside built the

Alan Patricof with Kenneth Clark, Founder of Northside Center for Child Development at his 90th birthday celebration.

Susan Patricof Head Start Center in a separate building to provide early-childhood education to two hundred students ages two to five.

The success and personal fulfillment we got from our connection to Northside led me to think about ways I could use my investing expertise to help impoverished communities. After some discussion with Susan, we decided that it would be a good idea for me to focus some of my time advocating for effective small business policies in developing countries as I was winding down the venture capital investments at Apax and thinking about what I wanted to do next.

As a first step, I called Trickle Up, a charity headquartered in New York with which Susan had been involved. Trickle Up issues micro-grants to the poorest of the poor in remote areas of Bolivia, Brazil, India, and various countries in Southeast Asia and sub-Saharan Africa. Recipients are usually so poor they don't qualify for micro-loans. Trickle Up grants start as low as twenty-five dollars and can grow to a hundred dollars for people living in poverty who want to start a business such as a fruit stand, a barber shop, a hair braiding shop, a service to sharpen knives, or other businesses like that.

Trickle Up provided the grants (and today, loans), as well as technical assistance in basic business management, like keeping records, calculating costs for raw materials, and determining a reasonable charge for the product or service in order to make a profit and grow the business. Trickle Up also teaches beneficiaries to save individually and in savings groups with other women in their village. I joined the board of directors and served in that capacity from 2001–2012. The annual Patricof Forum, which I underwrote, is still hosted by Trickle Up in New York one evening each year to highlight a single issue affecting the poorest of the poor. The married activists Nick Kristof (a journalist with *The New York Times*) and Sheryl WuDunn (formerly of *The New York Times*, and now an investor) were recent speakers at that event.

The second organization I got involved with around that time was TechnoServe. Peter Reiling, the CEO of the organization, and Paul Tierney, an investor and TechnoServe board member, approached me after hearing about my interest in international development. TechnoServe is based out of Washington, D.C., and had been operating for about twenty-five years when Paul called me. Its purpose was to encourage the development of small and medium-size enterprises and to help build infrastructure to support them in the poorest countries of the world.

The day I accepted a board position with TechnoServe has been memorialized in my mind for what also happened that day. At nine in the morning I had finished meeting with the organization's board in McKinsey's Manhattan offices, and was walking to my office, when I heard hysteria in the street—it was Tuesday, September 11, 2001, and the first plane had just crashed into the World Trade Center building. I rushed on foot to my home on the Upper East

Side, managing along the way to communicate with my office, which we closed, and my son Jamie, who lived one block from the World Trade Center with his wife and dog. When the planes hit, Jamie heard the noise and ran down to the street. As soon as he saw the smoke, he collected his family and headed north to our home on 76th Street. The interval between hearing from him and their arrival was one of the longest in my life. After grateful hugs, we spent the rest of the day glued to the television, shocked and mourning like the rest of the country.

DURING MY TEN YEARS AS a board member of Trickle Up and TechnoServe, I traveled to Mali, Mozambique, Uganda, Kenya—the list goes on. I probably visited a dozen or more countries to observe firsthand the activities supported by the organizations.

On one visit to Africa with Trickle Up I went to Ouagadougou, Burkina Faso, to visit several basket weaving factories and home-based clothing manufacturers. From there we set off by Jeep to Timbuktu, Mali. The road from Ouagadougou was unpaved dirt for most of the 450 miles, and took more than fifteen hours to traverse. It was a rough ride, and by the time we arrived, my back had gone out and I couldn't walk. Still, I gutted it out through visits to fishing operations located in a village outside the city—more Jeep rides—and meetings with business groups.

Our host was a woman named Judith Larivière, a foot soldier in the war on poverty from Montreal, Canada. Judith was a bundle of a woman with bright orange hair and a full wardrobe of colorful cotton dresses and pantsuits that you might expect to find in a place like Miami or Las Vegas. An entrepreneur herself, she went to Africa more than a decade before I met her to help poor women start small businesses that would help lift them out of extreme poverty and. then joined Trickle Up to run their operations in Mali. A day or two with Judith illustrated very well how a little capital and a little

Alan Patricof visiting with Trickle Up to Timbuktu to Mali in 2004.

technical assistance could change the lives of even the most disad-
vantaged people on earth.

On my last night in the country, I attended the wedding of the
cook who worked in the Timbuktu office of Trickle Up. One of
Mali's leading singers, Khaira Arby, gave a concert in a courtyard
attended by what seemed like the entire city. One of the customs
was for the singer to weave into a song the names of people in the
crowd, who are then obliged to come forward and dance with her
a bit. In my semi-crippled state, I was forced onto the dance floor
but did my part with goodwill. My pain and injury were so severe
that when I returned to New York I had to come off the plane in
a wheelchair, and I needed another week in bed at home before I
could walk.

At the same time that my activity started to pick up with Trickle
Up and TechnoServe, I connected with Jim Wolfensohn, a very old
friend of mine who is now deceased, but who at that time was president of the World Bank. I went down to Washington and asked

whether I could be helpful to them on a pro bono basis in the small and medium-size enterprise activities they conducted through the International Finance Corporation (IFC). To my delight and surprise, he arranged for me to meet with the head of the IFC, Peter Woicke.

As timing had it, the World Bank and the IFC were building out their programs for small and medium-sized businesses under a dedicated division. Peter greeted me with considerable enthusiasm, given his interest in producing value from the offices it was running, and from the IFC's Small and Medium Enterprise (SME) investment fund. Peter also introduced me to Harold Rosen, the man tasked with leading the formalized SME operation, and I started to collaborate with him. Over the next several years, Harold and I traveled together to India, China, Bangladesh, as well as multiple countries in Latin America and Africa.

I remember vividly my first trip to Africa with the IFC. Harold couldn't be at the first stop in Johannesburg, South Africa, so he planned for me to meet his deputy who ran the African operation. Before I arrived, the deputy sent me an email inviting me to his club for lunch and a round of golf, since I was arriving on a Sunday. But I don't really like golf, as I've mentioned, and wouldn't travel all that distance just to play. Instead, I wanted to meet his team and set up meetings, starting on that Sunday afternoon.

That set the stage for a productive two days in South Africa, where I met with the team and a number of start-ups in which the IFC was considering investing. I listened to the presentations just as I would to entrepreneurs looking for venture capital and asked the same kinds of questions I would of start-ups in the states: about the market, their product or service, the number and quality of people on their team, and so forth. I was direct with my questions, as I always am, unlike Harold and his team, who could not be due to their status as both investors and quasi-government employees.

I was not the first American businessman to try to help the African small business community. However, I am one of the few, according to Harold and others, to come personally with a hands-on, practical view of the financial discipline and basic management companies can apply. I helped enable opportunities for entrepreneurs and investors to share business knowledge with up-and-coming companies and form angel investor networks—the kinds of things we take for granted in the States. I demonstrated this personal involvement approach for the team in Johannesburg and I guess it made an impression, for when I arrived in Kampala, Uganda, the station chief greeted me with a smile on his face and a copy of an email he'd received from his boss in South Africa: "This guy is for real," it said.

From there I went to Ghana, and then to the Ivory Coast, which was in the middle of a true rebel uprising. I continued on to Lagos, where I had my first experience in Nigeria. Harold was with me by then, and on one of our days in the city our car got trapped in a pothole in front of the Central Bank. As we waited there for the driver to work out a solution, I asked Harold about the meeting we'd just left with the founders of a small business. Harold had awarded them capital from the IFC fund, and from what I'd heard during the meeting, it was to be delivered all at once.

"Why would you do that?" I asked him. "I'd never give an untested start-up all the money at once. I'd give them a little at first and see how they work with it. If they meet their goals, they get a little more, and so on." It was an approach Harold knew, of course, but the IFC had never operationalized, for a number of reasons. My suggestion offered a way to start. That form of incremental distribution of capital became standard practice for the small business program.

On another occasion, as part of an IFC trip to Lima, Peru, and Bolivia, I passed out from altitude sickness. I nonetheless made my way to Belem, Brazil—at the head of the Amazon—where I gave a lecture at a local university. When the lecture ended late in the evening and we left the building, we had to walk over a rudimentary wooden bridge that connected two buildings over a stream that flowed about five feet below. There were no streetlights, and we had to use our cell phone screens to see by. Still unsteady, I fell off the bridge and into the stream, and managed to tear open my leg. I lost a good amount of blood and had to go to a local hospital for stitches and to spend the night. When I returned to NYC, I had a follow-up with my orthopedic surgeon, who said it was a perfect repair. On reflection, it should have been no surprise given Brazil's popularity with Americans who travel there for plastic surgery. Today, I have no trace of a scar despite the ten-inch gash I received.

SHORTLY AFTER THAT TRIP TO Brazil, I attended a dinner in New York City at the invitation of the Vice Chairman of Citibank. I sat next to the president of Nigeria, President Olusegun Obasanjo. He was a huge presence, with his tribal finery and impressive demeanor. At some point during the meal, he asked me whether I'd ever been to Nigeria. When I told him that I had been to Lagos on a trip with the IFC and Harold Rosen, he asked about my experience. I said, "Frankly, it was one of the worst experiences I've encountered."

He asked why, and I described my experience of seeing visitors too afraid to walk out on the streets at night, that every place you went you were surrounded by guards with machine guns, the streets were filled with potholes deep enough to have been created by a bomb dropping and strewn with garbage, and that all the office buildings or complexes were surrounded by barbed wire and guards.

I also relayed how the World Bank group I was with had to leave the city three hours before our departing flight for what should have been a half-hour drive in a diplomatic car to the airport. When I had asked why, my escort had explained that we couldn't take the highway, but instead had to take a diversionary route to avoid marauders. As I told the president, these issues collectively don't leave a positive impression on a visitor.

I expected he would be taken aback by my candor, but instead he asked me to write him a letter and describe what happened. I was reluctant, but he pressed me hard and asked me to be thorough and honest. So I wrote and sent the letter and then heard nothing for several months, which both disappointed and embarrassed me. I eventually received a letter, ostensibly from the president. It said I must have been in Lagos under the wrong auspices and included an invitation to come back again and visit Abuja, the capital. I was taken aback and felt self-conscious that I had been so forthcoming, only to receive what read to me as a blow-off. I didn't take the invitation seriously until a month later, when I received a call and the woman on the other line said, "Would you hold for President Obasanjo?"

The president was incredibly friendly on the phone and thanked me profusely for my letter. He made no mention of the missive that I had received. He continued, "You're my kind of guy," referring to my directness and honesty, and he asked if I would consider joining his Presidential Advisory Council. The council included six or eight other people, including the presidents of Shell Oil, Siemens, CNBC Middle East, Ashanti Goldfields, and a few others—a prestigious group. At that point I realized the letter I'd received had been drafted by a functionary responsible for the president's correspondence.

I was reluctant initially to accept President Obasanjo's invitation because of ongoing concerns here in the US about corruption in Nigeria, as well as rebels in the oil region. I also had no prior or current business activities in the country, and so didn't know what I could contribute. In the end, however, I decided that it would be an interesting adjunctive experience, so I accepted the offer, and for some time served as a member of the Advisory Council. I served to the end of President Obasanjo's term in office in 2007 (Obasanjo had tried to have his country's constitution changed so he could serve a third term, but the effort was highly controversial and was rejected by the Nigerian Senate). I continued to participate during the term of the next president, Umaru Musa Yar'Adua, who died in office in 2010, and was still serving when President Goodluck Jonathan was elected. I attended one meeting with Jonathan, but the Council had lost its purpose and I stepped down.

While I participated, we met twice a year, once in London and once in Abuja with the president's entire cabinet. As an unsettling side note, one of the first Council meetings I attended in London in 2005 took place on the same day that there was a coordinated series of bombings on the London tube orchestrated by an Islamist extremist group. It stuck with me in particular because earlier that year in April, I had been in Cairo with the Council on Foreign Relations when an Islamist terrorist group detonated a bomb near the Khan El-Khalili souk, and I'd been in Madrid the year before in March on the day when Basque separatists orchestrated a subway bombing. Of course, I had also been in New York on September 11, 2001. For a while I felt like I was a bad luck charm—wherever I went, something bad happened. I felt lucky and grateful that I wasn't closer to the tragedies.

Many times while I served on the Nigerian President's Advisory Council, Obasanjo asked me to recount my experience in Lagos. I, embarrassingly, obliged. On one such occasion, the president had the governor of Lagos there to hear my experience. Together they decided on a plan to address different challenges in Lagos—one of them led an effort to tackle the problem of garbage, the other took the lead on the problem of security. They agreed to collaborate on the problem of transportation and infrastructure. The president at one point said to the governor, "We're not in the same political party, but we both want to see the country move ahead, so let's see if we can work together." It was not unlike the problem of a president here, who has to deal with each of the governors of the fifty states.

I am told the situation in Lagos is better now than it was in the early '00s, but I doubt my experience had much to do with it. It's encouraging to hear that there has been progress. Perhaps one of these days I will get back there. My time on President Obasanjo's Advisory Council was one of the most interesting experiences of my career, to see firsthand the openness and good intentions he had to improve the country.

My detours into politics as well as the time I spent with Trickle Up, TechnoServe, and the IFC gave me a fulfilling diversion during the early '00s as I wound down Apax's last venture fund and its investments. I have remained active in various social causes about which I feel passionate, and I encouraged Susan in her efforts to support organizations such as the Columbia School of Public Health and the International Rescue Committee, in all cases working to support women and children and alleviate poverty.

Most recently, I've gotten involved with prison reform after I attended the TED annual conference and met Robin Steinberg, a longtime public defender from The Bronx, New York. Robin spoke about the challenge of bail for minor offenders who otherwise might be incarcerated for months or years awaiting trial because they couldn't get their hands on $1,000 or $2,000. What a waste of taxpayers' money, with nothing really accomplished and no effort to set these individuals up for life back in society.

I have at least one personal experience with someone who got wrapped up in that bureaucracy. Hearing Robin speak gave me the impetus to do something broader through her organization, The Bail Project. Subsequently, I accepted a role as a director of The Fortune Society, a nonprofit that aims to help with one small part of the problem by providing prisoners who are transitioning back into society with training, work and professional licensing, and post-incarceration accommodations. I am also supportive of The Doe Fund, another nonprofit providing housing, training, and other services to people with a history of homelessness or incarceration. As a society, I believe we must do everything we can to keep people out of jail, and for those who do become incarcerated, to invest in integrating people back into a community to break the circular cycle of recidivism.

Rules of the Road: Lessons in Politics and Volunteering

Through my efforts in politics and global development I've learned a lot about how these worlds operate. In the case of politics, those of us who enter it as neophytes because we believe in a candidate usually do so through fundraising. Like many well-meaning people, I also wanted to be involved in substantive issues and policy making, but the lifeblood of a candidacy is fundraising, and if a person's entry point is through raising funds, they get pigeonholed into that corner of the campaign and hardly ever connect with the policy makers—the latter are often dismissive of the former, and take suggestions sparingly.

This is important to know for people who get involved in fundraising with their sights on a role in the administration: policy roles tend to go to traditional policy wonks. It's the reality of a campaign. For a limited few major fundraisers, ambassadorial appointments are the brass ring if one plays a significant enough role and is willing to fight for the plum, desired country positions in England, France, or Italy. For the less-important many, the best they can hope for is Malta, Latvia, Lesotho, or less attractive places where people are not particularly interested in living. Hot springs are nice, but they aren't enough to attract an ambassador to Iceland.

Another reality of a campaign is candidates tend to rely on a few trusted sources for strategy and it is very difficult, if not impossible, to change a strategy or inject new ideas once the train has left the station. Bill Clinton was fortunate from the outset to have an exceptional team around him that guided his strategy as a changemaker. Hillary's campaign for the presidency did not benefit from strategists as talented. As an outsider looking in, it appears that Donald Trump was his own strategist—as offensive as his views appear to those on the other side.

As for the inner workings of global development, my time with Trickle Up, TechnoServe, and the IFC gave me firsthand experience seeing how the lack of infrastructure and access to capital—as well as the skills gap possessed by the average start-up entrepreneur—present insurmountable obstacles, particularly in Africa. Wealthy people in many of the countries I visited do not have a mindset that encourages them to become minority investors, seed investors, or sponsors. This is in part because the systems of governance in many developing countries lack the financial controls that are embedded into US law, and into the laws of other developed countries.

I am referring to laws that protect minority investors and give them confidence to back new, privately held companies. The lack of legal protections means that in many developing countries, there is a small pool of successful entrepreneurs, each of whom owns multiple companies in multiple industries. If a young company interests them, they buy it outright and take it over. The limited minority investments that do happen go to family members or long-time friends—investing within a limited circle provides the control investors think they need but radically constrains capital flows and innovation. Interestingly, almost every successful venture fund operating in Africa until ten years ago could credit their success to one breakaway winner: CellTel, which was the leading cellular operator across Africa. Today, the continent is boasting multiple winners, such as Flutterwave and Jumia.

Fostering high-growth entrepreneurship in the developing world requires, in my view, systems that allow for a broader base of ownership, so that founders can reap the financial rewards. One thing I did while traveling there, sometimes with Julie Sunderland, was to encourage the formation of Angel Clubs to enable collective pooling of funds to sponsor individual entrepreneurs with good ideas. There are a lot of well-meaning people dedicated to similar objectives, and it is a challenging endeavor, but certainly worthwhile.

I am fortunate to have had many experiences through the organizations I served. I tried to make a difference and be effective. If there is one piece of advice I would give, it is to come prepared to actively participate and do more than just making a donation. People offering their time pro bono might be inclined to put the endeavor last on their list of priorities, but I don't think it's worth committing to something without really getting involved.

I approach my volunteer activities in the same way I approach my commercial ventures. Whether I'm an active board member or an observer, an investor or a volunteer advisor, I take it seriously enough to spend adequate time preparing for the meetings and reviewing all the materials and going to see the activities in which the organization is involved. I believe that approach has helped me make a difference where I could, and it definitely sends a message of respect to the people taking the time to present to you.

CHAPTER 7

Carving a New Path

The years between 2001 and 2004 were quiet for venture investing, and I kept myself busy by balancing my activities with Apax and the few remaining venture businesses in the portfolio with politics, international development, and philanthropy. The direction of the wind began to change sometime in 2004, when I started hearing again about young companies that piqued my interest. I wasn't in a position to do anything about them, as I was in an in-between state. I had mostly withdrawn from Apax and was no longer making venture investments from the Apax fund, yet I still kept an office at the New York headquarters and had started to think about my next move. At seventy-ish, I was of an age when many of my peers and friends were retiring, but I still had so much energy and curiosity and I wanted to use it. Given my history with media companies, I was particularly intrigued by the opportunities that the internet had started to present for digital media companies.

By 2005, a blog called *PaidContent* was gaining traction as the go-to source of information about the business of digital media. Rafat Ali, a young journalist and former managing editor at the *Silicon Alley Insider*, started *PaidContent* in order to demonstrate his writing and journalism skills for potential editors. Over time he attracted advertisers and hired a few freelancers to help create content. He didn't know how to expand his blog as a business, however, and he wasn't looking for capital when I called him, cold, to ask if we could meet. He was living in Los Angeles at the time, but was planning to be in New York to speak at a conference. We met at the Pierre Hotel and had a good conversation. He also shared some challenges he was facing running the business and editorial sides of the site as a sole proprietor.

I gave him a few ideas and we promised to meet again. A few months later, when I was in LA, I called Rafat to suggest we meet at his office. "Well, my office is in my bedroom," he said, "so I don't think we want to do that." Instead, we sat down at a café in Santa Monica and had another conversation, this time focused on my interest in becoming an investor. Rafat didn't yet have the proper structure or governance to accept investors, but we talked through what I would need to see him do. I also introduced him to Michael Cuniff, a financial executive who could help Rafat get his financial governance in order. I said I'd be in touch again in a few months.

Around that same time, I got a call from Brad Svrluga, founder of High Peaks Venture Partners. Brad's fund was an affiliate of Village Ventures, a fund network and back-office service provider founded by Williams graduates Bo Peabody and Matt Harris (Brad also went to Williams). The Village Ventures network focused on building high-growth businesses in smaller cities that didn't have much venture activity—places like Boise, Idaho; Burlington, Vermont; and Williamstown, Massachusetts (there were twelve smaller cities in all). Village Ventures later invited me to be chairman of their advisory board, which I have been ever since, but at the time of that phone call back around 2005, Brad's fund invested in early-stage firms in New York state. He was calling me about Steve Ellis, a media entrepreneur he thought I should meet.

Steve was a Wharton-graduate-cum-professional musician who'd formed one of the first internet-based music licensing business. It was called Pump Audio, and it worked in much the same way that iStock or Shutterstock work today for photos: musicians posted tracks to the site, and customers bought them through single-use licenses to use as background music for an animation, or intros and outros for television or radio programs.

I call the kind of music Pump Audio specialized in "sounds like" music, as in "That sounds like the Rolling Stones," or "That sounds like Don Henley." Even today, if a TV show or movie, or even a corporate training video, wants to use a clip from a Stones song, it can cost thousands—even *tens* of thousands—in licensing fees. But an unknown musician can compose and perform a track that *sounds like* the Stones and license it for a fraction of the price. That was the business model and market Pump Audio was pursuing.

This was years before protests from artists like Prince brought more widespread attention to the conflicts that can arise between labels and performers (Prince famously gave a live piano performance with the word *slave* written across his cheek). Yet Steve was motivated by the same issues. He had (and has) a natural suspicion of big business and had been bootstrapping Pump Audio from his house in the Hudson Valley for a few years until he met Brad, who then introduced him to me. Steve and I met at my office at Apax, and we hit it off right away. I immediately understood what he was trying to do and expressed my interest in investing, but he was still reluctant to take outside capital from investors.

I could respect that, but I also wanted to make sure Steve had the full picture, so we kept in touch over the next few months, and when the holiday season arrived, I invited him to join me at the Apax holiday party as my guest. He accepted and sat at my table, and I asked him to tell our tablemates about his business. Steve started by introducing himself and asked the same of my guests, who were all top executives at media companies that used services like Steve's. We spent a great dinner together and said our goodbyes at the end of the evening, and a few days after the holidays had passed, Steve called me and said, "I get it."

I DIDN'T HAVE A FUND to invest from yet, nor were Steve or Rafat raising money. My first interactions with them just validated that there was an opportunity to invest in digital media and served as my first efforts to seed a pipeline for the new venture capital firm I decided to form. I established Greycroft, named for my house that was built in 1894 in East Hampton, New York, and drafted a fundraising letter that I sent out in October of 2005 to private, high-net-worth individuals (investors and friends of mine). It wasn't a hard sell—just a simple letter with a form attached, explaining that I had formed a new entity and was inviting people to respond if they were interested in investing in the fund. People could respond, or not, and trust that if they didn't respond, they'd receive no further solicitation. It's a style I developed originally at Alan Patricof Associates and have continued to use to this day to initiate a new fund.

My assistant, Marie Jiha, remembers spending the days after Christmas of 2005 in the near-empty Apax offices preparing packages of legal paperwork for the investors who responded. I can't help but think of the similarly crucial help Carolyn Hearn gave me in 1969 as she typed my letter to the family offices that helped me form APA. There I was, starting all over again, this time with experience and insight that I wanted to build into Greycroft's operating model from the outset.

The first ground rule was to raise small funds—$40 million was my original max target for Greycroft, which grew to $75 million after I decided to bring on partners (a story I'll get to in a few pages). I imagined the fund would probably be one-and-done, as I would turn seventy-two the next year, and venture funds have a ten-year (or longer) life span. But if there was to be another, my thinking as of late 2005 was that any subsequent funds should be kept under $200 million to prevent the slippery slope I'd experienced with Apax of raising larger and larger funds and then needing to make larger and larger investments, and thus evolve from an early-stage venture fund into a private equity or buyout fund. I wanted a design that would stay venture-focused and I believed that raising only small funds would help, as would limiting the investor pool to only private investors.

The second ground rule was that Greycroft wouldn't require a minimum percentage ownership or minimum dollar investment in any company we supported. The average investment would be between $500,000 and $1 million, which at the time was slightly above the typical angel or seed venture capital round. I wanted to stay in a sweet spot of early-stage companies that had a commercial product in the market and some revenues—no pure start-ups, in other words, but also no late-stage deals. Constraining the investment size is a corollary to raising only small funds. In the same way that having a large fund forces a firm to make larger investments (since the money has to go somewhere), making a large investment comes with the expectation of a large percentage ownership to justify it—usually 20 percent. All that money in a young company drives higher valuations and outsized exit expectations. I didn't want to participate in that kind of run-up exuberance and sought to avoid it.

The third ground rule would be to concentrate only on companies which delivered products or services through the internet or a mobile device. There were a few reasons for that. The first was reputation: people still knew me as the founding investor of *New York Magazine*, and later of *Details* and *Scientific American*, as well as a major investor in AOL, Audible, Cellular Communications Inc., Emmis Broadcasting, LIN Broadcasting, and MedScape (now part of WebMD), among others. I had a long list of contacts in the media business and a deep understanding of how media operated. Focusing there would allow me to leverage my existing contacts and preserve bandwidth.

My second reason for focusing on firms with web-based businesses was that I believed it would allow me to build momentum within a market. If an investment did well, the firm would attract other early-stage businesses in the same area. The portfolio companies could also potentially help each other, since they wouldn't be competitors—I make it a point to try not to invest in two companies tackling the same market in the same way. My third and final reason for focusing on digital media was grounded in the economics of the internet, which allowed companies to establish themselves and build a customer base with relatively little capital. Compared to biotechnology or advanced manufacturing, digital media companies could do a lot with a little bit of money, which made them good investments for a small fund.

The fourth ground rule was that Greycroft would always include another firm as co-investor. This is an extremely rare approach for a venture capitalist, most of whom want as many exclusives as they can get. I had developed a friendlier view about partnerships after losing a big deal at Apax when an aggressive partner in the firm refused to participate in a syndicate, and as a result, we lost an opportunity to invest in Burt's Bees. I'd also seen firsthand the value in having another investor at the table to evaluate the potential of a start-up. When a co-investor uses their (ideally distinct) network and resources to do their own due diligence, you get two sources of data validating the company. If the deal goes through, that co-investor can also relieve some of the personal challenges that can arise when dealing one-on-one with an entrepreneur. Everyone benefits, including the entrepreneur, since it's much better for a young business to have at least two independent financial sources.

My last ground rule had to do with board seats: the new firm would only require a board observer role by contract. Observers got all of the materials distributed to board members and were present at every board meeting, but they didn't have a vote, which in my view didn't contribute much anyway. Though it had become common practice for venture investors to require a board seat, or even two, as a condition of investment, the seat rarely gave the investor enough voting control to affect the trajectory of a company—this contrasts with private equity, which in most cases controls the board and therefore can influence outcomes. By not requiring a board seat, Greycroft could eliminate conflict with other venture firms, which almost always required a board seat as part of their investment. It also got entrepreneurs excited, as we were the only one with that message.

Most of these ground rules remain part of the Greycroft investment ethos today. The exception is the size of the funds: they are getting much bigger.

All the other rules remain to guide how the firm operates—most importantly our commitment to syndicated investments. These ideas resonate extremely well with both entrepreneurs and investors, and remain a major differentiator for us. People are often surprised to learn that Greycroft doesn't require a minimum percentage ownership or a minimum financial investment, doesn't insist on having one or two representatives on their board, and welcomes other participants in the transaction. These rules make us good partners for the entrepreneur and send the message to other venture capital firms that we aren't competitors, but rather co-investors.

BACK IN 2006, WITH THOSE ground rules set up and the fundraising underway, I started to think more about the day-to-day reality of running the firm. I had two executive assistants who'd been with me at Apax and would be coming to Greycroft. Marie Jiha and Mary Gallivan had the skills and loyalty I needed in those early days—and still need today. (They're both still with Greycroft; Marie continues to be my administrative assistant, and Mary now handles human resources and recruitment for the firm's fifty or so employees.)

It occurred to me that I might want an investment analyst to work with me. I vacillated between absolute confidence in my ability to pursue a new path that condensed all my accumulated knowledge and concern that a potential contributor to the fund might be wary that I wouldn't live long enough to see the investments through to an attractive exit in ten years. I felt fit and had stayed involved, but I had seen my share of friends decline—some of them as healthy and vibrant as I was.

Having another investment colleague in Greycroft would require a number of changes I wasn't yet sure I wanted to make, however. For example, the firm would need a bigger fund to support salary and costs, and we would need to build the business with the idea that it would have a long-term legacy that other partners would continue when I stepped down. Still undecided, I nonetheless made some inquiries.

Given my history with the Columbia Business School, I reached out to the recruitment office, and Ian Sigalow's name came up. He'd served as a teaching assistant for Dean Glenn Hubbard, who I knew through my role on the Columbia Business School Board of Overseers. I called Glenn and heard raves. Like most people of his caliber, Ian had options: he had won a business plan competition for an online payments solution he hoped to commercialize and was raising money for that. He was also considering an offer from a prestigious management consultancy. During our first meeting we talked about his start-up, which didn't interest me for the new fund, though I introduced him to Tushar Maloo, an Apax associate who assisted me in managing the small amount of money still in the Apax venture fund. Ian and I also talked about his previous experience in venture capital before Columbia and about Greycroft and what I aimed to do.

I didn't extend an offer immediately after that conversation. From Ian's side, he later told me that he left the Apax offices thinking that if he ended up working with me to build the firm, it would be the best opportunity of his life.

In the meantime, my sons Mark, Jonathan, and Jamie—who were building their own careers outside of the venture business—knew I was considering bringing on a partner. Dana Settle's name came up once each for Jon and Jamie through different channels, and I called her. Dana had graduated from Harvard Business School and had spent about five years at the venture capital firm Mayfield Partners in San Francisco. She had just left to move to LA, but she was going to be in New York, so we met for coffee and talked about our respective views of where venture investing was headed. She was planning on raising a small fund she intended to run according to similar principles I had laid out for mine. After multiple conversations and meetings, Dana agreed to join me as a partner in forming Greycroft with the plan of moving to New York.

With Dana on board, I called Ian back. It was March by this point, and Ian was working on his start-up. He agreed to have lunch with me at the Friars Club. I told him about Dana and asked if he was interested in joining us. He agreed to think about it and talk to Dana, and he joined on the first of May, a week before his graduation from Columbia. We were all set to get rolling in New York, I thought, until Dana came to me to say for personal reasons, she couldn't move to New York. I briefly thought about going ahead with just me and Ian, but ultimately decided the firm would be better off with all three of us.

I hadn't originally wanted a California office, especially not while we were so young and small. Circumstance gave us one, and I was committed to supporting Dana's effort to make the firm bicoastal from the beginning.

RAFAT ALI'S *PAIDCONTENT* AND Steve Ellis's Pump Audio became Greycroft's first and second investments in the late spring of 2006. With additional capital and hands-on guidance from me and people I introduced to Rafat, *PaidContent* quickly expanded to other platforms and started running media-focused events. One of his first events in New York featured an on-stage interview between Rafat and Arthur Sulzberger Jr., the former publisher of *The New York Times*—a major win for a small media company. Rafat, with my assistance, identified and hired a CEO in late 2007 to run the business side so he could focus on editorial. The company continued to attract attention and was seeking its second round of funding in the summer of 2008 when *The Guardian* tendered an offer, which Rafat accepted.

In a funny side note, *The Guardian* deal was done in New York, and the day it closed, I had an evening event to attend for the presidential nominee-elect, Barack Obama. I thought it would be a fun surprise for Rafat to come meet the future president and his guests, including Hillary Clinton. I called him at his hotel and told him to meet me at the Loew's Regency Hotel, and he agreed. I guess I should have given him a bit more information, because he had been relaxing after the high emotions of the day and arrived in a rumpled T-shirt and sandals. Everyone else was in business dress. Rafat managed to smile for the pictures we took with Hillary and Barack, though he did say, "Next time you invite me to meet the future president, please let me know so I can at least take a shower."

Steve Ellis's Pump Audio experienced a similarly fast growth path. Together with Brad Svrluga of High Peak Venture Partners and Bo Peabody of Village Ventures, we participated in a $2.5 million venture round that allowed Steve to build up the content library and develop relationships with buyers. Fourteen months later, I organized a meeting in Seattle between Steve and John Klein, the CEO of Getty Images. A year later, Getty bought the company for $42 million.

I never tell entrepreneurs what to do, and I wasn't going to start with Steve Ellis. But I care about the entrepreneurs we support and feel a sense of responsibility to them. As Steve was mulling over the offer, I called with a piece of advice: "If you sell," I told him, "It's a lot of money and that is going to change your life, in part by removing something important from it. Be sure that's for you."

Steve ultimately decided to sell, but he remembers our conversation and it influenced him. He went on to start another company, Whosay, a social media and branding platform for celebrities, which he sold to Viacom in 2018—he's now Viacom's executive vice president of ad strategy and business development. For my part, I continue to counsel founders who are confronted with an early purchase offer that it's okay—and even tempting—to sell early, but to be wary of selling themselves or their opportunity short. It's one thing to sell because it's the right decision; it's quite another to sell due to lack of patience to play a longer game.

The first two investments and fast exits gave Greycroft some early momentum, but we were still chasing deals at that stage. We all spent significant time going to conferences and visiting incubators and attending product demonstrations to look for early-stage companies that interested us. I didn't just leave it to Dana and Ian. I had decided when I formed Greycroft that I wasn't going to be a dilettante who came in at ten and left at four and worked only four days a week. I wanted to be as active in the community of early-stage companies and investors as I had been in 1970 with my Wall Street and media connections.

More than that, I believed I *needed* to be more active to demonstrate to the youth-biased tech community that Greycroft was a serious company run by serious investors. As a consequence, I became a regular attendee at all the events and meetings related to technology start-ups and the venture industry. I'd be in New York one day, Las Vegas the next morning, and Los Angeles in the evening. I operated according to the belief—one I hold dear—that if you walk away from an event or meeting with just one new idea or contact, it is worth it.

Experience gives me a few advantages in this business. In recent years I have become known for saying whenever I attend a conference, panel discussion, or board meeting, "I assume I am the oldest person in the room, but I also have the longest time perspective."

(It was *usually* true at the advent of Greycroft; now it's *always* true.) I often follow that statement with a story relevant to whatever company we are talking about. It's a technique I have developed over the years to demonstrate that, in spite of my age, I'm not investing for a quick sale. The comment works for a lot of different purposes. It generates goodwill between meeting participants, and it helps a founder recognize I am not a get-rich-quick investor—I will stay with them for the long term.

These segues often seem like non sequiturs to meeting attendees who haven't spent much time with me. People who know me well, however, recognize what I am doing. They've seen it enough times to know that the discussion will often shift directions and become more open and relaxed. If it's an introductory meeting, it relaxes the inherent tension in a first meeting and makes me seem more human. If it's a board meeting, a story can help us all directly and openly discuss a sensitive problem with a softer reference. (Though I learned from all the conflict with *New York Magazine* never to bring up a controversial issue in a board meeting unless I had socialized it beforehand with the other board members and knew in advance the outcome, rather than waiting to see who raised their hand. If you can avoid it, you don't want to bring something up and have it voted down.)

One of my go-to non sequiturs is to tell the story of *Rashomon*, a 1950 film by the Japanese icon Akira Kurosawa. The film relays a violent event from the different perspectives of the participants, each version throwing the others into question. I'm usually trying to point out that different people can look at the same facts and draw different conclusions—most often in a context where I or my investors got a different impression from a conversation or a set of information than a founder did. "What is this, *Rashomon*?"

The concept reminds me of a joke I've heard many times about Admiral Johnson, the leader of a Navy battleship, who gets bad news over the wire one day and calls on Ensign Silver to deliver it. "Seaman

Jones's mother has died," the Admiral says, clearing his throat. "Can you please tell him gently." Ensign Silver says that he will and heads to the deck, where he blows his whistle to alert the crew. When he has their attention, Ensign Silver shouts through his bullhorn, "Seaman Jones, your mother has died." Seaman Jones collapses, and Ensign Silver pauses briefly before saying, "Dismissed."

Upon hearing how the Ensign handled it, Admiral Johnson pulls him aside and says, "Ensign Silver, you can't talk to people like that. When you have difficult news, you must deliver it gently." To which Ensign Silver nods gravely and says, "Yes, Sir, I understand, and I will do better on my next assignment. Please give me a second chance." The Admiral is hesitant, but says, "Well, Ensign Silver, Seaman Kelley's father has passed away. Please let him know. And this time do it more gently."

Ensign Silver returns to the deck, and again blows his whistle, and when the crew has collected, he shouts through the bullhorn, "Will everyone whose father is still alive please step forward." As the seamen all prepare to move, Ensign Silver shakes one finger toward the poor orphan. "Uh-uh, not you, Seaman Kelley."

My point? The right tone matters. Delivering a message or questioning a reference for due diligence requires some subtlety to reach your objective.

The mid-'00s provided many venture-focused event opportunities. One was NY Tech Meetups, a group founded by Scott Heiferman (the founder of Meetup.com) and Dawn Barber, the former director of the New York New Media Association (NYNMA). I knew Dawn, as NYNMA had organized of some of the first venture conferences for the New York tech community in the 1990s. With NY Tech Meetups, she and Scott formed the largest Meetup community in the world, with more than sixty thousand members at its height. Dawn became a good friend, who understood my interest in finding high-potential entrepreneurs and investing in them for the long-term. And I became the regular "senior guy" at the monthly Meetups of as many as a thousand entrepreneurs and venture capitalists.

Afterwards, a small group of the leaders would go to a post-Meetup dinner at Tio Pepe on Greenwich Street.

Another early investment was in *The Huffington Post* in 2007 (which was bought by AOL in 2011, bought again by Verizon Communications in 2015, and bought *again* by Buzzfeed in 2020). Near her launch, Arianna Huffington, who I knew socially, called me to ask if I'd write a blog post for her new publication. I did, and then asked her if I could join the venture round her cofounder, Ken Lerer, was raising. Thrive Global also entered the Greycroft portfolio in 2016 when Arianna became a repeat entrepreneur.

Greycroft's connection with *The Huffington Post* played a role in our decision to launch a seed fund in 2009 as part of Greycroft II. Our original concept of investing only in companies with a commercial product and some revenue had created a missed opportunity to invest in Buzzfeed when Jonah Peretti, the third *Huffington Post* cofounder, formed it. All *The Huffington Post* investors had been given a friendly pro rata opportunity to invest in Buzzfeed, but Greycroft passed on it because we weren't doing seed investments at that time.

We initiated the seed component as part of Greycroft II in 2009 so that we wouldn't again miss opportunities like Buzzfeed. We were not alone in our thinking: seed funds and angel networks had become more abundant and more relevant in the three years since we'd formed Greycroft. Though both had been around for a long time, the venture community hadn't paid much attention to either. Angels in particular had the reputation as alternative investment vehicles for successful doctors and lawyers or retired older entrepreneurs with time on their hands who wanted to dabble in investing but didn't know much about growth businesses. For that reason, professional venture investors tended to view angel-backed companies as more trouble than they were worth.

But by 2009, the market had begun placing more emphasis on seed investments, and angel networks increasingly got more sophisticated as second- or third-time entrepreneurs from venture-backed companies joined them. High-potential companies, that later went on to raise a Series A round, would often give their seed investors first dibs on the later round, so if we wanted to be in the running for later round opportunities, we needed to get in earlier.

In addition to content companies like *PaidContent*, Pump Audio, and *The Huffington Post*, we also started seeing more young firms with products that address various aspects of digital advertising, which was shifting to the programmatic model that is standard on digital platforms today. New York and LA had a lot of software companies in the ad space; their technology worked similarly to automatic trading platforms used by stock traders.

We made a number of investments in companies tackling that market. One was Vizu, which built software to profile customers and measure the impact of marketing campaigns—it sold to Nielsen in 2012. And in 2008, Ian brought in a company called Buddy Media, which started out in social games for Facebook. When it lost that space to Zynga, the company quickly pivoted to helping companies post social ads and drive "friends" to corporate Facebook pages. Greycroft made the investment, and Ian got hands-on working with the Buddy Media founders, husband and wife Mike and Kass Lazerow. When Buddy Media sold to Salesforce in 2012 for just shy of $700 million, our share of the proceeds was more than the value of Greycroft's first fund.

BUDDY MEDIA IS AN EXAMPLE of how Ian and Dana expanded their opportunity pool beyond digital media to include software developers, and eventually, fintech companies and ecommerce. Over time they also included mobility, analytics, AI, and other high-tech sectors. As the firm has grown and brought on new investors and partners, the mix of investments in our portfolios has evolved to reflect different interests and viewpoints.

Though some of the highest-profile investments by Greycroft were in media companies, including Maker Studio (which was bought by Disney), *The Huffington Post* (bought by AOL), and Axios, we also have many investments that are as well known in companies far afield from media, including Venmo, the person-to-person payment platform bought by PayPal; Shipt, an ecommerce delivery company that was purchased by Target; Thrive Market, an ecommerce organic grocer that delivered real food essentials long before Amazon bought Whole Foods; The RealReal, a luxury consignment company that went public in 2019, and many others. As these companies can attest, we were very much a national firm investing in early-stage businesses on both coasts, as well as in places further afield, like Indianapolis, Minneapolis, and Birmingham.

TheRealReal exemplifies the Greycroft ethos of always doing deals with other investors. Mathias Schilling, the co-founder of a San Francisco VC firm called e.ventures, discovered The RealReal in San Francisco and brought in Dana as a co-investor because of her knowledge and experience with fashion businesses. Mathias's connection to Greycroft was the result of years of trust and co-investing between our two firms—essentially since we formed. Dana had also gotten to know e.ventures and Mathias when she was still at Mayfield Partners, and spent time in the e.ventures offices after leaving Mayfield and before joining Greycroft. She introduced Mathias and his co-founders to me, and I agreed with her that there was a lot of natural synergy between us. In a funny coincidence, Mathias's father turned out to be good friends with Michael Hinderer, the co-founding partner of Apax in Germany.

I eventually advocated to have e.ventures join the weekly meetings we hold to talk about the early-stage companies that reached out to us for investment. We also attended theirs. Greycroft and e.ventures agreed that neither would compete against the other for a deal that came up in one of those meetings—and we haven't. Instead, we have co-invested in companies that interested both of us or supported the other with information or advice on companies that only fit one firm's portfolio. Mathias, who started his business when he was twenty-five, told me he never had a mentor, but he feels that the connection we have developed goes beyond deals to provide an important personal dimension of support.

It's a rare friendship between VCs, to the point that when Greycroft formed our growth fund, we did it as a joint venture between the two firms. We had a formal-informal understanding that we had to agree on any deals and invest in them in equal proportion. The relationship is now eleven years old, and though as a result of the growth and success of both firms we've had to disband the formal agreement, we've remained friendly and still do deals together from time to time.

I've tried in other ways to bring a diversity of ideas to Greycroft to prevent us from getting too insular. Over the years I have invited senior executives who've retired or left a previous role to join our weekly meetings and participate in the discussion. Attendees have included John Klein, the founder and chairman of Getty Images; Tom Glocer, the former CEO of Thomson Reuters; Michael Gould, the former chairman of Bloomingdale's; Tom Rogers of NBC and, more recently, TiVO, and Dan Shulman of PayPal.

Invitees tended to come only intermittently until David Stern—the retired commissioner of the National Basketball Association—started joining our partner meetings in 2016. I had only recently met him. As he was in the early stage of his retirement from the NBA, I thought he might find it interesting and energizing to see all the exciting new ideas, companies, and entrepreneurs that made a weekly parade to the office.

There's something infectious about venture capital. When people have a chance to see small businesses pursuing interesting ideas, it's exciting and engaging. David really caught that spirit. The more he joined us, the freer he became in criticizing and eventually participating in a number of deals, both in and outside of the sports area. He had an innate understanding of managing for growth. He and I also developed the idea that he was an "intern" and I printed Greycroft business cards for him that said "David Stern, Intern" to formalize it. He was as proud of that title as he was of "commissioner." I consider David to be a prime example of how I have mentored people in venture investing over the years, though most of my mentees are one-third David's age.

One day I had the crazy idea to introduce David to another friend, Robert De Niro, who had just released his movie *The Intern*. I sat together with the two "interns" at a 3:00 p.m. lunch (to accommodate DeNiro's schedule) at Sistina—a memorable meal between two giants in their fields, and me as the fly on the wall. We've all missed David at our meetings, me in particular, since his sudden passing in November of 2019. We were like a Mutt and Jeff team in the way we took turns bringing up the other side of an argument to stimulate discussion and offer up some historical perspective from our individual experiences.

I PERSONALLY CONTINUED TO FOCUS on digital media companies for the deals I led, even as Greycroft grew and our portfolio became more diverse. I had more than enough to keep my attention in the media space, given the new ideas made possible by the internet and later by new platforms and formats such as mobile apps and podcasts.

One of Greycroft's first mobile media investments was in a product called Pulse, an early app for aggregating news. Akshay Kothari and Ankit Gupta created the Pulse app as a Stanford design course project. They wanted to make it less cumbersome to read news on a smart phone or tablet and developed the app as a visual, skimmable, mobile way to do so. The app quickly rocketed up the charts in the App Store, earning a shout-out from Steve Jobs from the 2010 stage of the Apple Worldwide Developer's Conference. Dana and I went to meet Akshay and Ankit in Palo Alto and asked to participate in the Series A they were raising.

The round was almost fully subscribed by traditional Silicon Valley VCs by the time we got to them, but Akshay agreed to a small investment from us. He says now that he took the meeting without knowing much about me, but that it was "like destiny." His Palo Alto VCs understood product, he says, but I understood media, and could introduce him to media people he needed to know. Whenever Akshay was in New York, or I was in San Francisco, I would call him and invite him to dinner. He'd show up in his Palo Alto hoodie, and I'd be there with the publisher of Hearst or of *New York Magazine* or some other person in the media business.

I encouraged him to think long term about the business model of the company and the kind of media partnerships that could help him. He says now that despite our small stake, Greycroft was the "most helpful investor." Pulse and Akshay eventually caught the attention of LinkedIn, which bought it in 2013. Pulse became the foundation of LinkedIn's content strategy—now a revenue driver for the company. Akshay led the development of the content business for a time, before leaving to join a productivity and collaboration technology firm called Notion as COO.

NewsCred is another digital content delivery company in the Greycroft portfolio. NewsCred formed in 2008 with the goal of vetting and rating the credibility of news sources. Years before Donald Trump labeled any outlet that criticized him "fake news," Shafqat Islam and his two co-founders (all college friends from the University of Pennsylvania) tried to tackle the legitimate issue of reliability in the news media with a site that used qualitative and quantitative metrics to assess content.

Over time the company evolved into a software-as-a-service (SaaS) content marketing platform. I met Shafqat when NewsCred was still a content company. I liked the idea and brought in NewsCred for a presentation when it was raising a Series A round. The principal customers were publishers who were slow to make decisions and who had little money to spend on technology. Given that, there wasn't enough support for it at Greycroft to make the investment.

By the time NewsCred raised a Series B round the following year, they had dropped their focus on content and publishers as advertisers and shifted to consumer packaged goods firms and others that had more money and paid well. As a result, Greycroft invested. NewsCred has since rebranded as Welcome. After more than twelve years of ownership, I was overjoyed when the company was sold in late 2021 at a valuation that resulted in a modest but positive outcome for Shafqat and all the investors.

TheSkimm came into the Greycroft portfolio in 2014 after I reached out to the company. Similar to *PaidContent*, I had been hearing about theSkimm in meetings and at events, and after enough mentions I looked into what they were doing. I liked the approach they took to developing their audience of young, professional women with a smart daily newsletter that summarized what they needed to know. I sought out the founders, Carly Zakin and Danielle Weisberg, and asked to invest. Their Series A round was already fully subscribed, but they made room for Greycroft.

Later came Axios, a digital news site focused on business and politics started by three members of the leadership: Jim VandeHei, Mike Allen, and Roy Schwartz. Axios follows an editorial format of short, succinct, blog-style articles that sum up the gist of a topic in a concise format they refer to as "smart brevity." Axios also hosts panel discussions it streams on the site. Greycroft made that investment in 2017, and the company had already turned a profit by 2019—a major and rare achievement for a young media publication.

I HAVE MORE RECENTLY BECOME interested in podcast companies. I first cued in to the format a few years ago when I was walking on Madison Avenue and ran into David Carey, then the president of Hearst Publications. David wore headphones and seemed in another world. When I asked what had him so distracted, he said he was listening to a podcast. That interaction started me thinking that if a person as senior as David was walking down the street listening to podcasts, this media had reached a new level of maturity. Apple's launch of AirPods in 2016, further helped by enabling a better listening experience in almost all the ways that matter—size, sound quality, and fashion—led me to decide I should be looking at the audio space more carefully.

As a first step, I reached out to Betaworks, a business accelerator in New York City run by John Borthwick that in January 2017 held a "Voicecamp" accelerator for start-ups pursuing audio-focused businesses. I attended Voicecamp and got to know some of the start-ups there.

Later, my wife Susan was in the car on her way to an appointment and the driver was listening to a podcast by Wondery, an emerging producer of nonfiction, serialized stories about extreme events. One of Wondery's most famous productions is *Dirty John*, which tells the story of a serial con artist and exploiter of women, based on reporting from the *Los Angeles Times*.

I called Hernan Lopez, the former Fox International executive who'd founded Wondery, and asked if we could meet. He came to see me in my New York office. A meeting that was scheduled for an hour stretched to two as we talked about his vision of creating binge-worthy nonfiction audio stories. As it happened, he'd been bootstrapping the business for two years and trying to raise money with no luck. The VCs weren't interested, including my own—the Greycroft California office had looked at Wondery a year or two before and turned it down.

The reasoning at the time was that the overall market was too small, and the company was too early, too reliant on content and advertising, and too dependent on third-party platforms to reach its audience. Those reasons were sound, but Wondery had developed in the two years since Greycroft first considered it. I gave Wondery another look and ultimately led a small syndicate of investors to form a Series A round that closed in 2018. On December 31, 2020,

Amazon bought the company, creating a substantial return on our investment.

I've taken a holistic view of investing in podcasting by looking beyond content to the technology that supports it, and even further, to the whole field of audio, which after a hundred years of radio, is experiencing a vibrant rebirth as a new medium as a result of new content formats and new listener behavior. One benefit of my reputation as an early supporter of the medium is that a lot of early-stage companies in the space seek us out. As a result, Greycroft invested in Glow, which offers a solution for independent podcast creators to build their subscriber base; Chartable, which allows podcast publishers, as well as advertisers, to measure social media and ad performance on podcasts and attribute sales to the right source; Podsights, also an advertising attribution solution for podcasts; and Snackable, which has a natural-language AI solution that can search audio and video files for specific content.

More recently, we've invested in Veritonic, a company with an AI platform that analyzes the performance of audio used in brand marketing or in podcasts to identify the most effective sounds to capture audience attention. The company has already worked with major brands like Subway, Coca-Cola, and iHeartMedia, and almost all of the major platforms, including Audible—that has nostalgic resonance for me as one of Audible's original investors.

I made a few more podcast investments in 2021. One is in Podchaser, which aims to do for podcasting what Nielsen does for the television industry by serving as the ultimate source of information on listening traffic, content, people in the industry, and other data. Another is in Racket, a platform for user-created audio content lasting nine minutes or less—I think of it as a TikTok for mini-podcasters who want to "make a Racket."

I've also been exploring additional opportunities with unique audio content distribution platforms. I first started talking about distribution with Laura Walker, who I met at a summer party hosted by my friends, Peter and Susan Solomon (Peter, you'll recall, represented Lehman Brothers in the deal to finance LIN Broadcasting). At the time, Laura was the president of WNYC—one of the largest public radio stations in the US. Earlier in her career, she had worked for Sesame Workshop, the children's education nonprofit behind *Sesame Street*. While there, she had led an initiative to create the cable station Noggin. Laura and I waxed philosophical about the potential of podcasts to engage an audience beyond the public radio listener and how a nonprofit like WNYC could do it.

Shortly after that, Laura called me for advice about an acquisition WNYC wanted to make of an Australian podcast distribution platform called Pocket Casts (WNYC was part of an acquiring consortium that included NPR, WBEZ in Chicago, and *This American Life*—three of the biggest creators and radio distributors of podcast content). I happily shared my thoughts with her and offered to help her evaluate the candidates she was considering to lead the venture and to possibly finance the new spin-off.

After the acquisition took place, Laura and Owen Grover, the former General Manager of iHeartRadio and the ultimate pick to lead the entity, reached out again to have me help develop a proposal to spin Pocket Casts off into an independent entity. Laura believed that making Pocket Casts an independent, for-profit business partially owned by the public radio entities and expanded with venture investor funding would vastly broaden its potential to be a key platform for audio and create a revenue stream for the stations.

I agreed. Laura, Owen, and I created a strategic plan for the business. Greycroft committed to form an investor group to put $6 million in it—an equal investment to what the nonprofits would put in. Laura pitched the plan to the boards of the participating companies, but in the end, the consensus was that a for-profit business was too far afield from the ethos of public radio. The idea was rejected. Owen stayed for another year, but he hadn't signed up to run another nonprofit and moved on to become CEO of TrueFire Studios, a digital music education company.

Laura also left WNYC—she already had a plan in the works to leave the station before the spin-off idea was rejected, and unrelated to the failure of the venture, she departed the organization shortly after. She spent some time working on another podcast content idea which I hope to support once she gets it going, though it might be a while—in 2020 she announced she's putting the idea on hold to take a position as president of Bennington College, where I visited her in November 2021. She is living a much more bucolic life in Vermont.

As a coda to my voice-related adventures, in 2021 Greycroft invested in a unique team of AI engineers from Siberia to form a text-to-speech translation company known as Speechki. Their product purportedly has the ability to convert written text into audio (or vice versa) faster and cheaper than anything else on the market. Greycroft also went back into the audio content world to participate in the financing of Sonoro, a company producing Spanish and English content for the LatAm market; and in Lemonada Media, a women-led company focused on content for a mostly-women audience "turning lemons into lemonade" (e.g. making life better).

I WOULD BE REMISS IN relaying my experiences during the Greycroft era of my life if I didn't talk about Susan's illness, which she endured for more than a decade. Sometime in 2008 I became concerned about the frequency with which she asked me to repeat obvious numbers or letters. I might say, "I'll meet you at 20 West 15th Street," or, "Call Cathy," and she would respond, "Say that number again," or, "Call who?"

When it first started happening, I would admonish her for not remembering such basic information. She took it in stride, responding with something like, "You know I never had a good memory." We dismissed it (wrongly) as connected to a brain aneurysm Susan had developed years before as the result of a fall—the neurologist she saw every six months or so to monitor it always said it wasn't causing any problems (and it wasn't).

But the memory problems continued, and we decided to go see the neurologist Cathy Neeland, who referred us on to Dr. Norman Relkin, an Alzheimer's specialist at Weill Cornell Medical Center (known to native New Yorkers as "New York Hospital"). After taking an MRI and a CT scan, Relkin diagnosed Susan with aphasia, a communication disorder that occurs when a lack of blood flow causes neurons to die in specific regions. He showed us her brain scans and pointed out where she had lack of blood flow on both sides (unrelated to the aneurysm).

The damage on one side affected Susan's recall of words, and on the other side, her recall of numbers. Aphasia is one of the first symptoms experienced by people with Alzheimer's, with which Susan was eventually diagnosed after her illness progressed to include other symptoms beyond difficulties with language. (Neurologists say there are seven stages of Alzheimer's. Signs of aphasia appear in the first, but aphasia is not exclusive to Alzheimer's, which is why she received that somewhat less-serious diagnosis early on.)

One touching moment occurred years after Susan's initial aphasia diagnosis, when she and I attended a fund raiser for gun control, a cause we both felt passionate about. Gabby Giffords, the former US representative from Arizona and gun violence survivor, spoke at the event. Afterwards, Susan went to speak with Gabby about her experience with aphasia as a result of a gunshot wound to her head. Susan shared that she also had aphasia and they both got teary and embraced as they each shared the frustration they felt from losing the ability to communicate. For Gabby, time and therapy would allow her to reacquire some of her brain and verbal function. The same was not true for Susan.

Over the subsequent ten-plus years, Susan participated in a number of therapies and clinical trials in an effort to slow down or reverse the progression of her illness. For years she saw a speech therapist, who used puzzles and word games to help build secondary associations in the brain that could help Susan keep her memory and speech. Susan's neurologist, Dr. Relkin, also happened to be the chief investigator in a trial financed by Baxter Laboratories to see if intravenous immunoglobulin could reduce amyloid plaque buildup in Alzheimer patients. Relkin's team was analyzing the Phase III results when we first met him, and in the meantime, patients outside the trial could unofficially use the therapy.

Susan spent three to four hours every other week receiving the infusion, but around her tenth visit, Baxter released the results of the trial. Though some individual patients saw small benefits, the therapy failed to produce significant improvements. Susan didn't improve from using it, and we stopped the therapy. This was disappointing, but not entirely unexpected, as most drugs and treatments fail to make it through the trial period. Alzheimer therapies have a particularly poor track record, especially with more advanced patients.

Over the years, we had other disappointments. An experimental drug we considered for her was ultimately delayed by the FDA. We tried transcranial magnetic stimulation, which. had had some success in improving memory by stimulating the brain with electrical impulses, but Susan saw no results. In December 2016, a friend sent me an article that had appeared in *Nature* about a trial conducted by Dr. Li-Huei Tsai of the Picower Institute for Learning and Memory at MIT with mice using light impulses at 40Hz frequency.

The trial subsequently included sound inputs and was led by Tod Machover of the MIT Media Lab. The initial results were encouraging, but improvements in mice don't necessarily translate to humans, and I learned that there was no human trial planned at that time (but subsequently they have started). The non-invasive nature of the therapy still intrigued me. I got involved in supporting the research and convened a gathering of people to try to generate funding for human trials. I also found a way to recreate the system to use at home with sound. Susan sat in front of the light-and-sound machine for an hour each day for three years. I didn't observe any improvement, but who knows—perhaps her condition would have deteriorated even faster without the treatment. Such questions about impact are part of what research will eventually unpack through more randomized trials.

Susan saw different experts in the field for second and third opinions. I called Dr. Eric Kandel, the Nobel Prize winner in Physiology or Medicine and a professor at the College of Physicians and Surgeons at Columbia University, who I had known for years—we'd briefly worked together years earlier when I invested in a failed commercial venture involving serotonin receptors in the brain that Eric and another Nobel prize winner, Richard Axel, had started.

Eric reviewed Susan's scans and record and suggested that we meet with his number two, Dr. Scott Small, another leading researcher. (By that time, Eric was just doing research and writing and working on a six-part series about the brain for PBS). We visited Scott at Columbia and continued to see Norman Relkin at New York Hospital, but all they could offer was conversation as one drug after another failed in clinical trials.

In the spring of 2016, our problems got significantly worse. Though she was clearly declining, Susan had still attended the ballet, she walked the one-and-a-half miles around the Central Park reservoir several times a week with Ellen Thomas, her roommate from Cornell, and she also went to weekday matinees with a close family friend. Due to her high relative level of function, we had only employed a caregiver during the weekdays while I was at work. That all changed abruptly one Sunday afternoon. I had just left Susan resting on our bed, when I suddenly heard a loud thud. She must have gotten up and gone to the top of our stairs and somehow fallen, because now she was lying at the bottom. I called 911 and had her rushed to the trauma center at New York Hospital. She'd suffered a hematoma on her brain, a fractured vertebra in her neck, and a large gash over her right eye. As bad as it sounds, there apparently was no permanent damage after a week in intensive care and a subsequent period of healing. It was nonetheless clear we were at a new stage in the disease, and she would require round-the-clock care.

Courtney Dawson, our personal assistant at home, took on the role of recruiting caregivers and handling the schedule of activities, which at that time still included art therapy, music, barre dance, massages, and anything else we could think of to make her days more interesting and active as her level of functioning gradually continued to decline. Courtney also arranged for a family member or friend to come almost every day for lunch and also dinner if I had an evening appointment. Those visits eventually faded away as Susan became less and less communicative.

A few months after Susan's fall, I started attending a bi-weekly support group at the Alzheimer's Association on Lexington Avenue (the organization is now called CaringKind). They were ninety-minute support sessions for spouses and caregivers of people with Alzheimer's and other memory diseases. The attendees share their experiences from the previous two weeks and exchange information about services they have found useful, as well as techniques for dealing with common situations. Through that group I found a periodontist with a particular specialty of dealing with patients who have neurological problems, a painting program, a music therapist, and museum activities, just to name a few. The organization also offered classes to train caregivers, classes for early-onset patients, social work advice, and other resources.

Susan continued to decline and became dependent on full-time care. By the time we retreated in early 2020 to our East Hampton home to wait out the coronavirus lockdown, it had been years since she'd gone anywhere alone. She had periods during which she was very agitated, and her speech over time diminished, to the point that she stopped speaking at all. She needed help with everything—dressing, bathing, using the toilet, eating, and so on. We had four dedicated caregivers who worked in shifts over the four years of her final decline. Their care and concern made it possible for Susan to have some modest enjoyment in her day-to-day life. The caregivers and visitors used to wear name tags in the hope that a name would trigger a modest response. It used to, but then it didn't, so we stopped the practice.

We also played familiar music at all times, had family photos in a special frame that rotated all day. We hoped the pictures would assist in recall, and at one point they did, until they didn't. It was a profound luxury to have the resources to hire caregivers and a personal assistant—one I would have hated to do without. Susan's sister, Amy, spent much of her time with us as well, and sublimated her personal life for several years to assist in Susan's care and keep her company. I am very lucky to have had these great people around.

That message came home for me especially when I saw the different situations among members of my support group. Some became full-time caregivers. Others hired care during the day and provided care themselves at night—which is hugely exhausting, as Alzheimer's patients can often be active and agitated at night. Others opted for twenty-four-hour care, as I did. Still others found it impossible to keep their spouse or family member at home, either because the patient became unmanageable for the family, or the twenty-four-hour care became impossible to provide with the household resources. For my part, I was determined to have Susan at home. Not everyone can physically or financially do this. It's not a reflection of how much they care, but just the reality of their situation.

Alzheimer's is an insidious disease. It creeps up slowly without you noticing and gradually takes away every bodily function, one by one, and never in the same order for any two people. The worst part for caregivers and family members is that you never really know how the person suffering from the disease is feeling, since they lose their ability to communicate. Do they hear when you speak to them, since they no longer react to sound? Do they enjoy the taste of one food or another, since they may not express delight or distaste? Is the smile on their face a response to an experience, or is it just a reflex? Are they aware of anything around them, including the sun,

*Alan and Susan
Patricof at the
Northside Gala
in Manhattan
in 2005.*

the snow, or the cool breeze? It is frustrating to not know whether any actions you take for them have any impact.

At some point you have to ask yourself, "Am I doing the loved one a favor by working so hard to extend their life in some pleasurable way?" In my case, I took the attitude that Susan was still with us, and I wanted to do everything to extend her life even another month, without knowing if I was doing her a favor. I felt that she should be dressed each day as stylishly as she had been when she was well. We talked to her as if she understood and was part of the conversation. As long as we could, we fed her foods that resembled what she would have chosen when she was well. We took her to the ocean in the summer, and out in the snow in winter, and for long rides to visit friends. If I was invited to a party, I would bring her with me, if I could. If I had friends at home to visit or for dinner, she was always part of the group. In short, I tried in every way to keep her life as normal as possible, and to let others know she was still with us and she should be treated as such, not as someone who was seriously ill. Particularly with our grandchildren, I wanted them to experience her decline gradually. In order to keep my sanity, I also reestablished a limited social life for myself, motivated by a mantra I heard in my support group: "It's better to lose one person and not two." How true that is for one dealing with the long, steady decline of a loved one.

I say all of these things to benefit others who may unfortunately be confronted with a similar situation and to provide some guidance so that when the end ultimately comes, one can have the feeling of having done everything for your loved one with no residual regrets. In our case, Susan was at home with me until January 2021, when she began to have difficulty swallowing and ingesting food, usually the final sign of decline. She died peacefully with me, our sons, and grandchildren by her side.

AND AS FOR ME? I'm determined to live to be 114! I set that goal for myself after hearing a lecture many years ago by a Mount Sinai gerontologist who explained that the human body, absent major illnesses, was made to last 114 years (more recent research suggests the number is 120 for children born today). I liked that idea. I also like to say that if I don't make it, people can call me a liar at my funeral—if they're still alive to attend it.

Having a goal like that has had an impact on my psyche. Throughout these pages I have tried to offer perspective on the way I approach life, business, art, politics, volunteering—everything that I touch. If I am going to spend time on an activity, I do it with a positive attitude and a belief that obstacles can be overcome. If I have to be in Boston and Chicago on the same day, I'll find a way. If it's raining, I'll still go out without an umbrella. I still jaywalk against traffic. An optimistic outlook is a critical trait in a venture capitalist. It's also key to living the kind of active, charmed life that I believe I have led. Susan getting sick is the first truly terrible thing that has happened to me, but in this case, one is enough.

The only other situation that even comes close began seven years ago when my oldest son, Mark—then in his late forties—was having dinner one night with his daughter in a South Asian restaurant in Greenwich Village that famously served very spicy food. They received a certificate for ordering the hottest dish in the restaurant, but after the meal, Mark walked out feeling terrible and unable to breathe. He went home, took a shower, and drank some Pepto, but it did no good.

He then walked himself over to the emergency room of the Beth Israel Hospital a few blocks away, and within a few hours, he was on the operating table undergoing repair of a ruptured esophagus—a life-threatening event. They saved his life, though the recovery involved two weeks in intensive care and months at home under the care of a nurse. He continues to see a specialist to manage it. It's a bit of a sword of Damocles constantly hanging over him. Illnesses related to the original event still plague his health.

Doctors haven't restricted him from working, fortunately, and he recently created a new business advising sports stars on their investments. At the same time, my son Jamie, who became a film producer, keeps producing new movie and TV shows. John also has an exciting new venture that he began with Jonathan Soros, Athletes Unlimited, which is establishing a new concept in professional women's sports. Initially focused on fast-pitch softball, volleyball, lacrosse, and recently basketball, the games keep score according to the achievements of the individual athletes, not the team.

Building a cohesive family with three sons would be a challenge under any circumstances. The fact that Mark is also Bette's biological son, and Jon and Jamie are Susan's, presented its own specific issues. But I am most proud, more than any business accomplishment, of the fact that we are one family unit. Each of my sons treats each other with true brotherly trust, respect, support, and love. That feeling extends through their children, who act as true cousins, and to their wives and their wives' siblings, to create one cohesive unit in which everyone feels part of the larger group. We spend birthdays, holidays, and celebrations—and also sad events—together whenever possible. It didn't happen by accident, but through consistent effort to produce a bonded family. This gave Susan—and it still gives me—a great sense of pride.

I have become more aware (as if I needed the reminder) that my longevity isn't a given. I work for it. I have never smoked, I drink only a few glasses of wine in the course of a week, and I maintain my weight within a two-pound spread by weighing myself every morning and evening and adjusting my diet during the day to accommodate the numbers. I never loved to watch sports, but I do like exercise (ironically, all three of my sons are sports addicts and two of them are involved professionally in the sports industry).

Running became part of my life in 1970 when my close friend Stephen Wald convinced me to meet him every day at the entrance to Central Park to jog. I started participating in road races: half marathons and eventually in 1974, my first marathon. Back then, the NYC marathon involved running the full loop of Central Park four-plus times to cover 26.2 miles. In the first year I ran it, there were 127 competitors—my running partner and I purchased a truckload of apples to give out to the finishers. Today there are 61,000 participants, and the route now passes through all five boroughs. Prizes are in the millions of dollars.

Sadly, there's very little documentary evidence of my time as a runner, though not for lack of trying. By 1978, my running crew had grown into a group of five of us who ran as a "rat pack" for motivation and to help distract from the pain. We decided to run that year's New York City marathon as a group. We got T-shirts

Alan Patricof and friends at the 1980 NYC Marathon, driven to the start with a hired 1935 Rolls Royce.

made with the words "The Tourists" emblazoned on them, due to the practice we'd developed of wandering different parts of the city during our training runs. We rarely set a route, just a time objective. We'd run over the George Washington Bridge on Tuesday and then over the Brooklyn Bridge on Thursday, and down to Battery Park on Saturday—wherever the spirit led us.

On marathon day we hired a livery driver in a Rolls Royce to bring us to the race start point on Staten Island at the foot of the Verrazano-Narrows Bridge. We had arranged for a team of photographers to film us en route at predetermined places in Manhattan; the footage was to serve as our vanity souvenirs. Our family members and friends also placed themselves at various points along the route to cheer us on.

Despite the carefully constructed plan, the crowd proved too much for it. With twenty-five thousand runners flowing tight together on narrow streets and us in view for just a few seconds at any possible viewing point due to our eight-minute-per-mile pace, neither of the photographers were able to find us in the pack, and no permanent video exists! In the latter miles we began to split up and we finished at different times. (Today, everyone carries a chip so people can follow their position in the race.) I made it a personal point to slow down a touch so I could finish in three hours and thirty-one minutes; a three-thirty time would qualify me for the Boston Marathon, and I didn't want to be tempted to do it again!

I ran a total of five NYC marathons. That 1978 time still stands as my personal best (I have proof if anyone questions it!). There's a real euphoria and sense of accomplishment from finishing, but it's also tough—each year I said would be my last, but the elation is hard to give up. My true last time, in 1983, I ran as a partner for a person in a wheelchair as part of the Achilles Track Club, an athletic association for disabled runners. That race was the hardest; due to the starts and stops it took almost seven and a half hours to complete. I recently found four marathon T-shirts in my closet from 1975, '76, '78, and '79. I was so proud; I fit into '75 and '79, no change in thirty years. This past year, after standing on the sidelines watching the runners pass, I got a sudden urge to do it again myself. I have hired a track coach and am well into training to walk/run the 26.1 miles in 2022. If I make it, I hope you'll come cheer me.

I also ran the Beta Breakers on the West Coast and the West Point Run, with steep inclines down and back from the campus to the Hudson River. The most exciting run of all was from Falmouth, Massachusetts, to Woods Hole, where a group of us flew over in a private sea plane from East Hampton to Falmouth for the start, and back again after the race.

I started to deemphasize running when I was learning how to roller blade and went into a full split while learning to stop. I tore my hamstring so badly I had to go to the hospital in an ambulance. That knocked me out of running but had no impact on my roller blading. I kept that up until my workout partner, Leonard Gordon, asked that we switch to biking. I got very serious about biking, and we went on regular weekend tours around the Hamptons.

Then one day in 2008, when I was seventy-four, my friend Stephen invited Leonard and me to join him and his wife on a fifty-four-day cross-country bike tour. I didn't have the time or desire for the whole thing, but I thought it could be fun to join for a few days along the route. Leonard and I decided to take a forty-mile bike ride in the Hamptons to make sure we had the physical stamina to do it. The tour operator said that if we woke up the next day and said, "Let's go for a bike ride," we were in shape to join the tour. We took a Saturday ride from East Hampton to the Montauk Lighthouse, at the end of a very long hill, and back. It took us about four-plus hours, and both Leonard and I agreed it was a great day. But when I returned from dinner later that night, I found the following note pinned to the door of my house:

Dear Alan,

It was a great day today and I know we can make the ride—but I suggest you return the tickets.

Leonard

Needless to say, we never made the trek, and these days I spend my long weekend rides with Wayne Winnick, who is in his sixties and with whom I've now ridden with for fifteen years. For the last five or so, his new wife, Amy, has joined us. She's in her forties, so in the last few years I've had to find the secret of keeping up with her: a pedal-assist electric bike for long rides and the big hills, when I sheepishly turn on the electric switch to help me keep up.

I also exercise with a trainer three times a week. I read an article recently that said lifting sixty pounds or more three times a week increases life expectancy by 20 percent. I've been doing that for twenty-five years with Chris Schoeck, my trainer. I am certain that Chris and my training regimen are the reason I stand straighter and with more flexibility than most of my peers.

Despite how much I rely on Chris, I have encouraged him through multiple attempts to transition into another profession. He once trained as a chef at The Culinary Institute. He studied for the securities exam. He also studied to become a locksmith specializing in repairing and installing safes. None of these alternatives stuck, for various reasons. More recently, Chris taught himself the technique of bending steel with his bare hands, used by old-time strongmen in the Amish country around Lancaster, Pennsylvania. This naturally requires not only great strength, but mind control to take a piece of metal—whether a spike nail, a horseshoe, or a 1" or 2" steel bar— and bend it through sheer grip of his hands.

A cinematographer who lived in Chris's building saw him practicing and asked if he could follow his odyssey as he gained skills and began to appear in public performances. The resulting documentary, *Bending Steel*, has been screened in multiple film festivals around the country including Toronto, Telluride, and Tribeca, among others. It's now available on Amazon Prime. Chris had prospects for an aborted TV show and several modeling gigs. Nothing permanent developed, however, and he settled in to bending metal as a hobby and back into full-time personal training.

In the meantime, he still trains clients and specializes in people age sixty and older. I have recommended him to friends of mine, as I firmly believe that he will play a key role in helping me reach 114. My sons jokingly (and perhaps with the slightest envy) call Chris my fourth son, as I have watched him mature, seen him three times a week, and sometimes invited him for a meal or celebration. I am playing the surrogate role of father, brother, friend, and mentor. Twenty-five years of such close association is longer than most marriages.

He has certainly allowed me to enjoy a very high level of stamina and quality of life. I can sometimes still ski the blues at Deer Valley, and two years ago I went to Whistler with a much younger doctor friend and her twenty-five-year-old daughter and held my own. (Dr. Lisa, as everyone in my family refers to her, is the daughter I never had, as I was friends with her parents and may have been the first person after them and the doctor to see her when she was a baby.) I also ski every year at the Greycroft offsite we hold in

Deer Valley, Utah; the last one took place in January 2022. I walk faster than almost any of the under-thirties in my office. I ride the subway to work many days and take the NYC bus home, although in recent years I've also splurged on Via, the shared ride, when it was operating.

I have also retained the energy and enthusiasm to attend most of the venture industry events that take place in NY, and when I can in LA. I maintain an active travel schedule both for business and pleasure. I had planned in 2020 to attend Burning Man in the Nevada desert, determined to be the oldest person there. The COVID-19 crisis grounded those plans, but that just increases my chances of being the oldest next year when I go.

I am usually the first person in the office in the morning, but not always last to leave, as I often attend business or industry meetings or social events in the evenings. I am known for triple-booking social commitments into the same evening and working my way from one to another between the hours of six and nine at night. Even with that full schedule, I make sure to sleep between six and seven hours a night, though the recent pace of weeknight TV news is disturbing that pattern. I have unfortunately learned that the MSNBC news lineup from nine o'clock to midnight repeats from midnight to three in the morning! I also read the *Financial Times*, *The New York Times*, *The Wall Street Journal*, and most of the newsletters of Axios every day to stay informed and involved with business, family, and politics. During the pandemic I also became a dedicated hiker and long-distance bike rider.

Viewed together, the combined impact of a positive mental attitude, wide-ranging curiosity, physical activity, and engagement with people and activities have allowed me to live a rich, full life—and a long one. The span of my life—even including the experience of watching my wife enter her later years on a different trajectory from me—has gotten me thinking over the past few years about issues of aging and staying active and involved. I've contemplated the assumptions that exist about older people and how equipped we are to actively participate in business and life. I didn't have less energy when I formed Greycroft at seventy-one than I had when I formed APA at thirty-five, and at eighty-seven, I don't feel markedly less energetic than I did fifteen years ago. And now I have another idea—a business venture I am going to spend the last twenty-seven-years (at least) nurturing.

Rules of the Road: Lessons from a Second Turn at the Wheel

Though I was a seasoned investor when I started Greycroft, the market for start-up companies had changed dramatically from 1970 to 2006—and continues to change. Investors need to stay flexible and adapt, and yet there are a number of practices I developed early in my career that have only become more relevant the longer I stay in this business. One of the most important deals with forming a partnership that is built to last.

In the early months and years of Greycroft, I often thought about (Sir) Ronald Cohen and the strong bond of friendship, brotherhood, and mutual respect we have for each other. There was space for each of us to grow in our respective domains at the same time that we were sharing successes and collaborating to build something that would survive both of us.

I have tried to bring the same spirit to the partnership I have built with Ian Sigalow and Dana Settle. Though the difference in age between them and me created a different sense of partnership, there has still been mutual respect. They have been my partners in the fullest sense of the word, just as Ronald was before them. I credit Ian and Dana fully with helping build Greycroft's reputation. Dana deserves particular credit for building our reputation on the West Coast so that we were known from the beginning as a truly bicoastal firm. I know from building APA and the significant effort I put into hiring people and forging relationships to develop the APA San Francisco office that it is not enough to simply have an office somewhere. You need a reputation, and Dana developed that on the West Coast for Greycroft in a way APA was never able to.

Some of founding partners of Apax, Greycroft, and Primetime Partners in July 2021: (left to right) Ian Sigalow, Abby Levy, Ronald Cohen, Alan Patricof (missing is Dana Settle).

One of the keys to a successful partnership is to share both management decisions and profits on an equitable basis. If I hadn't done that, they wouldn't have been encouraged to remain with the firm and help to build it. Venture firms are known for operating with significant internal politics and winner-take-all policies. I think that's the wrong way to go. Investment firms that fail to share the pie, in my experience, lose their most talented partners, who move on to form competing ventures. I wanted to cut that off at the pass at Apax and at Greycroft. Mutual respect and sharing are key factors in building an organization that will outlast its founders. That sharing mindset is one of the reasons why I have initiated a four-year process to transfer my share of ownership in Greycroft to the other partners, as I did years ago with Apax Partners. The intimacy of the business that began as just me, Ian, and Dana has expanded far beyond my initial vision—as it should. A few of the investment professionals on our team are ready to become partners and need room to do so. My interests have also shifted beyond Greycroft, though I remain chairman emeritus.

Sharing and partnership is also why I instituted a policy, way back in the early days of APA, that every deal should involve two partners, a first and a second. Putting a duo behind every deal ensured from the get-go a degree of intellectual due diligence—two people had to believe in the company and the founders, not just one. Having two people also ensured a duplication of knowledge, so that if one was away or left the firm, the other still had the institutional knowledge. I encouraged people to form those partnerships with an eye on diversifying relationships. For example, if the first partner worked out of the New York office, I'd encourage them to choose a second out of the California office to encourage the feeling of a bicoastal firm. I particularly like to choose as my second investors people who are skeptical about an idea I like; it ensures robust due diligence.

I did that recently when I chose another Greycroft partner, John Elton, to be my second to look into a company that specializes in hormone supplements for longevity. John had recently considered and rejected a similar deal. I thought the research connections he had made for the previous product would help us understand the potential for this new opportunity. His negative conclusions about the space would keep me grounded, knowing that if my research led me to conclude there was potential, I would have to first prove it to him. I also took that approach a few years ago when I asked Chris Wallace, a junior investor with us, to help me with Lex Markets, a company that built a platform to sell fractionalized shares of commercial properties on a proprietary platform that allows the buyer to sell their shares right away if they want to. I liked the idea; Chris didn't. I invited Chris to do the due diligence to see if his negative view held when he had more information.

Though I have not been able to insist on this two-person structure for every deal at Greycroft because there were so few of us at first, I still encourage all of the partners to bring a junior associate along with them when they meet with one of our portfolio companies—just as I started doing with Pat Cloherty so many years ago and still do today with young investment professionals. One of the best ways to develop investors is to bring them with you and teach as you go. I never wanted either of my firms to operate like the Manhattan Project, with people involved in separate silos without any understanding of, or access to, the whole. I still like to build people up by giving them access and authority—and then let go. The best of our junior associates far exceed my expectations (which have always been, and continue to be, high), and I encourage them to express their opinion even if it's contrary to mine.

Within that context, it's nonetheless critical for a leader to project an identity for the firm that others will respect. In my case I have tried to encourage a culture of integrity, cooperation, and inclusion at Greycroft. I've encouraged practices that brought members of different offices together to work on a deal. I've encouraged partners to bring more junior associates with them to meetings so everyone could feel like they are involved and informed about the inner workings of the business. I've attempted to convey that family feeling to our investors, partner firms, and the companies we have financed.

This approach usually differentiates us in a venture capital market that has become highly competitive and more oriented toward "exclusives" than partnership. It has made us better, I believe, even if we sometimes get caught up in more negative dynamics. In fact, early in our evolution, I had to confront head-on a cutthroat VC that wanted to cut us out of an investment. Greycroft had just signed the deal led by a young associate to invest in a high-profile start-up selling a social media tool—we were one of two investors in the deal, consistent with our rules.

As the ink was drying, we learned that a very famous West Coast VC was courting the entrepreneur in a luxurious fashion. The entrepreneur shortly thereafter called me to say he wanted out of our arrangement. Greycroft was much smaller and less well known than the courting VC. Many in my position would have let it go, but I stand by my view that integrity in partnership matters. A deal is a deal (just as Ronald Cohen insisted to me years before when he paid the US APA office its share of the Lawry's fees). I made my views on the matter clear with the following email I wrote to the entrepreneur (I've suppressed the names of the participants):

In life, regardless of our age or experience, we have to establish for ourselves a set of values and ethics; I know mine and that of my firm. I believe that my principles have enabled me to have an untarnished reputation for keeping my word and consistently acting in an ethical manner.

This situation is purely about how one feels about signing term sheets with a no shop clause and then violating the terms. It is Ethics 101. I am particularly shocked by the behavior of [investor at the competing VC]. My understanding is that he is a member of the Bar and this certainly can't comply with his signing on to their Code of Conduct. Moreover, he has been around this business for many years and should be providing guidance, which would point this out. I feel very strongly about violating NO SHOP clauses. Sooner or later, if this term sheet is violated, someone, not us, will let this be known and it cannot reflect well on anyone involved. Ethics and honor are either something you have or you don't.

[Start-up company name] needs to make an effort to resolve the matter in an honorable fashion. I respect the desire to include [VC] in the deal, and I can understand the company making a best effort to do so. However, I cannot understand a total denial and disregard for an agreement, legal or otherwise. Clearly, [name of another VC investor at competing firm] is not aware of the implications of his actions on his own reputation and that of his firm.

...

If the Board and [VC] cannot work this out satisfactorily, the Board, in my opinion, has the ethical obligation to move forward on the terms as outlined in the term sheet as it stands.

Regards,
Alan Patricof

In the end, the entrepreneur did the right thing and readjusted the allocation to include the third VC, but not to the exclusion of those of us to whom he'd made a prior commitment. I should also add, he and I continue to have a good relationship to this day.

I pride myself on staying connected to the founders we support. The clearest endorsement of our approach at Greycroft is the fact that many of our founders come back to us when they set out to raise money for their second or third company. When I ask them why, I consistently hear entrepreneurs say they felt like Greycroft had always been committed to their success. They feel part of a family that transcends any one individual. They aren't just another company in the portfolio.

Steve Ellis, the Pump Audio entrepreneur, put it this way: "I never felt like you were saving your powder." When I asked him to elaborate, he explained that in his experience, I would talk about Pump Audio and introduce Steve to anyone I thought could help him grow his business or form an advantageous partnership. But if I thought the same media executive would be interested in both Pump Audio and, say, Pulse, I'd talk to them about both those firms. I don't actually believe it's possible to overuse a contact. On the contrary, relationships grow that way.

I like to believe all of our companies feel like we did everything we could to include them and promote their success—even the ones that don't achieve a successful exit. I have had the good fortune over fifty years in business to have seen some major successes. I have also had to learn the hard way to approach each round of financing as if it were the first. In other words, I apply the same fundamentals I use to evaluate an initial investment to decide whether to participate in a subsequent round.

Every time I find myself as an early investor in a promising company that needs more capital, I am reminded of an episode in Ernest Hemingway's famous story about big game hunting, *Green Hills of Africa*. In it, the protagonist and his guide are standing at the lip of a large natural bowl on the African savannah when they hear the booming report of a rifle. The protagonist waits to hear another, pondering a saying he'd heard from another guide he met in the hunting camp: "One shot, meat. Two shots, maybe. Three shots, heap shit."

As it applies to venture investing, many companies naturally need two and three rounds of capital to evolve from start-up to stable growth. This is especially true if the company needs to create a new market. In those cases, the first shot is the one that gets the investor an initial stake. The situation gets more complicated, however, if a company chews through an initial round or two of financing and fails to meet the objectives it set for itself. If you have to take a third (fourth, fifth, or ninth) shot on a company that keeps seeing delays or roadblocks that prevent it from reaching an inflection point, the potential to walk away with meat diminishes.

After many experiences of putting multiple rounds into a company that I should have walked away from, I gradually came to approach each round of financing as if it were the first, applying the same due diligence process I use to determine the initial potential of a business. I personally tell myself and encourage my partners to objectively reassess the four fundamentals of progress that I've referred to before in this book: Has the market grown as you expected? Has the product development progressed as you expected? Do you still think you have the right leadership? And are the capital needs appropriate to the earning potential of the business based on empirical data? That practice helps us take fewer third (or more) shots on companies that show no signs of turning around.

The same principles can be used by entrepreneurs to decide whether to continue pursuing an idea that isn't gaining traction. If you've tried multiple approaches and it still isn't working, you're often better off in the eyes of your investors giving the remaining capital back rather than running the bank balance down to zero. The recent decision by Jeff Katzenberg to fold Quibi despite $1.7 billion of raised capital is instructive. He quickly saw that the company wasn't going to be able to achieve the consumer subscription volumes he had anticipated to justify its overly high valuation. The quality of the videos was top notch, but viewers weren't paying. As we say in the trade, the dogs were not eating the dog food. He shut it down while he still had money to give back. If I'd been an investor, I would have clearly preferred to make a multiple of my investment, but second best is to get some back rather than losing it all.

Still, it's not easy to walk away. The decision to turn down participation in the next round of financing is fairly simple when a company is missing three or four of the four elements of market, product, leadership and economics. But when it still has three or even two of the four elements, we've had many cases of putting more money in when we shouldn't have. When we finally do make the decision to walk away or say no to an investment, I aim to do so in a way that is as direct but respectful as possible. Saying no so as not to offend anyone is a critical life skill for everyone.

The decision to stop investing can be harder than the decision to invest in the first place. And even when I do walk away from a business, sure that it has passed the point of no return, it doesn't always die. If you think you have buried a company and it has disappeared, go metaphorically to the funeral parlor, attend the burial, put a tombstone on the grave, and then come back a year later to make sure the corpse is still underground—and the headstone isn't rising. If it is, it wouldn't be the first. So many venture-backed companies have had a second or third life.

We've written multiple companies down to a dollar, only to see them come back from the dead to earn us a return. A recent example is AlphaDraft, an eSports company that we had written down due to poor performance and running out of cash, when out of nowhere it was snapped up and sold to a fantasy sports and online casino company, FanDuel, in exchange for stock. FanDuel itself was subsequently almost a failure, but had a miraculous recovery and was recently acquired by a UK firm, Flutter, at a valuation of around $11 billion. We'll end up with ten times our original investment cost in AlphaDraft. That is obviously a great recovery for a deal we thought was dead.

The ultimate examples of my axiom that venture deals don't die easily—and sometimes have nine lives—are two companies in similar businesses who went through similar experiences that almost led them both to crash and burn...until they didn't. Both companies were founded by totally inexperienced first-time entre-preneurs, each pair having the same simultaneous idea to create a new payment concept for millennials.

The first was New York-based Venmo—today practically a household name. Two graduates of the University of Pennsylvania started the company and walked into our offices on a hot summer day in 2011 wearing shorts and T-shirts (a bit casual, if not for the weather, certainly for the circumstances). The concept was to create a payment system that would work through SMS or the mobile web and allow consumers to pay for a restaurant meal or retail purchase. The iPhone had only been on the market for four years, so this idea was definitely early to market. Without going into all the details on the evolution of the technology, Venmo eventually morphed beyond the original idea of paying retail establishments into a peer-to-peer payment system so familiar today that the word *Venmo* functions as a verb. Beyond reimbursing a friend who bought tickets or paid for dinner, people regularly use Venmo to easily pay independent workers like their dog walkers and house cleaners, hairdressers and private music teachers.

Despite the obvious utility of the idea, Venmo almost went out of business due to the inexperience of its management, coupled with insufficient funds to handle the exploding growth in traffic. The founders had never been in the payments business before and had to learn about the regulations, such as Know Your Customer (KYC), and the different rules about obtaining banking licenses. Without the necessary anti-fraud provisions or compliance procedures in place, the company was on the verge of being shut down by the enormous, top-five US bank with which they had their commercial account—and which caught on, from looking at their transaction flows, that the company was running a payments business out of their standard business checking account and using their credit cards. This approach created a situation where Venmo actually saw the opposite of economies of scale: the faster they grew, the more they lost because of the need to pay transaction fees to third-party service providers; these fees were larger than the fees Venmo charged its customers.

At that point the choices were grim: Venmo was facing either being shut down, selling itself to another company, or letting itself fail due to an inability to cover expenses and payroll. Reluctantly, in July 2012, the founders decided to accept an offer from a Chicago company called Braintree—also in the payments business, but with better systems, more experienced management, and adequate capital. Venmo accepted an exchange of shares, and the preservation of the name Venmo. My usual view of selling one private company to another private company is not positive, since it is essentially "my cat for your dog"—of limited benefit for both parties. In this case, however, we got a Westminster Kennel Club champion (we even bought more Braintree stock after the sale). A few years later, in 2016, PayPal bought Braintree for cash, producing an enormous gain for all shareholders. PayPal has retained the Venmo peer-to-peer service and made it into a household word. Who would have thought that for one summer week in 2012 it had looked like all was lost?

Our experience seeing an upside with Venmo perhaps, unwittingly, made us too sanguine about payments companies, for in 2016 we got a call one day from a contact in Spain about a Spanish payments company very similar to Venmo, but for the Spanish market. Like Venmo, Verse was the brainchild of three young recent graduates, this time of the University of Barcelona, who wanted to set up a similar peer-to-peer payment system in Spain, with aspirations to spread across Europe. After a meteoric takeoff in traffic, the incompetence and inexperience of the founders also brought Verse to the brink of disaster.

In this case, Verse went through a corporate reorganization involving the installation of a more experienced management team, which took charge in 2018. After multiple rounds of financing to support the rejuvenated growth in demand, Verse also ran out of funds to support the growth, and reluctantly agreed to sell itself to Square, which aimed to use it as the basis for offering the "Square Cash" product in Europe. Square at first wanted to buy Verse for all cash, but because of the pandemic, decided at the last moment to execute a stock-for-stock exchange (this did not count as a "my cat for your dog" situation since Square was a public company). Lucky for us, we were required to lock up our Square stock under SEC rules for six months, during which time and beyond, the Square stock multiplied severalfold and produced a very positive return for Greycroft. Another example of us writing an investment down to $1 in our books, only to see it rise again. It only proves, as Yogi Berra once said, "It's never over 'til it's over."

I don't want to give the idea that these types of last-minute revivals are universal. They aren't. My point is that strange things happen in unpredictable ways—including that once-promising venture-backed businesses also truly collapse due to insufficient market demand, poor management, poor product concept, or lack of alignment between the costs to serve the market and what customers are willing to pay (at one point, Venmo was burning through $8 in overhead for each $1 in revenue!).

The reality of needing at some point to pay the shareholders back used to discourage entrepreneurs from taking more than they needed to evolve their concept in the market. But the promise of achieving massive scale fully dominates today's start-up environment and creates an impetus for small companies to take all they can get, rather than being strict about looking at the economics of their market and deciding what's viable. And if they still need more capital later, both the management and the shareholders will be reluctant to accept a lower valuation than it achieved in the previous round (known as a "down round"). The management doesn't want to raise at a lesser price for fear that it might cause the market to lose faith in their potential, and the shareholders are reluctant to write down their portfolio values, so they don't want to invest less than their pro rata because that can send a negative message to the market about the company's prospects and its market value. Market momentum then pushes for more, which perpetuates ballooning valuations that may not be grounded in reality.

There's also the fact that the more shots the investor takes, the harder it is psychologically to walk away. Motivations start to get muddy. Are you continuing to invest because the idea and its foundations are still sound? Or are you continuing to invest because you don't want to be the one to seal the doom of a company that you once had faith in? Investors tend to move in packs. If one signals support for a promising young venture, others follow. But if a lead investor defects—even if that investor has a relatively small stake after multiple rounds—it can lead to a cascade of defections. No investor wants their decision to foreclose other options for a company; the possibility can lead them to hang on longer than the evidence suggests they should. I've even seen partners in my own firm conveniently "forget" their previous assumptions about valuation in order to justify staying in for another round. It's hard to stay rational when you've gotten to know the management of a company intimately.

And what about the situations that produce a positive exit for the firm? Be self-aware about the risk you took and whether it was worth it. I always say to myself and people working with me, when you go home tonight, look in the mirror. Don't kid yourself and get too self-congratulatory, especially if the results are only on paper and not yet realized. Be honest and realistic about results you have achieved. Measure your successes in relation to the risk you took to achieve them. Maybe you earned two or three times your initial investment, but consider whether at the outset you were betting the ranch and got lucky with a modest multiple, when you should have returned ten times or more to justify the risk. If you had not gotten lucky you might have lost everything. Be hard on yourself in equating risk to reward.

This applies as well when opportunities come to merge an existing portfolio company with another private company. Entrepreneurs and investors can get carried away when a private firm offers shares in its company to acquire yours. There's a momentary feeling of exultation if the pricing seems on the face of it to represent a good exchange. But the fact is that no one really knows what one private company is worth versus another private company. This is another example of a "my cat for your dog" transaction. Selling to a public company whose price is established through daily trading offers a more objective exchange of value.

Even as I have continued to have varied experiences and learn, my time at Greycroft has reinforced lessons I learned at the beginning of my career. The most foundational is that I still don't drive alone. Getting out, getting involved, and making connections is as critical an ingredient for success today as it was more than sixty years ago when I started at Naess & Thomas. What it literally means to get out and make connections for any given person depends on the business they're in. For me, getting out of the office now has morphed from my days attending the Brimberg Lunches, to more recently attending NY Meetups and Voicecamp, as well as conferences, trade shows, and product demos. Staying active and involved has allowed me to keep my ear to the ground and hear about new companies while they're still on the rise—ideally before everyone else knows about them.

For an entrepreneur, getting out of the office is a key practice promoted by Steve Blank, the lean start-up guru, as a way to learn about customers and their needs. Steve tells entrepreneurs to go see with their own eyes and ears how people use their product. I passed on that tip to the founder of one of Greycroft's portfolio companies recently, a software company in the Midwest that had a highly automated sales process that limited person-to-person interaction with customers.

As the company grew, it started getting questions it couldn't answer about the pricing formulas, the competition, product functionality, and so on. At my suggestion, the CEO went on the road for a couple of weeks to see firsthand how customers used the service and find out what needed to be fixed. He returned with a deeper and more nuanced understanding of how his product needed to evolve. Nothing beats meeting face-to-face—a lesson that long months stuck at home during the coronavirus pandemic has only confirmed.

A final lesson brings me full circle to one of my first observations, which is that life is cumulative. The thirty years I spent with my partners growing APA into Apax Partners, and watching it morph and change, provided me with a set of experiences that informed the guiding ethos of Greycroft. It also gave me a list of contacts and a reputation as an investor that was invaluable when it came time to start the firm. Back in 2006, people marveled that it took just two months to raise the first Greycroft fund. My response is that it actually took thirty-six years and two months—what came before directly affects what comes after.

I confronted the cumulative nature of life in a more personal vein in 2015, when I was invited to go to Kiev, Ukraine, to give a talk to the Ukrainian Venture Capital and Private Equity Association. The meeting was to be held in the local indoor soccer stadium. Knowing that my father was born about a hundred miles from Kiev in Smiela, Ukraine, I decided to accept the invitation and take a side trip.

Kiev is a thriving cultural and business center, and the venture capital event had more than a thousand attendees, including young entrepreneurs displaying their products with as much excitement and energy and modern concepts as you'd find in Silicon Valley. That impression did not hold, however. After the event, I rented a car and driver and took the quick trip on a four-lane highway to Smiela.

When I entered the town, I was transported back to another century. The main square and surrounding streets were empty. I couldn't even find a sandwich or a cup of coffee, or for that matter, a person to direct my Ukrainian driver to the synagogue or cemetery. When we finally found the Jewish cemetery, every headstone was broken, making it impossible to read the Hebrew script. On the drive back to Kiev, I wondered what the place had been like in 1907, when my father had left the area, and realized how different life would have been for him—and how unlikely my birth—if he had not made the trek as a young boy to Rotterdam. Life is cumulative, indeed.

Greycroft's investor-friendly approach, our non-insistence on a minimum investment or percentage, and no requested board seat differentiated us when we formed, and continue to do so today. Time has added a number of defining practices. For example, we place a strong emphasis on repeat entrepreneurs. Running a prior business gives a founder perspective that first-time entrepreneurs lack—they too have accumulated lessons that a second, or third, business allows them to apply. Greycroft likes to support people with some experience under them—they often exceed our expectations. Experienced founders get bonus points if their proposed leadership team includes one or two people they've worked with before. We view it as a big show of confidence in the founder when a colleague votes with their career and follows the founder into a new venture—it confirms belief in the concept.

My ongoing interest in experienced, repeat founders is one reason why I have again set myself up to distill what I've learned into another turn at the wheel. My latest adventure is a new venture firm called Primetime Partners, which my new partner Abby Levy and I have launched, even as I continue the four-year transition from Greycroft that I initiated in 2018.

What is the secret to leaving while not leaving the firm you founded? The answer is to give up authority. If anyone comes to you with a complaint, or asks you to reverse a position, you defer.

Offer advice when asked, and accept any alternate decisions. Get comfortable with the fact that actions will be taken with which you disagree. If you have suggestions, make them privately, and with deference to the fact your opinion no longer counts as it once did. For me, those guiding principles have worked out very well and I have felt very comfortable in my new role as the éminence grise. It may be why I was able to start Greycroft while still a resident in the Apax offices. It may be why almost every partner of Apax invested in Greycroft, and every partner of Greycroft invested in Primetime Partners, the focus of my latest adventure.

CHAPTER 8

My Next Trip

When I consider the span of my career in venture capital from 1970 to the current day, I am often in awe of the large number of technology "firsts" I have touched, especially given the fact that I hung up my shingle in New York and not in Silicon Valley.

In the early years of APA, Datascope was the first company to build a cardiac monitoring device. NAC was the first company commercializing the technologies that would provide the foundations of the internet. Periphonics was the first company to sell the voice response solutions that are now standard in call centers. A company called Computer Identics was the first to use bar codes on freight train cars to track the locations of certain shipments or cars and redirect them when needed.

Later, in the 1980s and 1990s, Apple Computer was one of the first personal computers; Cellular Communications, Inc. was one of the first twenty-five companies awarded the initial batch of cellular service licenses; AOL was the first peer-to-peer communications tool using the internet for more than game play; Virtual Reality, Inc. was the first to seek a market for virtual reality technology; Audible was the first large-scale producer and distributor of audiobooks; Agouron was the first pharmaceutical company to produce an anti-retroviral drug to treat HIV; Life Time Fitness was the first large-scale fitness studio chain. At Greycroft, Venmo was the first peer-to-peer social payment provider; Buddy Media was among the first companies offering social marketing tools for businesses; Lex Markets was the first SEC-approved marketplace for small investors to trade fractional shares in real estate or alternative assets, something that was not available before for non-accredited investors.

I could make the case that I saw a lot of firsts because there have been a lot of firsts to see since 1970, given the explosion in technology innovation, and adoption. But I don't think that our capture of early winners is simply a function of being in the right place at the right time, or of being in the venture business a long time. Rather, I see it instead as a function of being prepared to see potential and go after it. It's not enough in any field of endeavor to simply stand around and wait for chances to come. I've had to inform myself, do my research, explore my interests, engage with ideas and people, and then say yes when an offer came. And when the offers didn't come—because often they don't—I had to be willing to hustle. Approach the entrepreneur whose company I kept hearing about. Call the potential business partner I could help. Pitch the investor whose philosophy and approach jives with my values.

I admit, there have been other "firsts" that I could have gone after but didn't. When I first heard of Starbucks, I couldn't see the market need it was addressing and passed on it. Travis Kalanick came to see me when he was early on with Uber to talk about the nuances and potential of the New York market. The meeting wasn't about money, but I could have expressed interest in investing. I chose not to—shame on me. I can rationalize my decision, since I couldn't at the time see how the business model would eventually turn a profit and operate under its own power. In the case of Uber, I still can't, but I admit I apparently missed an opportunity. I also toured a WeWork location when it had one building. I interpreted the We Company as a real estate deal and so didn't raise my hand, since Greycroft didn't invest in real estate. I did introduce my friend

Mort Zuckerman, CEO of Boston Properties, to WeWork, and he became an early investor.

Most people at my age would look at our track record and say it's enough—they've earned their nickel and made their mark. Not me. If you've read this far, you know by now that I like having multiple balls in the air. Call it a compulsion, or just simply who I am. I still have a lot of energy. I still have connections and interests. I still feel as energized and excited by the potential I see in new companies as I did fifteen years ago at the beginning of Greycroft, or fifty years ago at the beginning of APA. I am now channeling that energy into yet another "first" that will serve as the cornerstone of my newest adventure. At the age of eighty-five, when most people think their biggest contributions are behind them, I started a new fund.

The idea started to germinate in 2018, when I approached Dana and Ian, my co-founding partners at Greycroft, and worked out a plan for a four-year transition, which allowed me to remain actively involved in the firm, but not in the day-to-day management. As part of the plan, I assumed the role of Chairman Emeritus.

For the first year it was mostly business as usual, except that for the first time since I entered the venture business, I began to make a few direct investments outside of the Greycroft portfolio (to avoid the reality or appearance of conflicts of interest, I had established with the first APA fund the personal practice of never investing in any private company outside my firms' venture portfolio). My first extracurricular investments were interesting, but not terribly satisfying because my head was not yet out of Greycroft.

But then in early 2019, I began to get interested and gradually to focus on the subject of aging and the different needs that arise for people later in life. Susan's illness definitely provided a catalyst for this line of thought, but my interest extended far beyond chronic illness or any specific disease. On the contrary, I am less interested in illness than I am in the conjunction of older people and health and longevity.

When I look around, I see many of my friends and acquaintances reaching retirement age—or at least transitioning from their
chosen profession—with significant stores of energy and vitality.
Few of them consider starting another professional chapter (and I
am not saying they have to), but they could, and in doing so would
bring a wealth of knowledge and experience with them. Yet society
as a whole doesn't tend to view older people as entrepreneurs, and
the investment business definitely doesn't. Instead, conventional
wisdom has myopically pushed venture investors to focus on
young entrepreneurs, despite the fact that few have the necessary
experience to bring their ideas to operational scale. I myself have
sometimes fallen into that mindset trap.

These observations motivated me to do some research on the
subject of aging. According to the last US Census report from October
2019, by 2034 there will be 77 million people over the age of sixty-
five, and 76.5 million under the age of eighteen. The under-eighteen
demographic as of 2016 was 22.8 percent of the population, and
the over-sixty-five group represented 15 percent, but over the next
few decades, the age groups will cross over, with the over-sixty-fives
becoming the largest age demographic in the country.

I also came across several authoritative research studies that
examined the relative success of older entrepreneurs compared with
younger founders and discovered that older business founders gener-
ally achieve better outcomes. One study by academics Pierre Azoulay
(MIT), Benjamin Jones (Northwestern), J. Daniel Kim (the Wharton
School), and Javier Miranda (the Census Bureau) reported in the
Harvard Business Review in July 2018 found that the likelihood of
experiencing success as an entrepreneur increases with age up until
the entrepreneur is in their late fifties. The top 0.1 percent of successful
start-ups were founded by entrepreneurs forty-five years of age and
older. That evidence convinced me that there was an opportunity in
the field of aging. It was no small motivation that I could also serve
as a poster child for the venture given my own age and vitality—if I
could start a new career, so could others in my age group.

The more I explored the idea, the more I realized, again, that I am looking at a virgin field with many white-space opportunities for products, services, technologies, and adaptive experiences for the aging. I have my eye out for serial founders developing products for that space. If those founders are themselves older adults, all the better. The opportunity is simply so tempting that I decided it would be the focus of my third business. I quickly learned there were others who shared my vision. Abby Levy, formerly the founding president of Thrive Global along with CEO Arianna Huffington—which is how I knew her given my role as an investor on behalf of Greycroft and a board observer—was also looking at opportunities to amplify the availability of start-up funding for founders and early-stage businesses focused on older adults.

Abby and I decided to join forces to create one of the first venture funds solely dedicated to everything about aging—or as I like to call them, "the ageless generation." The concept has resonated with almost everyone we have approached with the idea, and in July, 2020, we formed Primetime Partners. The company is operating a ten-year fund focused on the over-sixty market— by far the fastest-growing segment of the US population. We had already invested in twenty early-stage companies (as of December 2021). They include e-commerce platforms specifically for seniors, a company offering training and entertainment content over Zoom for consumers aging at home or in senior facilities, software for healthcare agencies, specialist telemedicine for senior living facilities, financial services for the aging, including a firm providing an alternative to reverse mortgages retirement planning, and the list goes on.

In just over a year and a half we have been exposed to over seven hundred investment opportunities as a result of our aggressive positioning to become the thought leader in the space. We are determined to be the go-to source for capital. This is a major untapped opportunity, and I am as excited and personally engaged with this new fund and the portfolio companies we are investing in as I was in *New York Magazine*, Datascope, AOL, Audible, Pump Audio, Wondery, or any of the hundreds of companies that my firms have helped grow over the years. I still intend to live to 114 and spend at least part of the next twenty-seven years building Primetime Partners into a business with as much staying power as Apax or Greycroft. It's sure to be a hell of a trip—with no red lights. Keep your eye out for Primetime Partners II.

Acknowledgments

No book could be completed without a lot of assistance along the way. My journey began many years ago when the late Tom Ginsburg, then head of Viking Publishers, prompted me to write a memoir. Many other friends and business associates encouraged me along the same line. But it was probably Margaret Carlson, my very good friend, currently a reporter for *The Daily Beast* and for many years a key writer for Time, Inc., who convinced me it would be worthwhile to share my story and how I have pursued the many offshoots of my life. Along the way to publishing, Margaret has read and reread many versions and offered constructive inputs. Her guidance has been instrumental in my efforts to complete the project.

Another turning point occurred almost three years ago when my close friend Mort Janklow, one of the country's leading literary agents, convinced me to put pen to paper. I wrote 80,000 words freehand, had it typed up, and then sent him the preliminary version in hard copy. "This is definitely a book I can sell," he said. I wasn't convinced everyone would feel that way—Mort is my friend, after all—so I reached out to another agent with Janklow & Nesbit, Richard Morris, who agreed with Mort and took the role of agent. Both Mort and Richard have been invaluable in the process of bringing the book to fruition. Richard ultimately connected me to Debra Englander, my editor at Post Hill. She and her colleagues have tirelessly worked to bring the book to print.

Richard also suggested early in the process that I engage a professional writer/editor to help me take my initial writings and shape it into a full manuscript I could present to a publisher. After interviewing several candidates, I was introduced to Laura Starita, a professional writer and editor who's had her hand in more than twenty published books and countless articles and blog posts.

After an initial meeting in person, I made the decision to bring her on board even though we had to develop a structure of working remotely (she lives in Baltimore). We met in person every few weeks or so in New York City and used Zoom meetings weekly or bi-weekly for one to two hours. Who would have dreamed that in our COVID world this would be normal for everyone? I never could have imagined it. Laura has been my co-writer (she denies this and says it's all me), my critic, my confidant, and my researcher for the past two years, and in the process has become a very good friend. I can't overstate her support through every step of the process, delivered without a single outburst of frustration or discouragement.

Along the way Laura and I have called on people—friends, family members, colleagues, founders my firm supported, associates, and others—for help remembering facts and events, or just to reminisce and hear their perspective. They include Ian Sigalow and Dana Settle, my co-founding partners at Greycroft; my long-time assistants Marie Jiha and Mary Gallivan (the latter now runs HR for Greycroft); investment professionals Marisa Campise, Teddy Citrin, Zander Farkas, Weston Reynolds, and Chris Wallace; and Mathias Schilling, the co-founder of San Francisco VC firm e.ventures. I must also thank Abby Levy, my current partner in Primetime Partners, and Ray Jang, a Primetime investment professional.

There were also many people from my years at Apax Partners (née Alan Patricof Associates) who agreed to help Laura and me piece together long-past events, including my assistant from the early years, Carolyn Hearn, and a number of partners, investment professionals, and entrepreneurs from that era, including Patricia Cloherty, who started with me on day one in 1970, Bill Bottoms, Robert Chefitz, George Jenkins, John Megrue, Adele Oliva, Jackie Reses, Russ Steenberg (at AT&T, an investor in the fund), Paul Vais, and Jason Wright. Ronald Cohen and Maurice Tchenio shared their recollections of how we combined our efforts to bring venture to the U.K. and France, and Michael Hinderer weighed in on how we expanded our reach into Germany and Austria.

Thank you as well to the founders who helped provide details about how we met and worked together, including Rafat Ali of PaidContent, George Blumenthal of Cellular Communications, Inc., Steve Ellis of Pump Audio, Peter Frischauf of MedScape, Chad Halvorsen of When I Work, George Heller of Datascope, Shafqat Islam of Welcome, Akshay Kothari of Pulse, Hernan Lopez of Wondery, Howard Meyers of Quexco, Roy Schwartz of Axios, Laura Walker of WNYC, and Danielle Weisberg of theSkimm.

Julie Sunderland shared her memories of the time we spent traveling in Africa as volunteers trying to make a difference to the small business community; Harold Rosen told Laura about my work with the International Finance Corporation; Erica Payne recalled our collective time volunteering for Bill Clinton's first and second presidential campaigns; Steve Marriotti recalled advice I gave while he was developing the nonprofit Network for Teaching Entrepreneurship (NFTE); and Dawn Barber reminded me about the NY Tech MeetUps.

A special thank you goes to my family and their support throughout the process. Marcia and Jaclyn, my sisters, provided key insights of what it was like to be siblings. Others, including my sons Mark, Jon, and Jamie, offered helpful suggestions on early drafts. Last, I must acknowledge Susan, my wife for more than fifty years. She did not live to see this book in print, but she was there as my chief companion and supporter for all of it. She would have been excited to relive many of the stories in the book.

Special thanks go as well to Courtney Dawson, my assistant at home, who has kept everything on track through the whole process; and Marie Jiha, my assistant in the office, who pulled documents and coordinated my conversations and meetings. It truly does "take a village" to put out a book. To all of the above I give my warmest appreciation.